Midlife Transformation in Literature and Film

In this book Steven F. Walker considers the midlife transition from a Jungian and Eriksonian perspective by providing vivid and powerful literary and cinematic examples that illustrate the psychological theories in a clear and entertaining way.

For C.G. Jung, midlife is a time for personal transformation, when the values of youth are replaced by a different set of values, and when the need to succeed in the world gives place to the desire to participate more in the culture of one's age and to further its development in all kinds of different ways. Erik Erikson saw "generativity," an expanded concern for others beyond one's immediate circle of family and friends, as the hallmark of this stage of life. Both psychologists saw it as a time for growth and renewal. Literary texts such Virginia Woolf's *Mrs Dalloway*, Shakespeare's *Antony and Cleopatra* or Sophocles' *Oedipus the King*, and films such as Fellini's *8½* and Campion's *The Piano*, have the capacity to represent, sometimes more vividly and with greater dramatic concentration than actual life histories or case studies, the archetypal nature of the drama and in-depth transformation associated with the midlife transition.

Midlife Transformation in Literature and Film focuses on the specific male and female archetypal paradigms and presents them within the general context of midlife transformation. For men, the theme of death of the young hero presides over the crisis and the transformative ordeal; whereas for women, the theme of tragic abandonment acts as the prelude to further growth and independence.

This book is essential reading for anyone studying Jung, Erikson or the midlife transition. It will interest those who have already been through a midlife transition, those who are in the midst of one, as well as those who are yet to experience this challenging period.

Steven F. Walker is Professor of Comparative Literature at Rutgers University. He received his Ph.D. in Comparative Literature from Harvard University and has published a number of essays using Jungian perspectives in order to interpret literature and film. His publications include *Jung and the Jungians on Myth* (Routledge, 2002).

Midlife Transformation in Literature and Film

Jungian and Eriksonian Perspectives

Steven F. Walker

Routledge
Taylor & Francis Group

LONDON AND NEW YORK

First published 2012
by Routledge
27 Church Road, Hove, East Sussex BN3 2FA

Simultaneously published in the USA and Canada
by Routledge
711 Third Avenue, New York NY 10017

Routledge is an imprint of the Taylor & Francis Group, an Informa business

British Library Cataloguing in Publication Data
A catalogue record for this book is available from the British Library

Library of Congress Cataloging in Publication Data
Walker, Steven F., 1944-
  Midlife transformation in literature and film : Jungian and Eriksonian
perspectives / Steven F. Walker.
       p. cm.
  Includes bibliographical references and index.
  ISBN 978-0-415-66698-5 (hardback) − ISBN 978-0-415-66699-2 (pbk.)
1. Middle age−Psychological aspects. 2. Middle-aged persons in literature.
3. Middle age in motion pictures. 4. Jung, C. G. (Carl Gustav), 1875−1961.
5. Erikson, Erik H. (Erik Homburger), 1902−1994. I. Title.
  BF724.6.W35 2011
  155.6′6825−dc23

                                                        2011021737

ISBN: 978-0-415-66698-5 (hbk)
ISBN: 978-0-415-66699-2 (pbk)
ISBN: 978-0-415-15576-9 (ebk)

Paperback cover design by Andrew Ward
Typeset in Times by Garfield Morgan, Swansea, West Glamorgan
Printed and bound in Great Britain by TJ International Ltd, Padstow,
Cornwall

MIX
Paper from
responsible sources
FSC® C004839

Printed and bound in Great Britain by
TJ International Ltd, Padstow, Cornwall

Diis Manibus Cedric H. Whitman

Contents

Introduction

In classical Jungian theory, all human capacities, including the potential for transformation at midlife, are based on the archetypal nature of the collective unconscious, which is common to all human beings and which is what makes all human beings recognizably members of the same species. Human beings are, so to speak, hardwired instinctually to grow and change in ways that can offset some of the pressures exerted by culture, society and individual psychological make up. Consequently, the so-called midlife crisis—the period of transition between what Erik Erikson called the stages of life of "young adulthood" and "adulthood"—would seem to be inevitable and irresistible. However, transformation at midlife can come at a cost: the pain and even the agony of leaving the old self behind and becoming, to some degree, a new person. In addition, human beings are not so driven by archetypal and instinctual programs that they cannot resist and even forestall the archetypally generated process of transformation. Both C.G. Jung and Erik Erikson, approaching the problem of midlife transition from very different perspectives, recognized the possibility of arrested development—of a failure, for whatever reason, to make the transition successfully.

Culture certainly plays a key role in the resolution of this problem. Nature must be seconded by nurture, if what is prompted by nature is to be fully realized in an individual's life. But what happens when proper nurture is lacking? In his seminal essay "The Stages of Life," Jung lamented the absence of social institutions—of "colleges" for the middle aged—which would facilitate the transition to full maturity (Jung 1989b: 32–33). The underlying assumption of my book is that, in the absence of such "colleges," literature and film can help fill part of the cultural gap. Visionary artists have the power, which Jung celebrated in his essay "Poetry and Psychology" (Jung 1966: 89–105), to provide powerful transformative images and symbols that can awaken the latent archetypal capacity for transformation at midlife. I will present and discuss a few examples of what I call *oneiric* texts—texts whose symbolic depth makes them somewhat analogous to archetypal dreams and which have the capacity to deeply move the reader and to provide insights into the midlife transformation process. Marcel Proust compared the effect of such texts on the reader to that of the various lenses that an optician would try out on a client during an eye test: how do things look with this lens? How about this one? Such oneiric texts ultimately encourage the reader to become the reader of his or her own life. I thus hope that the younger reader will be able to imagine a midlife transition still to come, the middle-aged reader to relate with confidence and optimism to one that is in the process of unfolding, and the older reader to discover the specific contours of one that has already completed itself. And, of course, I hope that all readers will gain some appreciation for the potential miracle that is midlife transformation.

But a few words of caution and qualification are necessary. Some surveys have questioned whether many or even most people actually experience a "midlife crisis."[1] So it is possible that some people consciously undergo a dramatic midlife crisis, with accompanying anguish and despair, and that others do not. Recent focus on the problems of midlife may itself be a sign that the midlife crisis may be a phenomenon peculiar to, and even restricted to, modern culture. If that were the case, one would not expect it to be represented—as I have found that it is—in any recognizable form in the literature of past ages. Furthermore, one could argue that the midlife crisis may not only be culture bound, but also context bound in terms of a specific individual's life choices. From such a perspective it would have nothing about it that one could label archetypal, being simply a process of conscious management, within the framework of a culture's norms and an individual's life, of conflicts involving family and professional life in the second half of life. Of course, the midlife crisis would still be of major interest and concern for those who undergo it, for better and for worse, and of no less interest for the analysis of its reflection in modern literature and film. However, even the word "crisis" itself may be taken as suspect. For instance, *A Critical Dictionary of Jungian Analysis,* under the entry for "stages of life," raises the issue as to why "the midlife transition" should be "regarded as so traumatic and crisis-ridden," and suggests the answer, as regards the universality of the idea of a difficult midlife transition, that "Jung generalized too freely from his own personal experience of breakdown following the separation from Freud when he was in his late thirties" (Samuel, Shorter and Plaut 1986: 142).[2] But, even when the midlife crisis is viewed as rooted in an archetypal pattern, and not as a purely personal period of creative disorientation, it is possible that the unfolding of the archetypal process of midlife transformation may be experienced more consciously by some people and less so by others, and that for others it may even be totally unconscious—a natural process that perhaps can proceed without much in the way of conscious reflection at all.

All these are certainly significant issues. But, having acknowledged their importance, I do not intend to resolve them. As a literary scholar, I can only present a few possible ways of viewing midlife struggles from both Jungian and Eriksonian psychological perspectives, in terms of their applicability to a few carefully chosen texts from various time periods and from various cultures, without engaging with the question of the ultimate scientific validity of these paradigms. With no experience as a practicing therapist, I must defer to the authority of those who, like James Hollis and Murray Stein, have found in their years of therapeutic experience ample confirmation of problems that they feel can be categorized as problems of midlife crisis and transformation.[3] When I find midlife patterns seemingly well reflected in a few major works of the creative imagination from different cultures and from different time periods, it does seem to me that they can be theorized in Jungian terms as manifesting a significant archetypal dimension. More than that I cannot assert.

One perhaps controversial position taken by this book is that archetypal patterns of midlife transformation may well be gender specific, at least to a degree. Female patterns of initiation have already been investigated by such Jungian authors as Bani Shorter (1987), Sylvia Brinton Perera (1981) and Virginia Beane Rutter (1994). My argument that the male archetypal model of midlife crisis involves the tragic mythological theme of the death of the young hero, and that the female model centers on the tragic myth of abandonment, is something that I cannot prove exists in real life, but I can demonstrate that it is a useful hermeneutic tool for analyzing certain works of the imagination. Thus, as regards the hypothesis of somewhat divergent male and female archetypal patterns of midlife transformation, I must leave the argument to be persuasive in terms of the analysis of the literary and cinematic examples presented, rather than conclusive as regards ultimate scientific validity. In all events, I most certainly do not wish to promote what would be a contrarian position, in our age of aspirations for gender equality, namely, that men and women are fundamentally different and live lives that manifest radically different concerns. But I do find plausible the classical Jungian assumption that the archetypal nature of the human psyche is very slow to change. Thus many modern problems remain rooted in humanity's history and indeed prehistory as a species, during which relative gender social differentiation has been the rule. But I am quite willing to admit that, if many men were to spend their young adult years caring for infants, just as many women today often spend their earlier years fighting to impose themselves heroically in the public arena of profession and politics, the archetypal rules of the game could change—or at least bend. On this issue, and as regards possible variations in midlife transformation paradigms in the case of people with gay identities, it seems to me that, even within the parameters of archetypal constraints, the human psyche can be considered as enormously flexible. Since the interaction between the archetypal and the social and the personal is always a complex interaction, it would be hazardous to try to tie everything involved in midlife transformation down to a few simple archetypal patterns. In all events, the two primary gender related paradigms for midlife transformation that I have proposed are not to be taken as psychologically normative, but only as potentially useful frames of interpretation.

Finally, I need to provide a bit of justification for my occasional use of Eriksonian as well as Jungian paradigms for midlife transformation. I am reluctant to assume, as Jung seems to have done frequently, and as David Tacey seems to do now, that the midlife crisis, as "a moment of deep transition," necessarily involves a "turn towards the spiritual" (Tacey 2001: 192).[4] Although in the case of Proust's narrator Marcel, discussed in Chapter 7, this certainly seems to be the case, it does not seem to be so in some other cases. Rather, it is Erikson's concept of *generativity*— an enlarged capacity for concern for the world and for the welfare of others—that seems to me to have a broader applicability to the problems of midlife than the idea of a move towards spirituality, which seems to me to be needlessly restrictive to the case of budding mystics. Whatever the specific content of the realizations that can occur at midlife, and whether they can be typed as spiritual or as simply psychological and social, they would generally seem to stand in contrast to the values of youth, or, at the very least, to involve a less ego-centered extension of these earlier values. In short, spiritual crises and spiritual transformation are no doubt admirable things, but they do not seem to me to be necessarily stage of life related.

I have published preliminary approaches to some of this book's material in various journals and collections (see the bibliography under my name), and my thanks go to the editors and readers who helped me at the time. Some material in Chapter 8 concerning the *Bhagavad Gita* was first published as part of an article in two parts ("Arjuna's Eunuch Problem and the *Gita's* Epic Frame") in *American Vedantist* 14.1 (summer 2008), 9–14, and 14.2 (fall 2008), 8–16, and is reprinted here in a revised version with the kind permission of Vedanta West Communications. My thanks also go to the many people who have discussed with me the problems of midlife, both practical and theoretical, and in particular to Mathew V. Spano, who has given the manuscript his kind and insightful attention. Christianne Cain did some valuable research for me on the female midlife crisis, for which I am grateful. Robert Bly read a few of the earlier essays I had published on midlife topics, and gave them a nod of approval I much appreciate.

Finally, this book is dedicated to the memory of Cedric H. Whitman, who many years ago responded with enthusiasm to a seminar paper I wrote at Harvard concerning midlife issues in the *Odyssey*. He urged me to publish it, but I put it aside and went on to other things. In retrospect, it seems to me that it is he, more than anyone else, who has been the "ghostly guru" presiding over the writing of this book.

Notes

1 See the online Wikipedia article "Midlife Crisis", http://en.wikipedia.org/wiki/ Midlife_crisis (accessed June 2, 2011), for a brief presentation.
2 For an extensive analysis of Jung's own midlife transition, see Staude 1981.
3 See in particular Hollis 1993, 2005 and Stein 1998, 2003.
4 See also, on this point, Tacey 2006: 48–52.

Chapter 1

Jung, Erikson, midlife transformation and the oneiric text

C.G. Jung's 1931 essay "The Stages of Life" (Campbell 1976: 3–22) defined the entry into midlife as a transition period fraught with drama and even tragedy. Jung's focus on midlife had much to do with the development of his own originality as a psychologist in the wake of his break with Freud in 1912, when he was in his late thirties and had enjoyed for a number of years his status as the young heir apparent of the Freudian movement. This painful break was followed by what Anthony Storr has called a "near psychotic breakdown" (Storr 1991: 15), in the course of which Jung confronted a flood of images from the unconscious of almost overwhelming intensity. Having experienced the power of what he would later call the "collective unconscious," Jung originated a theory of the unconscious in its deeper archetypal dimension that expanded Freud's conception of the psyche to include more—much more—than the purely personal contents described by his erstwhile mentor. Whereas Freud's theory of the unconscious had assumed that all its contents derived from repressed personal memories, Jung posited that beyond this personal unconscious lay a "collective unconscious," whose "archetypal" contents were not the result of repression, but rather preexisted the birth of the individual and constituted the psycho-instinctual substratum common to all humanity. Jung viewed the psychic growth and creative transformation he experienced at midlife as archetypal in nature, in that the images that triggered his transformation were not only associated with personal memories and associations, but were also linked with disturbingly powerful mythic images.

In Jungian terms, midlife transformation can be seen as programmed in the psyche in the same way as the transformation processes associated with adolescence or young adulthood. It has no doubt an extremely important personal dimension—people live out their midlife transitions in their own particular ways—but it also manifests archetypal patterns which are based on a template in the psyche that involves the individual at midlife in a process that is recognizably similar to what all other individuals undergo, regardless of the specific cultural milieu in which their lives are embedded. In order to illustrate clearly the nature of a few of these patterns, I have chosen examples from literature and film and especially from the type of texts I call *oneiric*, that is, those which present significant mythological and dreamlike characteristics. They are texts that can be read as dream-texts, but dreams metamorphosed, polished and clarified by art, and made more accessible and entertaining for those who might be understandably bewildered and put off by the complexity and apparent confusion of personal accounts of actual dreams.

In the course of this book I will present not only examples drawn from literary and film texts of our own time, but also examples taken from the literature of other times and places, in order to highlight what they have to offer in terms of powerfully symbolic representations of the midlife transformation process. Such oneiric texts may be said to constitute a treasure house of symbolic representations of human experience. My assumption, which is shared by most Jungians, is that the archetypal characteristics of the human psyche are slow to change. Jung has written that

> the collective unconscious, being the repository of man's experience and at the same time the prior condition of this experience, is an image of the world which has taken aeons to form. In this image certain features, the archetypes or dominants, have crystallized out in the course of time. They are the ruling powers, the gods, images of the dominant laws and principles, and of the typical, regular occurring events in the soul's cycle of experience.
>
> (Jung 1956: 105)

For that reason, even ancient texts, such as some Greek tragedies or ancient myth narratives such as the Sumerian myth of the Descent of Inanna, remain relevant to the problems of the midlife transition in modern times, and, in spite of their cultural specificity, may provide precious insights into its archetypal foundations.

It was Jung's personal experience of a quasi-initiatory midlife ordeal involving mental anguish and even the threat of insanity and death that turned him into a creative and original psychologist in his own right, and not merely a brilliant follower of Sigmund Freud. A "midlife crisis" is thus not a sign of neurotic regression—although it can certainly involve neurotic regression—but a sign of the ongoing growth and transformation of the psyche. In fact, writes Jung, neurotic regressiveness at midlife is primarily the result of *resisting* change and transformation: "the very frequent neurotic disturbances of adult years all have one thing in common: they want to carry the psychology of the youthful phase over the threshold of the so-called years of discretion" (Campbell 1976: 14).

Jung's essay "The Stages of Life," particularly as regards what it has to say about the challenges of midlife transformation, would have been a good place for him to have brought up the case of Oedipus, had he not, throughout his later career, been consistently gun shy of the Freudian master myth, which saw in the myth of Oedipus a paradigmatic symbolic representation of a young boy's fantasies of murdering his father and marrying his mother. Jung might have pointed out that the later story of Oedipus, as dramatized in Sophocles' great tragedy *Oedipus the Tyrant*, could be taken as an equally powerful symbolic representation of a man on the brink of midlife transformation. Sophocles shows Oedipus not only as resisting knowledge about his own past (the murder of his father and his incestuous marriage with his mother), but also resisting midlife transformation and the new identity it will be his fate to realize and live out in the second half of his life. As I will demonstrate later, in Chapter 3, Oedipus' tragic willfulness and pigheaded stubbornness in Sophocles' tragedy can be taken as symbolic of the rigidity of midlife resistance to new values and to the process of assuming a new identity—a resistance to change all the more intense if, as was the case with Oedipus, the values of youth have led to what seems to be unqualified worldly success. At the height of his power as tyrant of Thebes, Oedipus seems to have done it all, and done it very well. He has vanquished the monstrous sphinx and saved the people of Thebes, thus becoming a heroic legend in his own time; he has married the widow of the former king and has had sons and daughters with her; he is respected and even idolized by his people; he is at the apex of his social achievements and at the zenith of his strength and glory.

But the great hero Oedipus, having risen so high, is soon due for a fall. Jung compared the course of life to the journey of the sun from dawn to sunset, with the moment when youth begins to give way to middle age being equated symbolically with the sun's highest position in the sky. At that moment things get dramatic: "at the stroke of noon," writes Jung, "the descent begins. And the descent means the reversal [*enantiodromia*] of all the ideals and values that were cherished in the morning" (Campbell 1976: 15). Jung found this solar analogy very meaningful, and expanded on it as follows:

> Our life is like the course of the sun. In the morning it gains continually in strength until it reaches the zenith heat of high noon. Then comes the *enantiodromia*: the steady forward movement no longer denotes an increase, but a decrease, in strength . . . The transition from morning to afternoon means a re-valuation of earlier values. There comes the urgent need to appreciate the value of the opposite of our former ideals, to perceive the error in our former truth.
>
> (Jung 1956: 74–75)

For Oedipus, the experience of this descent is particularly tragic, since by the end of Sophocles' play he has lost everything (his high position, his wealth, the respect he enjoyed) and everyone (his wife, his children, his people) that he valued in his life. And he was almost totally unprepared for this tragic catastrophe. All the qualities that had served him so well in his youth (cleverness, self-assertion and youthful heroism) are of little use to him now. That is why Sophocles' tragic and dramatic portrayal of a maturing Oedipus, as opposed to the more youthful heroic Oedipus as he appears in the traditional myth utilized to great effect by Freud, can be taken as symbolically paradigmatic of the midlife crisis faced by many people today. Modern people are sometimes as unprepared as Oedipus for this *enantiodromia*, this midlife reversal of values. Jung deplored the absence of "schools for forty-year olds" (Campbell 1976: 16), which would educate them and prepare them for the inevitable descent, since

> whoever carries over into the afternoon the law of the morning . . .
> must pay for so doing with damage to his soul just as surely as a
> growing youth who tries to salvage his childish egoism must pay for
> this mistake with social failure.
>
> (Campbell 1976: 18)

In "The Stages of Life," Jung emphasized that

> we cannot live the afternoon of life according to the programme of
> life's morning; for what was great in the morning will be little at the
> evening, and what in the morning was true will at evening have become
> a lie.
>
> (Campbell 1976: 17)

As we have seen, Jung's concern with midlife, which he felt began typically "between the thirty-fifth and fortieth year" (Campbell 1976: 8), although its onset can occur well into a person's fifties, was partly the result of his own personal experience of an unusually transformative midlife passage, which led him to distinguish his own analytical psychology's goals and objectives from those of Freud's. Freudian psychology was mainly concerned with enabling the individual "to love and to work"— achievements no doubt valuable at any stage of life, but of most specific and crucial value to youth and early adulthood, when marriage, acquiring friends and professional success are traditionally of prime concern. However, it is not such personal goals, but rather "culture" that Jung wants to assign as the task of the second half of life:

> Money-making, social achievement, family and posterity are nothing
> but plain nature, not culture. Culture lies outside the purpose of nature.
> Could by any chance culture be the meaning and the purpose of the
> second half of life?
>
> (Campbell 1976: 18)

Jung felt, however, that modern culture tended to ignore and even to discourage the potentially momentous shift in values and psychological orientation that can occur at midlife. He had visited the United States on two separate occasions, during which he had had the opportunity to become acquainted with mainstream American culture and the dominant social values of the early twentieth century, when the modern cult of youth and youthfulness had become well established. In America, he wrote:

> For the most part our old people try to compete with the young. In the United States it is almost an ideal for a father to be the brother of his sons, and for the mother to be if possible the younger sister of her daughter.
>
> (Campbell 1976: 18)

But Jung had also had the opportunity of getting acquainted with the tribal society of the Taos Pueblo in New Mexico, and its respect for traditional values and the wisdom of the elders made a great impression on him. Jung thus felt able to make the following comparison between modern culture and traditional tribal culture:

> In primitive tribes we observe that the old people are almost always the guardians of the mysteries and the laws, and it is in these that the cultural heritage of the tribe is expressed. How does the matter stand with us? Where is the wisdom of our old people, where are their precious secrets and their visions?
>
> (Campbell 1976: 18)

His conclusion was that modern culture was tending more and more to identify with the goals of youth as the only goals worth realizing, and so to ignore that momentous *enantiodromia* of midlife where these youthful goals begin to lose their value and change their valence.

It was—somewhat paradoxically—the Freudian Erik Erikson, in close collaboration with his wife, Joan, who was to shed light on the period of the onset of midlife as a major stage of growth and transformation, thus taking a giant step beyond the Freudian emphasis on the problems of childhood, adolescence and young adulthood. Without specific reference to (and perhaps without knowledge of) Jung's earlier essay on the stages of life, Erikson in the late 1940s began to describe mature adulthood as a stage of life in which *generativity* came into conflict with what he termed *stagnation*; a successful resolution of this conflict would endow the individual with a broadened sense of concern for others and for the culture at large.

But it is interesting to note that, in their first formulation of his theory of the stages of life, the Eriksons almost omitted the stage of midlife! In her preface to the extended version of *The Life Cycle Completed* (1997), Joan

Erikson tells how the couple was on the way to Los Angeles, where her husband was to present their recently elaborated theory publicly to a gathering of psychiatrists and psychologists, along with a chart showing clearly seven successive stages of life. Suddenly they remembered that in his comedy *As You Like It*, Shakespeare had presented the "seven ages" of man, just as in their sequence, but realized that in Shakespeare's listing there was a glaring omission as regards the flowering of mature adulthood. They then asked themselves whether they too had skipped a stage. Joan Erikson later remembered that "in a shocking moment of clarity I saw what was wrong: the seven chart stages jumped from 'Intimacy' (stage six [Young Adulthood]) to 'Old Age' [at that point stage seven]." Realizing, she wrote, that "we surely needed another stage between the sixth and the seventh" (Erikson 1997: 3), they quickly developed the idea of a stage of life in which the conflict between generativity and stagnation would be the dominant characteristic.

Shakespeare's evocation in *As You Like It* (Act II, scene 7) of a parade of representative figures of the Seven Ages of Man does in fact include a figure who could be taken as symbolizing mature adulthood, but in anything but generative terms:

> Then a soldier,
> Full of strange oaths and bearded like the pard,
> Jealous in honor, sudden and quick in quarrel,
> Seeking the bubble reputation
> Even in the cannon's mouth."

The satirical and negative cast of Shakespeare's portrayal of his midlife figure as a violent and braggart soldier (*miles gloriosus*) corresponds nicely, however, to what Erikson called the negative (dystonic) "ritualism" that is "potentially rampant in adulthood," and is "authoritive" and linked to the "antipathetic trend" of "rejectivity." "Authoritism" he defined as "the ungenerous and ungenerative use of sheer power for the regimentation of economic and familial life" (Erikson 1997: 70)—a kind of bullying that is brutal and self-seeking in its use of force. "Rejectivity" is defined as "the unwillingness to include specified persons or groups in one's generative concerns—one *does not care to care* for them" (Erikson 1997: 68). Rejectivity can even lead to the hybris of pseudospeciation, a term Erikson later devised to designate hostile behavior towards other human beings, treating them as though they belonged to a different and lower species. "Stagnation" is the result of seeking to prolong youth beyond its normal bounds, thus resisting midlife transformation, and of the failure to become generative and generous-minded.

One must be careful, I feel, in making too broad a use of the term "stagnation," which is associated in Erikson's mind with the term "self-absorption," as the main pitfall in the attainment of midlife generativity. This is where Eriksonian and Jungian theories of midlife begin to clash. Erikson's theory is mainly concerned with an individual's level of functioning in the outside world, whether for better or for worse. In terms of social adaptation, generativity is good, and stagnation is bad. But, in the Jungian perspective, stagnation can also represent a long stage of liminality, of a slow psychic preparation for transformation. Jungian theory is also rather more open than Eriksonian theory to the idea that contemplative and spiritual values may play a large role in midlife transformation. The midlife crisis can also be a spiritual crisis, and Jung was prone to see it, at least for the analysands he had to deal with, as primarily that. In addition, the introverted and introspective aspect of Jungian analytical psychology contrasts vividly with the extroverted and socially concerned slant of Eriksonian theory. Jung was prone to speak of inner transformation and introspective depth, whereas Erikson stressed social adaption and responsibility. But I see their two approaches as wonderfully complementary, and in the course of this study will turn to one or the other, depending on which one seems most illuminating for the particular hermeneutic context.

Like Jung's discussion of midlife transformation, Erikson's theory of the stages of life is presented as gender-free, equally applicable, at least in principle, to either sex, even though Erikson's examples are drawn almost entirely from the lives of men. Jungian theory, by contrast, thanks to its stress on the important contrasexual dimensions of the anima and the animus, is, at least potentially, more open to the possibility that there will be differences and even major differences between a male paradigm of midlife transformation and one that would apply specifically to women; my analysis in Chapter 5 of the midlife transformation of Penélopê in the *Odyssey*, is one of my attempts to sketch out what those differences might be in terms of divergent archetypal paradigms. But, at least in the case of the *Odyssey*, however much Homer's imagination might have been richly androgynous, there is always the possibility that the figure of his Penélopê might deserve the strictures of Virginia Woolf, who argued that many of the great female characters created by male authors "are by no means what they pretend to be." Some of them, she argues, "are plainly men in disguise; others represent what men would like to be, or are conscious of not being" (Woolf 1979: 42). The same problem exists with other figures that seem to provide rich material for the analysis of the female midlife transformation, such as Shakespeare's Cleopatra. In Jungian terms, such a female character might be the result of a male author's anima projection or might serve as an example of Woman as Other; in both cases such a distorted image would be unreliable, as Woolf reminds us, when it comes to illustrating "the truth about women."

In her introduction to Jung's *Visions: Notes of the Seminar Given in 1930–1934* Claire Douglas (1998) has shown how Jung's own gender bias significantly distorted his presentation of a long sequence of visions experienced by an American woman, Christiana Morgan, who "at age twenty-eight and during a period of personal crisis set out on an imaginal quest similar in many respects to the one Jung had undertaken after his traumatic break with Freud" (Jung 1997: x), which had constituted for her "a personal but also archetypal rite of initiation" (Jung 1997: xiii). Douglas adds that "many of her images offer a view of women's psychological development that is only now becoming generally recognized" (Jung 1997: xiv). Douglas's remark suggests correctly that it is becoming more common today to recognize the possible unreliability of men's views of women—and, I would add, of women's views of men. That is why I have taken care to analyze texts by both male and female authors, assuming that writers are more likely to have accurate psychological insights into characters of their own gender. I have also tried to maintain a balance between the analysis of texts representing male, and those representing female, transformations at midlife.[1]

It would be impossible to formulate new archetypal approaches to midlife crisis and transformation without giving full credit to Murray Stein's pioneering book *In Midlife* (1983); my early investigation of the topic was greatly indebted to it, and so, even more, was my need for guidance during my own midlife transition. But in Stein's case also the question of gender focus does need to be addressed. Although his recent book *Transformation* (1998) opens with the interpretation of a thirty-five-year-old woman's dream that provides one of its leading images (the emergence of a butterfly from a cocoon), it is, for all its gender-free language, mainly oriented around a description of the male midlife process, illustrated first of all by a lengthy analysis of the German poet Rainer Maria Rilke at midlife. Some of the understandable ambivalence Stein may feel about setting up a male model of transformation as paradigmatic and applicable to women as well, for whom there may exist a separate and distinct pattern of midlife transformation, may be manifested in his decision to limit his subsequent discussion of midlife transformation via biographical vignettes to three men (Rembrandt, Picasso and Jung), and then in his somewhat unconvincing attempt to justify this decision not to discuss at least one woman (he mentions in passing Eleanor Roosevelt, Georgia O'Keefe and Frieda Kahlo as possible candidates) by referring to "limitations of time and space" (Stein 1998: 109). In fact, the question of whether there is a specifically female initiatory process is never broached in his book, and its references to "adult" imago and "human" transformation avoid the issue, even when he uses women's dreams as material for discussion.

Yet Murray Stein's recent book, however problematic its gender-free universalism may be, has many merits, including the marking and naming of a key element of midlife metamorphosis: the *transformative images* that preside over inner change at midlife. Stein defines them as "images [that] arise from the archetypal collective unconscious—whether 'inner' or 'outer' is immaterial"—that "create the bridge between the old psychological constellation and the new one" (Stein 1998: 109). His idea seems to me to be a refinement of Jung's theory of the transcendent function, according to which the unconscious can spontaneously provide a compensatory symbolic image, which can serve as a catalyst for the resolution of a near intolerable conflict in an individual's psychic life. Stein gives a striking example of this from the life of William Mellon, heir to a great family fortune, who at age thirty-seven read in a magazine article about the life work of Albert Schweitzer, and immediately became inspired, deciding that he too wished to found a hospital caring for people in the Third World. He then wrote Schweitzer a letter, followed his advice, went to medical school and dedicated the rest of his life to founding and fostering the growth of the Albert Schweitzer Hospital in Haiti. It was thus a transformative image of Albert Schweitzer that was to become the catalyst for the radical reorientation of William Mellon's life and its extraordinary transformation at midlife (Stein 1998: 39–40). In Mellon's particular case, the origins of the image came from the outside world: a magazine article, probably some photographs of Schweitzer at work, and then a letter from Schweitzer himself. This outer image created in his mind a powerful corresponding inner fantasy concerning Schweitzer, which was to change his life completely.

But transformative images can equally well arise from the inside, and thus may appear first in significant dreams, or in the practice of deliberate fantasy generation—what Jungians call "active imagination." In Jung's own case, the account, in his autobiography *Memories, Dreams, Reflections* (1963), of a sequence of transformative images, will be of great usefulness for my analysis of literary works representing symbolically the inner psychic drama of the male midlife process. This particular section of Jung's autobiography constitutes a prime example of an oneiric text, that is, a description of a dream or fantasy sequence organized around striking transformative images. Oneiric texts are narratives of a special sort, with a high symbolic hermeneutical potential. They can be found not only in accounts of actual dreams and fantasies in psychoanalytical studies, but also in literary narrative and cinematic texts. In the latter, the raw, unvarnished quality of the case study descriptions of dreams is given esthetic elaboration, which may mask to some degree the archetypal dimensions of the description. Oneiric texts thus include not only write ups of such archetypal dreams, but also literary and film texts that recreate the visionary effect of this type of dream in the context of an ongoing narrative or dramatic sequence. Reading such texts as oneiric texts highlights the presence within them of the archetypal subtexts that give them their visionary power—their sometimes almost hallucinatory effect.

We will now turn to Jung's key midlife oneiric text—the much later write up in his autobiography *Memories, Dreams, Reflections* of the sequence of dreams and waking visions that had propelled him almost fifty years before into a full blown midlife crisis and a near psychotic breakdown. The sequence is invaluable for the way it sets up via powerful transformative images five potentially major themes of male midlife transformation:

1   The demise or diminishment at midlife of the youthful and blindly self-assertive heroic attitude.
2   The problematic coming to consciousness of the shadow (the repressed contents of the personal unconscious).
3   The resurgence of a man's feminine side (his "anima," in Jungian terms).
4   The appearance of a midlife mentor.
5   The acquisition of a new sense of identity.

I will assume—and this is perhaps a controversial assumption—that Jung's visionary experiences indicated symbolically not only what was going on in his own psyche at that time, but also provided valuable insights into the psyche of men in general (whether of women in general is another question). In other words, if one accepts the possibility that Jung's archetypal dreams constituted objective knowledge of certain aspects of the psyche—that is, that they were visions into the objective, collective nature of the psyche, the collective unconscious—then Jung's oneiric text and the transformative images it contains may be taken as a paradigm or template for the archetypal, quasi-instinctual process of the male midlife transformation, not just for Jung himself, but for men in general. One would then expect to find other oneiric texts—literary and film texts that can be read and interpreted somewhat as though they were dreams—that would confirm, to some degree at least, the general validity of Jung's descriptions. (I will assume that the corresponding template for a woman's midlife transformation may differ, perhaps in significant ways, from the male paradigm, and will consider this topic later.)

One major transformative image presiding over Jung's entry into a full-blown midlife crisis is that of the murder of the Germanic hero Siegfried. Jung's dream occurred on December 18, 1913, and he later described it as follows:

> I was with an unknown, brown-skinned man, a savage, in a lonely rocky mountain landscape. It was before dawn; the eastern sky was already bright, and the stars fading. Then I heard Siegfried's horn sounding over the mountains, and I knew that we had to kill him. We were armed with rifles and lay in wait for him on a narrow path over the rocks. Then Siegfried appeared high up on the crest of the mountain, in the first ray of the rising sun. On a chariot made of the bones of the dead he drove at a furious speed down the precipitous

slope. When he turned a corner, we shot at him, and he plunged down, struck dead.

(Jung 1963: 180)

In Jung's later interpretation of his dream, he saw Siegfried as symbolizing two things. First of all, he symbolized "what the Germans [just before the opening of World War I] want to achieve, heroically to impose their will" (Jung 1963: 180)—thus far, nothing of great psychological interest.[2] But his second interpretation of his Siegfried dream can be said to mark a moment of discovery in the history of analytical psychology. Jung believed he had discovered, first for himself, but also by extension for other men, that the heroic myth, however necessary it may be in a man's youth (since a young man must struggle to "impose himself"—to win his way in the world—or remain always in a state of infantile dependency), can turn sour at midlife.

Jung's emotional reaction to the dream murder of Siegfried was at first fraught with guilt and anxiety:

> After the deed I felt an overpowering compassion, as though I myself had been shot: a sign of my secret identity with Siegfried, as well as the grief a man feels when he is forced to sacrifice his ideal and his conscious attitudes. This identity and my heroic idealism had to be abandoned, for there are higher things than the ego's will, and to these one must bow.
>
> (Jung 1963: 180–181)

In Jung's personal case, the analogy between the figure in the dream of the Germanic hero Siegfried and himself (his "secret identity with Siegfried") seems clear enough: as the heir apparent of the Freudian movement, his fellow Freudians had called him their "gigantic blond Siegfried" (Wehr 1987: 180), and it was this privileged role of the young hero of the Freudian movement that he had relinquished by breaking with Freud earlier that year. In the dream's symbolic language, he had "killed Siegfried."[3]

Once Jung had awoken from this dream, he found himself unable to make sense out of it and tried to go back to sleep:

> but a voice within me said, "You *must* understand the dream, and must do so at once!" The inner urgency mounted until the terrible moment came when the voice said, "If you do not understand the dream, you must shoot yourself!" In the drawer of my night table lay a loaded revolver, and I became frightened.
>
> (Jung 1963: 181)

Thus Jung's experience of this transformative image of the murdered Siegfried was also accompanied by the threat of death to himself, and this in itself is highly significant. Transformation means not only the acquisition of a new identity but also the loss of an old one—metaphorically, the death of the older self in the form of Siegfried—and this threat of death points to an obvious initiatory element in midlife transformation. In youth initiation rites, as described by the anthropologist Arnold van Gennep in his now classic *The Rites of Passage* (*Les rites de passage*, 1908), the element of symbolic death can play a significant role, even to the extent that

> in some tribes the novice is considered dead, and he remains dead for the duration of the novitiate. It lasts for a fairly long time and consists of a physical and mental weakening which is undoubtedly intended to make him lose all recollection of his childhood existence. Then follows the positive part: instruction in tribal law and a gradual education as the novice witnesses totem ceremonies, recitations of myth, etc. . . . When the novice is considered dead, he is resurrected and taught how to live, but differently than in childhood.
>
> (van Gennep 1960: 75)

From a Jungian perspective, there is good reason to think that all rites of passage organized collectively as rituals by archaic societies as well as the inner experiences of modern individuals without such ritually structured scenarios are based on an archetypal template that is activated when there is a need to move from one stage of life to another, including the midlife transition from youth to mature adulthood, and from an already established type of identity to a new one. Thus Jung's first visionary experience, which was the prelude to his vision of the murdered Siegfried six days later, was clearly initiatory in character. Jung had sat down alone at his desk and allowed himself to feel himself dropping into dark depths; eventually he saw the vision of a corpse floating by:

> A youth with blond hair and a wound in the head. He was followed by a gigantic black scarab and then by a red, newborn sun, rising out of the depths of the water. . . . I was stunned by this vision. I realized, of course, that it was a hero and solar myth, a drama of death and renewal, the rebirth symbolized by the Egyptian scarab.
>
> (Jung 1963: 181)

The next set of Jung's fantasies (accompanied this time by active imagination[4] on his part) concerned a *katabasis*, a descent into the underworld of the unconscious—and a *nekyia*, a journey to the Land of the Dead. In its intriguing symbolism and images are found two more themes of great potential importance for a man facing the transition to midlife: the coming to consciousness of his inner femininity (the anima) and the appearance of a midlife mentor. After what seemed like a descent of about one thousand feet, Jung felt as though he were on the edge of a cosmic abyss:

> First came the image of a crater, and I had the feeling that I was in the land of the dead. The atmosphere was that of the other world. Near the steep slope of a rock I caught sight of two figures: an old man with a white beard and a beautiful young girl. I summoned up my courage and approached them as though they were real people [a primary technique of Jungian active imagination being active engagement with fantasy figures as though they were real], and listened attentively to what they told me. The old man explained that he was Elijah, and that gave me a shock. But the girl staggered me even more, for she called herself Salome! She was blind. . . . They had a black snake living with them which displayed an unmistakable fondness for me.
>
> (Jung 1963: 187)

The image of Salome, a figure from the New Testament represented in Jung's vision as blind, embodies a resurgence of the feminine at midlife, that feminine side of the man that, in the process of constructing his male gender identity and social persona, has been repressed and left undeveloped. Given the biblical origin of Salome in the figure of the female nemesis of John the Baptist, whose head she had demanded on a platter, it is understandable that Jung adds that he was "distinctly suspicious" of her (Jung 1963: 181). The *anima*, Jung's term for such an image of a man's own repressed feminine side, is grounded in the psychobiological contrasexual archetypal feminine, and is thus both individual—a female subpersonality whose specific characteristics vary from man to man—and collective, that is, a representation of what Goethe called the Eternal Feminine (*das Ewig Weibliche*), whose ultimate function is to serve as a bridge to the collective unconscious. The *anima* is potentially many sided. She can be helpful, like Dante's Beatrice (a transformative image for Dante based on a memory of a young woman with whom he had never even had a conversation); she can be tricky and devious, like Kirkê in the *Odyssey*; and at her worst she can be a *femme fatale* of the psyche, who may lure a man into madness and death. But in whatever form she may appear, she teaches a man something about the femininity he has locked up inside himself and has only until then experienced through blind projection onto the world and through the subsequent infatuation with women, who can appear to him as sweetheart angels or demon bitches or as both at the same time, according to the positive and/or negative nature of the projection. Jung's "suspicion" regarding Salome underlines this ambiguous status of the psychic feminine in a man's life. Her blindness may also point to something lacking in her from the standpoint of reliable wisdom and guidance.

Jung's Salome appeared in the company of an old man with a white beard, who identified himself as Elijah; Jung felt he was worthier of trust than Salome. "Elijah and I had a long conversation" (Jung 1963: 181), he wrote later, adding, somewhat humorously, that it was a conversation he could make no sense out of. The figure of Elijah represented the first appearance in Jung's psychic life of a midlife mentor, a figure who can communicate (if only one can understand him!) the wisdom necessary for a man's trans-formation at midlife. Such a figure, as we have seen, was represented for William Mellon by Albert Schweitzer, who was both a real doctor who wrote him a short handwritten letter that urged him to go to medical school, and an inspirational figure—a secular saint, not only for Mellon, but for many people in the modern world. For Mellon, he was also a transformative image that helped unleash the energy and resolve that changed his life.

But Elijah was not enough of a mentor for Jung, since Jung was unable to understand anything he said. So another figure, Jung recounts, devel-oped out of the Elijah figure, this time pagan rather than biblical. (Jung's distrust of the value of his family's ingrained Protestantism is perhaps evident here.) He called the figure Philemon (a classical Greek name) and, writes Jung, "he brought with him an Egyptian-Hellenistic atmosphere with a Gnostic coloration." Philemon became a genuine mentoring figure for Jung: "in my fantasies I held conversations with him, and he said things which I had not consciously thought" (Jung 1963: 182). Philemon was the one he credits with teaching him about the objective nature of the psyche, and this resulted ultimately in Jung's theory of the collective unconscious, a theory that challenged the assumptions of the erstwhile mentor of his youth and early professional success, Sigmund Freud, for whom unconscious contents of the psyche could only be the results of the repression of an individual's memories of conscious experiences. In relation to Freud, the mentor of his earlier years, Philemon represented for Jung "superior insight" (Jung 1963: 183)—"superior" in the first instance, one imagines, to Freud's. But the whole experience of this first encounter with the collective unconscious was still painful for Jung, who felt himself to be awash in powerful images from the unconscious that nearly overwhelmed him. Anthony Storr, as we have seen, has characterized this period as a near psychotic breakdown, and Jung's ordeal should be a reminder that the midlife crisis, like any crisis leading to transformation, can have painful and even excruciatingly painful dimensions. "In my darkness," wrote Jung,

> I could have wished for nothing better than a real, live guru, someone possessing knowledge and ability, who would have disentangled for me the involuntary creations of my imagination. . . . In the absence of a living figure who could pick up where Freud left off, this task was undertaken by Philemon.
>
> (Jung 1963: 184)

But this salutary midlife mentoring task was undertaken for Jung's benefit not only by the "ghostly guru" Philemon, if the truth were told, but also by a woman in flesh and blood. Toni Wolff, first Jung's analysand and student and then lifelong friend and lover, played an equally important role as his midlife mentor, especially as regards the practical side of surviving a near psychotic breakdown. Jung, like many European men of his class and generation, was careful to hide his private life from public gaze, although his lifelong liaison with Toni Wolff was an open secret for his entourage in Zurich. She was later known as an extraordinarily good therapist in her own right. Although she had herself not ventured deeply into the unconscious, she had an extraordinary mediumistic ability to guide others into it and back again safely. She was as instrumental as Philemon, if not more so, in pulling Jung out of the dangerous situation in which he felt he was near to drowning in an apparently endless flood of images from the collective unconscious.

Although Jung avoids all mention of her in his autobiography, Toni Wolff's "rescue" of Jung is alluded to covertly in one of its most fascinating episodes. The section of *Memories, Dreams, Reflections* that recounts a trip Jung took to Ravenna, Italy, with an unnamed friend, describes in detail his visit to the fifth-century tomb of Galla Placidia and the Baptistery of the Orthodox, where he was especially impressed by four wonderful mosaics that he did not remember having seen in an earlier visit twenty years before in 1913.The fourth mosaic, he later wrote,

> was the most impressive of all. . . . It represented Christ holding out his hand to Peter, who was sinking beneath the waves. We stopped in front of this mosaic for at least twenty minutes and discussed the original ritual of baptism, especially the curious archaic conception of it as an initiation connected with real peril of death. Such initiations were often connected with the peril of death and so served to express the archetypal idea of death and rebirth. Baptism had originally been a real submersion which at least suggested the danger of drowning.
>
> (Jung 1963: 285)

As they soon found out, the particular mosaics they had admired so much together did not actually exist. After his return to Zurich, Jung asked another friend, who had also scheduled a visit to Ravenna, to bring back postcards of these mosaics, since he had been unable to find any himself. But his friend returned and reported that, not only were there no postcards, but the mosaics themselves were simply not there! Although this explained why Jung had not noticed the mosaics during his first visit in 1913, Jung was still quite astonished, since his visual memory of them was so vivid, and, he recalled, "the lady who had been there with me long refused to believe that what she had 'seen with her own eyes' had not existed" (Jung

1963: 285). This lady was in fact Toni Wolff (Molton and Sikes 2011: 244)[5] and what she and Jung had experienced together in the Baptistery of the Orthodox had evidently been a vision or hallucination *à deux*. "It was," wrote Jung much later in his autobiography, "among the most curious events in my life," adding that "it can scarcely be explained," after which he starts to run on about mosaics that might have burned in the early Middle Ages, without adding anything in the way of psychological interpretation at all. He mentions only—intriguingly and tantalizingly—that "I had actually had a brush with those perils which I saw represented in the mosaics. I had come close to drowning" (Jung 1963: 286), but says nothing about who might have played Christ to his drowning Peter. But the explanation, once one knows who the lady was and what her earlier role had been in Jung's desperate years twenty years before, is obvious to the reader and must have been obvious to Jung as well, although he chose not to make his interpretation public in his autobiography. It is clear that the vision of the mosaic concerning Christ's rescue of Peter drowning had represented symbolically for both of them the fact that it was Toni Wolff who had rescued Jung from drowning in the flood of unconscious images which had brought about his near psychotic breakdown starting in 1913; and that, in so doing, she had played a major role as a midlife mentor for him.

By way of providing a striking parallel with Jung's experience of the simultaneous appearance of both an anima figure and a midlife mentor, I would like to turn to an episode recounted in the fourteenth-century Italian poet Petrarch's book *The Secret* (*Secretum*). In it he evokes the arrival of the beautiful young virgin whose name is Truth, who brings with her "an aged man, venerable and majestic" (Petrarch 2003: 86), a mentoring figure he calls "Saint Augustine," who both resembles and differs from the actual historical figure of one of the chief fathers of the Church. Petrarch's narrative stands as a clear antecedent for Jung's description of his waking vision of Salome and Elijah, and Petrarch's conversations with Augustine provide a startling precedent for Jung's own conversations with Philemon (although there is no evidence that Jung was acquainted with this particular work of Petrarch's). The Italian poet wrote down these conversations as a kind of memorial for the help he received from a "ghostly guru" at a critical moment of his midlife *enantiodromia*. Although the text is a literary fantasy, and modeled on the philosophical dialogue form originated by Plato and carried on by Petrarch's great Roman culture hero Cicero, it surely has its roots in Petrarch's inner psychological life and experience. *The Secret* was written between 1346 and 1353, but refers back to the period around 1342–3, when the poet was almost forty years old. Until that time, he had been obsessed night and day with his beloved Laura de Noves, dedicating an immense amount of youthful energy and poetry to an attempt to win her affections. But, however enriching all this amorous enthusiasm and anima infatuation were for his poetic genius, any expectation of a flesh and blood relationship was ultimately doomed to frustration. As he reached the age of forty, he increasingly felt that he was wasting his time with Laura, and fell into a deep depression.

Petrarch's account of his midlife transformation in the *Secretum* begins with an account of this depression, which his mentor figure and ghostly guru Saint Augustine labels *acedia* (listlessness or torpor) or *aegritudo* (grief or sorrow), but which had symptoms that went beyond mere lethargy and spiritual dryness. Petrarch has his namesake Franciscus describe its effects in this way: "everything is sad, hard, miserable and horrific." It is a disease, he says, where "the road to despair beckons relentlessly, and [where] everything colludes to push unhappy souls to self-destruction" (Petrarch 2003: 90). Saint Augustine's first task as midlife mentor is thus to lighten the burden of Petrarch's depression and suicidal despair. By the end of the second chapter Petrarch can claim that, thanks to their philosophic dialoguing and spiritual conversations, he is ready to live more philosophically, accepting the necessary sorrows of life with better grace.

But chapter three opens up a totally new and unexpected perspective. A deeper analysis of the cause of his depression, according to Augustine, leads to the conclusion that it lies in his love for Laura. Franciscus defends himself vigorously against this accusation:

> Whatever worthiness you see in me I possess because of her, and I never would have attained whatever reputation or glory I now have if she had not nobly cultivated the fragile seed of virtue that nature had placed in my breast.
>
> (Petrarch 2003: 110)

In the end Franciscus is forced to yield to Augustine's insistence that this noble love was merely disguised enslavement to a woman's charm:

> this claim that she taught you to focus on higher things and that she took you away from the common lot of humans really means only that you sat at her feet, captivated by her sweetness alone, assiduously neglecting and utterly contemptuous of everything else.
>
> (Petrarch 2003: 111)

Petrarch is thus brought to a near total reversal of his youthful values—values that were oriented around his love for Laura and the poetic career for which he experienced her as the primary inspiration, given the role of creative anima figure and Muse that he had projected onto her. Now, at midlife, he sees his new life's path as one of spiritual struggle, and of a new concern for the life of the soul that is introspective and meditative in nature. Abandoning the role of the young lover he had celebrated in his verse, he declares that "I will collect the scattered fragments of my soul, and I will diligently focus on myself alone" (Petrarch 2003: 147).

To the extent that we take Jung's midlife initiation as potentially paradigmatic for many men at midlife—in other words, to the extent that it was a personal experience rooted in an archetypal and collective initiatory pattern that included the peril of death and the appearance of a mentoring figure or guide—it is clear that a man's midlife mentor can be a female figure like Toni Wolff just as well as a male figure like Jung's Philemon, Mellon's Albert Schweitzer or Petrarch's Saint Augustine. This should come as no surprise, for midlife initiations are likely to turn out to be different from the familiar patterns of traditional and more ritualized initiations of youth into adulthood. Since the establishment of a solid social and gender identity is the main goal of these earlier youth initiations, it is not surprising that, in traditional societies where male and female worlds demanded different skills and presented different challenges for young adults, the mentors for boys would be older men and the mentors for girls would be older women. At midlife, however, the major goal for an adult is not to forge a primary social identity (this would already have been done), but rather to develop cultural capacities that would bring into functioning aspects of human potential neglected in youth, especially generative and contrasexual qualities. For this purpose, a female mentor might well play as important a role for a man at midlife as a male mentor. Such, for example, seems to have been the case with Socrates as he is represented in Plato's *Symposium*, where he tells his circle of male friends and associates that his great teacher when it came to understanding love and sexuality had been the woman Diotima. Since he is talking about something that was obviously of great importance to his development as a man and as a philosopher, one can easily see the parallel with Jung and Toni Wolff.

In most pre-modern societies there was a need for young people to assume the status of adults as soon as possible; given the many dangers threatening the welfare of a tribal society, there could be no delay in young people assuming their roles in adult society. So it made sense that youth initiations would be carried out over a relatively short period of time and would be marked by dramatic and often perilous ritual activity. We can assume that midlife initiations, by contrast, might occupy a longer time frame, since the goal is culture building and not adaptation for survival; in that case, it would be likely to involve gradual process rather than quick transition. The process could well extend even over years, and would contrast vividly with the rather quick and abrupt initiation of youth into early adulthood.

The goal of any stage of life initiation is the establishment of a new identity, and as regards this new identity, Jung's autobiography does not make explicit this final and key element in its long description of the transformative images that presided over his midlife transformation. But

Stein (Stein 1998: 43–45) points out how Richard Noll (Noll 1994) had called attention to the fact that the sections in Jung's autobiography *Memories, Dreams, Reflections* dealing with his near psychotic breakdown after he had ceased relations with Freud do not tell the whole story of the images and fantasies that began his own process of midlife transformation, a process that began in 1913 and would not be complete until about 1920 (that is between ages thirty-eight and forty-five), when Jung finally emerged from the pain and confusion of his midlife crisis and emerged as the generative psychologist he was to continue to be for the rest of his life. The particular fantasy, which the autobiography omits and which Noll has highlighted, occurred in December 1913, a few nights after the initial fantasy of Salome. Jung was to describe it at length over ten years later to a group of his students in a seminar given in English, notes of which were later published as *Analytical Psychology: Notes of the Seminar Given in 1925*:

> Then a most a most disagreeable thing happened. Salome became very interested in me, and she assumed that I could cure her blindness. She began to worship me. I said, "Why do you worship me?" She replied, "You are Christ." In spite of my objections she maintained this. I said, "This is madness," and became filled with skeptical resistance. Then I saw the snake [the black snake of the first fantasy, who reappears with its head now turned white after being defeated by a white snake] approach me. She came close and began to encircle me and press me in her coils. The coils reached up to my heart. I realized as I struggled that I had assumed the attitude of the Crucifixion. In the agony and the struggle, I sweated so profusely that the water flowed down on all sides of me. Then [the blind] Salome rose, and she could see. While the snake was pressing me, I felt my face had taken on the face of an animal of prey, a lion or a tiger.
>
> (Jung 1989a: 96)

In his interpretation of this fantasy, Jung draws a comparison with the "mysteries of deification" that gave the reborn initiate a sense of immortality. The actual transformation the snake induced in him through its pressure was both a transformation into the crucified Christ as well as into the lion-headed god (*Deus Leontophorus*) of the Mithraic mysteries, "the figure which is represented with a snake coiled around the man, the snake's head resting on the man's head, and the face of the man that of a lion" (Jung 1989a: 98). Jung underlines the Mithraic context of the fantasy, but it is possible to seek a more specific explanation of the meaning that this adult imago would have had for him personally, whose significance is underscored by the care with which he presented to his seminar group in 1925, about twelve years after the event. The process of midlife initiatory death and rebirth is certainly inherent in the crucifixion motif. Jung wrote later in his autobiography that this "integration of unconscious contents made an essential contribution to the completion of my personality" (Jung 1963: 286), but remained vague as to what specifically that completion entailed for him personally, stating only that "we have a particular feeling about ourselves about the way we are" and "we convey a particular feeling to others" (Jung 1963: 287). Murray Stein has gone into great detail concerning the process of how "the adult imago functions to express and orient the manifestations of psychic energy" at midlife (Stein 1998: 108). In the case of the lion-headed crucified god in the coils of a snake, the iconographic significance may be both Christian and Mithraic in origin, but what might have been the exact personal relevance for Jung of this powerful image? I would speculate that Jung was to come into his own as a psychologist for whose system the religious instinct (emblematized by the crucifixion) was to become as important as the sexual instinct was for Freud's; for Jung, transformation at midlife frequently involved an awakening of this need to find a spiritual orientation. As for the "lion-headed god," the self-imposing heroic attitude that Jung had let go of in the form of the youthful hero Siegfried is replaced in the fantasy by a mature form of spiritual heroism symbolized both by Christ and by the lion. It is an "adult imago" that combines spirituality, generative suffering, and a new kind of midlife heroism. It represents rather exactly Jung's new identity at midlife.

If Jung is correct in asserting that the structures of the deep unconscious are common to all human beings, then one would expect there to be a great deal of evidence concerning midlife transformations and its associated psychic imagery in cultures distant in time and/or in space. But although modern anthropology has uncovered an enormous amount of material associated with youth initiation, it has almost totally neglected the topic of midlife initiation. The reason for this is primarily the apparent absence of midlife rituals corresponding to those of youth initiations. But here anthropology has perhaps overlooked the possibility that the rituals designed to initiate young people also involved the active participation of older people in a way that was initiatory for them as well, but in a different way. The adults' participation has been viewed only in terms of its relevance to the initiated youth, not in terms of its transformational potential for the older people themselves, who presided over, and directed, the ritual process. I would maintain that these youth initiation rituals thus had a hidden or at least less obvious dimension, which was the significant effect of the ritual on the older people themselves. Initiating young people into adulthood was preeminently a *generative* act. It confirmed not only the new young adult status of the children, but also the older adult status of the initiating elders. Thus a midlife ritual is present but invisible in the rituals seemingly associated only with the initiation of youth. The elders themselves were active participants in a ritual celebrating change and transformation, but were they not themselves changed and transformed in the process? Was the youth initiation not also a midlife initiation for the elders and the mentors?

There is of course another possibility, which is that the midlife transition was simply less heavily ritualized than that of childhood to adulthood in archaic societies, and that much of what took place in the men's secret societies and other such adult groupings constituted a kind of ongoing process of initiation over time, as for example in the rites and rituals of Freemasonry in modern times. If the transformation at midlife involved a slow process of maturation rather than a quick transition from boyhood to manhood, its ritual context would be much more spread over time and less dramatic and intense.

There is also a third possibility, one that does not exclude the other two, but the one that this book will tend to foreground, namely, that midlife has traditionally been the great age of culture building, and the much of its archetypal transformative imagery is to be found in cultural performances such as epic recitation and theater, rather than in ritual per se. Of course, both types of performance, both epic and dramatic, have a ritualized dimension, and although the listeners and spectators may seem to play a more passive role than participants in a ritual, this is not in and of itself a problem. In discussing the effect of ritualized performances, Jung had the following to say concerning "experiences induced by ritual":

> In these mystery-dramas the transcendence of life, as distinct from its momentary concrete manifestations, is usually represented by the fateful transformations—death and rebirth—of a god or godlike hero. The initiate may either be a mere witness of the divine drama or take part in it or be moved by it, or he may see himself identified through the ritual action with the god. In this case, what really matters is that an objective substance or form of life is ritually transformed through some process going on independently, while the initiate is influenced, impressed, "consecrated," or granted "divine grace" on the mere ground of his presence or participation. The transformation process takes place not within him but outside of him.
>
> (Jung 1971: 51)

Thus the audience of epic recitation, like the spectatorship of drama, may itself be theorized as the potential beneficiary, to some degree at least, of the represented transformational experience, without having to undergo the near psychotic breakdown and eventual radical change that might characterize an inner experience of the sort Jung described in his autobiography and in his 1925 seminar. If Alain de Botton (de Botton 1998) entitled his book amusingly *How Proust Can Change Your Life*, he was not altogether tongue-in-cheek, and it would be to lose faith entirely with the value of literature if one were to deny its potentially life-changing power. So we can assume that if Proust can change your life, at least to some degree, so can Homer or Shakespeare. Having granted the possibility of this kind of potentially transformative effect of a text upon its audience, we can feel confident in analyzing literary works and films as regards their oneiric representations (frequently in mythic and symbolic terms) of transformative images leading to midlife transformation. In other words, their effect on auditors, spectators, or readers may not only be esthetic, but also (if only indirectly) psychologically transformative, in that they have the power to awaken or "constellate" some of the structures of the psyche that preside over midlife transformation.

Of course, it would be to exaggerate the effect of literature on life to claim that literature can be a sufficient cause of radical transformation. Jung felt that the effect even of highly significant archetypal dreams was not in itself transformative:

> the most beautiful and impressive dreams often have no lasting or transformative effect on the dreamer. He may be impressed by them, but he does not necessarily see any problem in them. The event then naturally remains "outside," like a ritual action performed by others. *The more aesthetic forms of experience must be carefully distinguished from those which indubitably involve a change of one's nature.*
>
> (Jung 1971: 52, my emphasis)

However, even if one continues to doubt that literature can really *change* one's life, it is still not totally outlandish to expect that literature can *enlighten* one's life—that there is at least a potential cognitive benefit even when the transformative benefit may be weak or nonexistent. When a person is ready for change, literature and film may become contributive causes, if not sufficient causes, for midlife transformation. So learning something through literature and film about the nature of the archetypal structures of midlife transformation is certainly worth the trouble, although there is much pleasure as well. It may be easier to read about midlife transformation than to experience it, but psychological armchair tourism of this sort may wind up stimulating and informing the actual journey.

It is also possible that oneiric texts, myth related as they are, may have a real advantage over theoretical disquisitions, when it comes to stimulating change. Jung had reservations about the ultimate value and effect even of the theoretical terminology of his own analytical psychology:

> The protean mythologem and the shimmering symbol express the processes of the psyche far more trenchantly and, in the end, far more clearly than the clearest concept, for the symbol not only conveys a visualization of the process but—and this is perhaps just as

important—it also brings a re-experiencing of it, of that twilight which we can learn to understand only through inoffensive empathy, but which too much clarity only dispels.

(Jung 1968: 26)

The idea that a certain kind of literary or film text can be analyzed at times as though it were roughly analogous to the account of a dream, daydream or fantasy is found already in Freud's 1908 Essay "Creative Writers and Day-Dreaming" Freud's basic idea was that while a writer is indeed a daydreamer presenting his audience with personal wish fulfillment fantasies, it is the writer's esthetic talent that allows us to enjoy his personal fantasies as though they were our own, the formal qualities of the work serving as a means to overcome our reluctance to make contact with the private fantasies of another human being. Freud explains that "the essential *ars poetica* lies in the technique of overcoming the feeling of repulsion which is undoubtedly connected with the barriers that rise between each single ego and the others." (Gay 1995: 443).). The question still remains, however, as to how a private fantasy can not only be made palatable to another, but also convey meaning in such a way that the other feels enlightened and instructed. For Freud, this is not the issue; literature gives pleasure, and that is enough, since "our actual enjoyment of an imaginative work proceeds from a liberation of tensions in our minds." (Gay 1995: 443). Freud's idea is a somewhat trivializing restatement of Aristotle's theory of catharsis (according to which the goal of tragedy was the purging of an emotional overload of pity and fear), which he makes applicable to the imaginative arts in general. Literature, in other words, has nothing to teach, but it does make one feel more relaxed, since it enables us to enjoy daydreams that, if they were our own, would frequently prove embarrassing, and that, if we took as someone else's private fantasies, would frequently repulse us. Freud does, however, entertain the possibility that some fantasy is less personal in origin, since it would derive "from the popular treasure-house of myths, legends and fairy tales" (Gay 1995: 442) in which case all a writer has to do is to "re-fashion" this ready-made material. For Freud, this material is probably no more than "distorted vestiges of the wishful fantasies of whole nations – the *secular dreams* of youthful humanity" (Gay 1995: 442).

But Jungians would call such material "archetypal," and would value it highly for its capacity to stimulate awareness of the collective unconscious and of its fateful effect on human life and transformation.

Jung's analysis of his own 1913 dream in which he murdered Siegfried illustrated in fact both of the possibilities that Freud discussed several years earlier. Siegfried was on the one hand a negative wish fulfillment of Jung's anguished sense, after his break with Freud earlier that year, that he was finished as the young hero of the psychoanalytic movement, and that he had to abandon or "kill" any hope of continuing as a Freudian Siegfried.

On the other hand, Siegfried is ready-made material, part of the treasure-house of Germanic mythology, and as such represents the dangerous power drive of the Germans near the opening of World War I. But Jung took the analysis of the dream a step forward when he asserted that Siegfried represented "higher things than the ego's will"; in other words, an archetypal force "to which one must bow" (Jung 1963: 180), and not merely a figure symbolizing what Freud called sarcastically "His Majesty the Ego, the hero of every day-dream and every story" (Freud 1958: 51). Freud's position in 1908 that "we must separate writers who, like the ancient authors of epics and tragedies, take over their material ready-made, from writers who seem to originate their own material" (Freud 1958: 50) is also something that Jung took up and transformed in his 1930 essay "On the Relation of Analytical Psychology to Poetry," with his distinction between "psychological" and "visionary" writers. It is the second category that attracts his interest, and he attributes to it a function that goes far beyond simply refashioning ready-made material or creating material spontaneously. Visionary writers are the keepers of the gates of horn, and thus we all owe them a tremendous debt of gratitude for revealing the presence of the archetypal structures of the human psyche.

Oneiric texts are of almost infinite variety, but they have in common that they shed light on the deeper structures of psychic life. They provide a kind of vicarious experience of the archetypal world, and for that reason have not infrequently been taken as guides to living human life in depth. These are the types of texts I will be presenting in the following chapters, with the hope that my analysis will encourage readers to understand through the prism of art the emotional and intellectual dimensions of midlife transformation, and to experience, if only vicariously, some of its agony and wonder.

Notes

1 This is especially necessary now that recent research has begun the process of differentiating the two. *The Breaking Point* by Sue Shellenbarger (2004) was the book that first revealed to a larger public the growing consensus among professionals that women may have midlife crises and periods of midlife transformation that have some different characteristics from those of men.
2 In my opinion, it is one of Jung's more questionable procedures to present psychological material from his dreams and fantasies as prophetic of collective world historical happenings.
3 For an extensive interpretation of the Siegfried dream, see S.F. Walker 2002: 42–45 and 63–71.
4 "Active imagination" is a Jungian term for the conscious development and elaboration of a fantasy initially supplied by the unconscious.
5 See also Bair 2003: 729–730, n. 34.

Chapter 2

The shadow and the contrasexual side at midlife

Jung's midlife dreams and visions of December 1913, which we have been taking as a plausible paradigm for some of the archetypal structures of the male midlife transformation process, especially as regards the theme of the death of the young hero, included the figure of a "dwarf with a leathery skin, as if he were mummified" (Jung 1963: 179), along with the corresponding figure of "an unknown, brown-skinned man, a savage" (Jung 1963: 180). Jung identified both figures as symbolic representations of his shadow, the personified repository of everything his ego had repressed in his life. The two figures served as gatekeepers, so to speak, for the mysterious and dramatic core of the two visions: the appearance of the corpse of a youth with blond hair floating in the water, and then the murder of the Germanic hero Siegfried. The dwarf guarded the entrance to a dark cave, and Jung described how he had to squeeze past him in order to enter the cave. He also described how the savage was the one who had taken the initiative in plotting the death of Siegfried, a mythic scene that, as we have seen, was of crucial importance for Jung's coming to terms, not only with his traumatic break with Freud, but also with his relinquishment of the role of the young hero of the Freudian movement. Although the figures of the dwarf and the savage appeared primarily as unpleasant and disturbing figures, they also supplied a kind of wisdom (the mummified ancient Egyptian aspect of the dwarf) and a kind of fierce energy (the savage's murderous plot) that symbolized the new kind of wisdom that enabled Jung to discover things that Freudian psychology could not explain, and to finalize his break with the mentor of his youth and with his status as the crown prince of the Freudian movement.

Jung frequently emphasized that dealing with one's shadow is a work of moral self-examination—of being honest with oneself about oneself—that can be painful, boring or stressing, but is always necessary in order to maintain one's psychic equilibrium through the recognition in oneself of repressed unconscious contents. The continuing need to know oneself better, especially as regards the dark corners of one's personality that one would be happy to ignore and to have others ignore as well, is part of good psychological hygiene, and is appropriate at all times and at any age. But there is another side to the shadow that has specific reference to midlife, which can lie in discovering new perspectives on life and new energies with which to engage with life more vigorously. The appearance of the shadow releases repressed shadow energies that can propel a person into a new stage of life. Jung himself was to say later that, thanks to these dreams, "new forces were released in me which helped me to carry the experiment with the unconscious to a conclusion" (Jung 1963: 181).

A similar influx of new psychic energy at midlife was occasioned for Robert Louis Stevenson by a nightmare he had had in the fall of 1885, when he was almost thirty-five. The resulting novella *The Strange Case of Dr. Jekyll and Mr. Hyde* (1886), a powerful oneiric text about an encounter with the shadow that turns disastrous, has a back story that one might entitle "The Strange Case of Robert Louis Stevenson." Stevenson's health had always been fragile, and he had been sick and confined to his room when he had the nightmare that inspired him to write what turned out to be his most popular piece of fiction. When writing the tale based on the original dream, he found himself borne along by an unusual influx of energy that allowed the bedridden author to produce over ten thousand words of text per day over a period of three days. The case gets stranger still, however. According to the later account of his stepson, Lloyd Osbourne, the nightmarish tale so offended the moral sensitivities of his wife, Fanny, that Stevenson threw the manuscript furiously into the fire, and then rewrote it over the next three days at an equally feverish pace, but now as a moralizing allegory warning of the dangers of recklessly experimenting with human nature. The amount of energy that the composition of this tale released in the sickly author was truly extraordinary. Lloyd Osbourne recalled the whole episode years with wonder:

> The writing of it was an astounding feat from whatever aspect it may be regarded. Sixty-thousand words in six days; more than ten thousand words a day. To those who know little of such things, I may explain that a thousand words a day is a fair average for any writer of fiction. Anthony Trollope set himself this quota; it was Jack London's; it is— and has been—a sort of standard of daily literary accomplishment. Stevenson multiplied it by ten; and on top of that copied out the whole in another two days, and had it in the post on the third! It was a stupendous achievement, and the strange thing was that, instead of showing lassitude afterward, he seemed positively refreshed and revitalized; went about with a happy air; was as uplifted as though he had come into a fortune; looked better than he had in months.
>
> (Stevenson 1999: 135)

It is this rewritten version of the tale that we have today, and to some degree one misses in it what one imagines must have been the raw amoral energy of the original version based directly on the nightmare. Still, toned down and domesticated as it was, Stevenson's tale was immediately success-ful, partly because it spared its Victorian readers' sensibilities in a way that his wife Fanny rightly felt would be necessary. It even became a topic for some ministers' sermons! But *The Times* reviewer also correctly saw in it "a flash of intuitive psychological research, dashed off in a burst of inspiration" (Stevenson 1999: 136). Reading the tale today as an oneiric text has the advantage of restoring to it some of its original shock value as a text inspired by a nightmare of great psychological intensity and significance. In fact, Stevenson's text encourages a kind of reading between the lines that brings out the latent psychological symbolic content as opposed to the overt moral dimension of the work. It is a text that gives a mythological representation of the shadow that, in spite of its overlay of Victorian moralizing, has kept its capacity to shock the reader into an awareness of the highly problematic nature of one man's encounter at midlife with his shadow. It provides a useful psychological lesson through negative example. If, like Dr. Jekyll, a man were to become aware of his shadow at midlife and then, unlike Dr. Jekyll, does not persist in identifying himself with it, but rather thoughtfully integrates some of it into his life, the results of such an encounter with the shadow at midlife could be revitalizing and beneficial rather than, as in Stevenson's tale, depressing and catastrophic. However, since depression and catastrophe at midlife are not uncommon, *The Strange Case of Dr. Jekyll and Mr. Hyde* turns out not to be so strange after all.

In a letter to a friend, Stevenson revealed that Dostoevsky's novel *Crime and Punishment* and its hero Raskolnikoff had had an almost visceral impact on his imagination:

> Raskolnikoff [*Crime and Punishment*] is easily the greatest book I have read in ten years; I am glad you took to it. Many find it dull; Henry James could not finish it: all I can say is, it nearly finished me. It was like having an illness.
>
> (Stevenson 1999: 127)

And one can easily see why Stevenson was so disturbed. In the Russian novel, the young man Raskolnikoff succumbs to the idea that he is somehow beyond good and evil, and so he kills his avaricious landlady in order to prove to himself that he is capable of committing murder without suffering the pangs of conscience. In the end, however, the memory of this remorseless crime is not something he can live with, and so he is eventually driven to repent and to confess the murder publicly. One could say that Raskolnikoff had identified himself initially with the psychopathic side of his shadow, and so had acted out a shadow-inspired crime in a spirit of total amorality that he could not wind up maintaining for long. His ambition to go beyond the all-too-human concern with morality was doomed to failure, precisely because he was *not* a psychopath, but rather someone whose shadow contained a strong psychopathic streak.

Like Raskolnikoff, Dr. Jekyll aspires to transcend the normal human condition. He believes that, through a chemical potion he has devised in his private laboratory, he can change himself temporarily into another person, that is, Mr. Hyde. As this other person, he can sally forth into the streets of London and do all kinds of immoral things without jeopardizing his social reputation as a respectable doctor. Unfortunately, Mr. Hyde, in spite of his suggestive name, turns out not to be as well hidden from public view as Jekyll had hoped. In fact, Hyde is all too conspicuous a figure, and inspires immediate fear and loathing in the people who cross his path. One of them says, after Hyde has been surrounded by a small crowd of witnesses after he accidentally knocked over a young girl in the street, "I never saw a man I so disliked, and yet I scarcely know why" (Stevenson 1999: 36). Yet Hyde does offer the middle-aged doctor the opportunity of feeling young again, and of sowing his wild oats again as he did in his youth. This is what the good doctor will miss most, he confesses: "the liberty, the comparative youth, the light step, leaping impulses and secret pleasures, that I had enjoyed in the disguise of Hyde" (Stevenson 1999: 84).

Thus Mr. Hyde does have a positive side, since he contains, as a representation of Dr. Jekyll's shadow, a kind of youthful vitality and *joie de vivre* that the good doctor repressed as he grew older and identified himself increasingly with his work and status as a respected physician. For Dr. Jekyll, the initial effects of living out this fun-loving side of his shadow were fairly innocuous. "The pleasures which I made haste to seek in my disguise," states Dr. Jekyll, "were . . . undignified; I would scarcely use a harder term" (Stevenson 1999: 81). Up to that point, at least, his collusion with Mr. Hyde—in psychological terms, his identification with his shadow—seemed to be a harmless game, with no serious personal repercussions. Dr. Jekyll had simply allowed him to become, as Hyde, a bit more relaxed and fun loving, and his time spent in the disguise of Mr. Hyde might have seemed a welcome and rejuvenating release of vital spirits for the good doctor encased in his mantel of Victorian respectability. As Jung wrote, the shadow, as the repository of repressed feelings and impulses—repressed in the interests of morality and social adaptation—should by no means be viewed as entirely evil:

> The shadow is merely somewhat inferior, primitive, unadapted and awkward; not wholly bad. It even contains childish and primitive qualities which would in a way vitalize and embellish human existence, but convention forbids!
>
> (Jung 1969: 134)

But this brief period of reliving the freedom and pleasures of his youth through the disguise of Mr. Hyde soon takes the good doctor far beyond the mere flouting of social convention. There is psychopathic cruelty lodged in the depths of the good doctor's shadow, and the plot thickens rapidly when a distinguished member of London high society, Sir Danvers Carew, is found brutally murdered in the street, his body dreadfully mangled. It is Mr. Hyde who is the perpetrator of this ghastly crime, as the reader finds out shortly, and Dr. Jekyll's shadow problem suddenly becomes tragically unmanageable. The figure of Mr. Hyde contains not only pleasure-loving impulses that can be satisfied without too much embarrassment (Stevenson, forced to observe Victorian proprieties, does not reveal what these might be: music halls? a bit of bordello hopping?), but also rage, aggressiveness and psychopathic indifference to the sufferings of others—exactly what one would naturally expect a good, caring physician to have repressed, since they would have interfered with his professional work and damaged his respectable social persona. Increasingly unable to prevent himself from metamorphosing unexpectedly and involuntarily into his nemesis, Mr. Hyde, Dr. Jekyll finally takes his own life in order to avoid discovery and disgrace.

But this melodramatic ending, morally uplifting as it is, nevertheless is not entirely satisfying from the psychological standpoint. One wonders whether suicide was really the only way out for Dr. Jekyll. The fantastic nature of the story (Jekyll can no longer control his chemically produced alter ego) does indeed set him up for this inevitability, but not without hinting at alternative perspectives on the problem of human evil and how its presence in the psyche can be managed. The key would be the careful integration of the shadow as opposed to its brutal repression or reckless expression. Jung, although he never downplayed the moral problem posed by the shadow, also insisted that the careful integration of some of its aspects could foster new psychological growth, especially at midlife.

Stevenson's anatomy of the shadow in *The Strange Case of Dr. Jekyll and Mr. Hyde* appears especially masterful, if one allows oneself to read between the lines of his text and to detect the presence of psychological insights the author only hints at prudently. The murder of the highly respectable Sir Danvers Carew may benefit in particular from this type of reading between the lines, as Stevenson's text suggests that this distinguished old gentleman may not have been as entirely respectable as he appeared to be to the naive and sentimental maid who witnessed his murder late at night from her moonlit balcony:

> Never (she used to say, with streaming tears, when she narrated that experience), never had she felt more at peace with all men or thought more kindly of the world. And as she so sat she became aware of an aged beautiful gentleman with white hair, drawing near along the lane; and advancing to meet him, another and very small gentleman, to whom at first she paid no attention. When they had come within speech

(which was just under the maid's eyes), the older man bowed and accosted the other with a very pretty manner of politeness. It did not seem as if the subject of his address were of great importance; indeed, from his pointing, it sometimes appeared as if he were only inquiring his way; but the moon shown on his face as he spoke, and the girl was pleased to watch it, it seemed to breathe such an innocent and old-world kindness of disposition, yet with something high too, as of a well-founded self-content.

Mr. Hyde, whom she had seen before, and "for whom she had conceived a dislike," had listened silently to the old gentleman's words, she remembers, "with an ill-contained impatience," and then

all of a sudden he broke out in a great flame of anger, stamping with his foot, brandishing his cane, and carrying on (as the maid described it) like a madman. The old gentleman took a step back, with the air of one surprised and a trifle hurt; and at that Mr. Hyde broke out of all bounds and clubbed him to the earth. And, next moment, with ape-like fury, he was trampling his victim under foot and hailing down a storm of blows, under which the bones were audibly shattered and the body jumped upon the roadway. At the horror of these sights and sounds, the maid fainted.

(Stevenson 1999: 46)

In what seems at first reading to be a piece of pure sensationalism, Stevenson has nevertheless loaded the dice against accepting the maid's story as the whole story. The maid is possibly as much of an unreliable narrator as the governess in Henry James's near contemporary tale *The Turn of the Screw*. Stevenson has emphasized throughout, and rather gratuitously, it would seem at first reading, that the scene is known to us only through how it had appeared to a moonstruck maid on her balcony. The phrases "she became aware," "it did not seem," "it sometimes appeared," and "it seemed to breathe" indicate the tentative and possibly unreliable nature of her perceptions. The maid herself is so clearly in a mood of wishing to see everything and everyone as bright and beautiful, especially the "aged beautiful gentleman," that the reader readily shares her point of view. But if one reads between the lines, it may be that she is wrong about some crucial aspect of the scene she has witnessed. If so, and if she is in fact an unreliable witness, what might actually have happened?

In his now classic study *The Other Victorians* (1966), Steven Marcus had revealed with great wealth of example what respectable Victorians—men, especially—wished to keep hidden about themselves, especially their secret lives of sexual indulgence and perversion. With Marcus's perspective in mind, the reader can speculate as to what the respectable white-haired gentleman, Sir Danvers, might have been doing out very late at night, when he accosted a young man in a lonely, dark London street. What was he asking him, or what was he proposing to him? Why was he pointing? Why did the young man—the "very small" gentleman—get into such a fury? Of course, the maid can only see this as a horrifying and unmotivated attack on a polite old gentleman who, in her fantasy, was probably only asking for directions. But Stevenson has her lay it on a bit too thick for the reader not to suspect that something may not be quite right with the old gentleman whose face, as far as the moonstruck maid is concerned, "seemed to breathe such an innocent and old-world kindness of disposition, yet with something high too, as of a well-founded self-content." The reader reading between the lines may thus glimpse in Sir Danvers the presence of "the other Victorian," prowling the London streets at night in a search for illicit sex. The beautiful old gentleman could just as well be an old degenerate who has learned to hide his forbidden desires carefully behind a mask of respectability; and the very small gentleman could be someone he mistakes—tragically—for a rent boy, who responds to his sexual proposition with indignant (and psychopathic) rage.

In this key scene of *The Strange Case of Dr. Jekyll and Mr. Hyde*, the respectable Sir Danvers may be suspected of acting out his shadow side just as much as the good Dr. Jekyll is acting out his, but without the benefit of an alter ego like Mr. Hyde to rely on as a near perfect disguise. Of course, it was Sir Danvers's tragic misfortune to have fallen on Mr. Hyde, who was not the rent boy he thought he was, and who was an aggressive young psychopath to boot, indifferent to the pain he could inflict, and even indifferent to committing murder. With its intimations of a pleasure-seeking nocturnal excursion gone terribly wrong, Sir Danvers's tragic death thus prefigures the tragedy of Dr. Jekyll's imminent death. For both respectable Victorian gentleman, but for different reasons, Mr. Hyde proves to be a fatal attraction. But the story of the murder of Sir Danvers Carew also allows Stevenson to make the point, at least for those readers who can read between the lines (and Stevenson does this without offending those Victorian readers who wish to see no more than what the maid thinks she has seen), that the shadow world is all around us, even in the most respectable of gentlemen. If even Sir Danvers can be suspected of having his own dark shadow, which he indulges as an "other Victorian," then so must everyone else. Thus what seems at first to be the "strange case" of Dr. Jekyll and Mr. Hyde turns out to be a "typical case," although Stevenson's oneiric text does not analyze it, but rather mythologizes it in a vividly symbolic mode.

If Sir Danvers may be said to represent the risk involved in living out shadow impulses, the lawyer Mr. Utterson represents a much more hopeful case of a man who seems to have managed to come to terms with his shadow and to integrate some of it harmoniously into his life. Mr.

Utterson cultivates an odd sort of friendship with his distant kinsman Mr. Richard Enfield. Many of those who know the two men wonder what they see in each other, as they take their weekly Sunday walks together, hardly speaking to each other and appearing rather bored with each other's company. Stevenson describes at length the nature of the bonds that have created this "odd couple" in the opening pages of his text, although it is not clear at first what this lengthy evocation of an unusual type of male bonding might have to do with his main subject. But, in retrospect, it is clear that their friendship is mutually beneficial, and that it provides in the text a counterbalancing example for the ill-fated Jekyll and Hyde relationship, for its dominant characteristic is to facilitate the integration of shadow contents, and not their repression or identification with them.

Utterson himself is described as rather frosty in temperament, but in his inner attitudes is said to be actually kind and benevolent towards his fellow human beings:

> He had an approved tolerance for others, sometimes wondering, almost with envy, at the high pressure of spirits involved in their misdeeds, and in any extremity inclined to help rather than to reprove. . . . it was frequently his fortune to be the last good influence in the lives of downgoing men.
>
> (Stevenson 1999: 31)

Utterson is thus presented as an "other Victorian" in a positive sense, that is, as someone who has so integrated his own shadow that he is able to avoid manifesting the mindless Victorian moralistic condemnation of others—one of the least pleasant results of unconscious shadow projection. Having accepted and come to terms with his own shadow side in his own dryly ascetic way (he is, for example, a potentially gluttonous lover of fine wines who consciously makes himself drink gin instead), he has ceased to be censorious towards others. For that reason, "lean, long, dusty" and "dreary" though he appears to be, he is "yet somehow loveable" (Stevenson 1999: 31). He is, in short, a man who has done well with the process of integrating his shadow, and who consequently not only feels at ease with himself, but also able to deal with others in a humane and tolerant manner.

Jung once evoked the intrapsychic figure representing the accumulated mass of repressed contents of an individual's personal unconscious as

> your brother, your shadow, the imperfect being in you that follows after and does everything which you are loathe to do, all the things you are too cowardly or too decent to do.
>
> (Jung 1984a: 76)

Utterson's friend and kinsman Mr. Enright can be said to embody symbolically just such an "imperfect being." He is described as a "well-known man about town" (Stevenson 1999: 31), and hence we may assume that he is pleasure loving in a way that contrasts vividly with the self-controlled and somewhat puritanical Mr. Utterson. We do not learn much more about him, although we do learn that he was one of those who witnessed the scene of Mr. Hyde apprehended after he had apparently trampled a young girl in the street. But his account of this incident reveals that, like the beautiful old gentleman of the moonstruck maid's narrative, he was probably out and about late at night for morally dubious reasons—reasons he delicately does not specify:

> I was coming home from some place at the end of the world, about three o'clock of a black winter morning, and my way lay through a part of town where there was literally nothing to be seen but lamps. Street after street and all the folks asleep—street after street, all lighted up as if for a procession and all as empty as a church—till at last I got into that state of mind where a man listens and listens and begins to long for the sight of a policeman.
>
> (Stevenson 1999: 33)

His words might suggest to an alert reader who can read a bit between the lines, that Mr. Enright, like Sir Danvers, may be one of those "other Victorians" prowling the midnight streets of London in search of illicit pleasures, and hence someone who is apparently the opposite of his quiet-living and even ascetic bachelor-lawyer friend Utterson, who, "though he enjoyed the theater, had not crossed the doors of one for twenty years" (Stevenson 1999: 31). But opposites frequently attract. For it is clear from Stevenson's description that Enfield lives out Utterson's own more disreputable "other Victorian" shadow side, just as Utterson lives out Enright's repressed respectable and ascetic side—the more positive dimension of his kinsman's shadow. Each gentleman has repressed in himself shadow qualities which, if carefully integrated, could have done much, as Jung asserted, to "vitalize and embellish" their lives. However, in the absence of the process of such conscious shadow integration, both do some of this shadow integration, however indirectly and unconsciously, through their carefully ritualized relationship—ritualized through their regular Sunday walks together (they observe the Sabbath in their own fashion, so to speak), which

> they counted the chief jewel of each week, and not only set aside occasions of pleasure, but even resisted the calls of business, that they might enjoy them uninterrupted.
>
> (Stevenson 1999: 32)

These dominical walks seemed to have been for a long time wonderfully therapeutic for both of them—better than going to church, Stevenson perhaps is intimating. Simply silently strolling together allowed them to participate in a dim awareness of their own shadow sides as embodied in a friend, and then to return to their workaday lives refreshed and invigorated. Even though in terms of ordinary social intercourse these walks may have seemed boring to others and even to each other as well, the two men speaking nary a word to each other during their excursions, it is no wonder that they valued them so highly. If only Dr. Jekyll had had such a friend! Instead, his shadow came roaring into his midlife solitude and ultimately destroyed him.

Albert Camus's novella *The Fall* (1956), written when the author was in his early forties, bears comparison with Stevenson's *The Strange Case of Dr. Jekyll and Mr. Hyde*, in that it concerns another strange case of a man at midlife, whose life has also been radically transformed by identifying with his own shadow, although with less completely tragic results. Rather than Victorian moralism and allegory, cool cynicism and irony dominate the narrative, which takes the form of a long confession, a "full statement of the case," like the final section of Stevenson's novella.

Both Stevenson's Dr. Jekyll and Camus's Jean-Baptiste Clamence had been eminently respectable and successful men at the peak of their profession, the one as a medical doctor and the other as a trial attorney, when fate, or rather midlife *enantiodromia*, suddenly struck. In the case of Camus's character, his midlife transformation is initiated by a kind of fall from grace. Up to this point, he has led a charmed life; everything has seemed to go the way he wanted. He is a bachelor, and, like Stevenson's Mr. Enright, a man about town, but not in the context of Victorian England, but rather in the very different context of postwar Paris, where love affairs with single or married women (including the wives of his friends) could not even be called unconventional. Jean-Baptiste Clamence thinks very well of himself, as he "soars" (to use his metaphor) over life and the rest of humanity, considering himself to have made a success of his life; he even admits that he looks upon himself as "something of a superman" (Camus 1956: 28). He is both a narcissist (the great love affair of his life, he avows, was always with himself), and what the Jungians would call a *puer* (someone identified with the youthful energies of the archetypal Divine Child or *Puer Aeternus*), an eternal adolescent who has never grown up. In this he is somewhat typical of his period. If bearded Victorian gentlemen tended to identify with the respectable ideal of the *senex*, the elderly man with his high moral standards and devotion to tradition, mid-twentieth-century clean-shaven men tended to identify with the ideal of the *puer* with his charming amoral innocence and fun-loving temperament. But just as the Old Man/*senex* of Victorian culture had his shadow side, so did the mid-century *puer*. Jung's close associate Marie-Louise von Franz wrote a classic anatomy of the *puer* personality, in which she characterized the typical *puer*'s shadow as a "gangster" shadow (von Franz 2000: 52); it is interesting to note that Camus's *puer*-like protagonist asserts rather provocatively at one point in his confession that "every intelligent man . . . dreams of being a gangster" (Camus 1956: 55). In fact, by the end of the tale, that is close to what he has become, playing the role of an informal legal counselor for the Amsterdam underworld that gathers nightly in a dive named Mexico City, and harboring in his apartment a stolen (and priceless) painting, Van Eyck's *The Just Judges*.

The story of his "fall" into an awareness of his own disreputable shadow (the book's title is an allusion to the Judeo-Christian myth of the Fall from the Garden of Eden as the origin of sin and evil) turns out to be quite unusual. As he explains the matter to the fellow French lawyer whose acquaintance he has just made in his usual nighttime haunt, the bar Mexico City, his "fall" began with a strange auditory hallucination:

> it was a fine autumn evening, still warm in town and already damp over the Seine. Night was falling; the sky, still bright in the west, was darkening; the street lamps were glowing dimly. . . . I had gone up on the Pont des Arts [a pedestrian bridge] deserted at that hour, to look at the river . . . I felt rising within me a vast feeling of power and—I don't know how to express it—of completion, which cheered my heart. I straightened up and was about to light a cigarette . . . when, at that very moment, a laugh burst out behind me. Taken by surprise, I suddenly wheeled around; there was no one there. I stepped to the railing; no barge or boat. I . . . heard the laughter behind me, a little farther off as though it were going downstream. I stood there motionless. The sound of the laughter was decreasing, but I could still hear it distinctly behind me, coming from nowhere unless from the water.
>
> (Camus 1956: 37–39)

The laughter, he says, was "hearty, almost friendly," and yet it made his pulse race. His view of himself suddenly began to change. He began to lose confidence in himself and to slide down the slippery slope of self-criticism—that is, to become increasingly and uncomfortably aware of his shadow side.

The event that had first catapulted him into the midlife transition phase in which years later he still seems stuck occurred "two or three years" before the laughter. It was no hallucination . . . or was it? One November night, returning from the bed of his latest mistress, he was returning home and crossing the Pont Royal, the next bridge downstream from the Pont des Arts (the idea of a passage between two stages of life is symbolically present in the image of a bridge in both episodes):

> It was an hour past midnight, a fine rain was falling, a drizzle rather . . . On the bridge I passed behind a figure leaning over the railing and seeming to stare at the river. On closer view, I made out a slim young

woman dressed in black. The back of her neck, cool and damp between her dark hair and coat collar, stirred me. But I went on after a moment's hesitation.

(Camus 1956: 69–70)

But then the momentous event occurs that will reveal to him some of the turbid depths of his shadow:

I had already gone some fifty yards when I heard the sound—which, despite the distance, seemed dreadfully loud in the midnight silence—of a body striking the water. I stopped short, but without turning around. Almost at once I heard a cry, repeated several times, which was going downstream; then it suddenly ceased. The silence that followed, as the night suddenly stood still, seemed interminable. I wanted to run, and yet didn't stir. I was trembling, I believe from cold and shock. I told myself that I had to be quick and I felt an irresistible weakness steal over me. I have forgotten what I thought then. "Too late, too far . . ." or something of the sort. I was still listening as I stood motionless. Then, slowly under the rain, I went away. I informed no one.

(Camus 1956: 70)

As to what followed this strange event, he replies to his drinking companion's implied question that he simply does not know—that he did not read the newspaper the next day or indeed the following days.

The shadow element that through this experience he began to become aware of—his cowardice and lack of concern manifested in his unwillingness to take a risk in order to possibly save someone's life—reveals a side of himself that was the opposite of the persona of the caring, crusading lawyer with which he had identified himself. He prided himself on being an attorney dedicated to helping the unfortunate and oppressed obtain justice. However, when put to the test outside of his usual protective professional context, his vaunted concern for others was found to be criminally lacking, since he had failed to come to the aid of someone in distress, or even to call for help, when a young woman was presumably attempting suicide by throwing herself into the Seine. This incident apparently meant little to him at the time, however (i.e., he repressed the memory), until the hallucinatory laughter on the bridge a few years later reminded him of the fact that (like Dr. Jekyll) he had a double nature: his conscious social persona of the crusading lawyer, and his unconscious shadow who could not give a damn about other people's welfare, and was cowardly to boot.

His reaction to this disturbing psychological discovery, as he makes clear in his long confessional monolog, was to analyze himself and his ambiguous situation obsessively, until he had found a theory that justified the existence of his less than perfect divided self. It is a clever theory, which does not help him come to terms with his shadow so much as it provides a rationalization that protects him, in the short term, from succumbing to self-doubt, which might have eventually developed into a healthy critical self-awareness. Through a devious equation between the actual guilt of all human beings, and the need to protect himself from his own share of it (once again, given his *puer* narcissism, he clings to his image of himself as a special person who soars above common humanity), he redefines himself as a "judge-penitent." This novel identity he has created for himself, and which has led to his taking on the pseudonymn of "Jean-Baptiste Clamence" ("John the Baptist crying [Latin *clamans*] in the wilderness"), enables him to loudly proclaim his own moral failings in order to entangle the rest of the world in a net of suspicion and collective guilt from which they cannot escape. It is a perverse attempt to escape from his own shadow:

> I had to find another means of extending judgment to everybody in order to make it weigh less heavily on my own shoulders . . . Inasmuch as one couldn't condemn others without immediately judging oneself, one had to overwhelm oneself to have the right to judge others. Inasmuch as every judge some day winds up as a penitent, one had to travel the road in the opposite direction and practice the profession of penitent to be able to end up as a judge.
>
> (Camus 1956: 137–138)

His technique of obsessive public confession, he admits near the end of his long confessional monolog, allows his scathingly critical self-portrait to morph into a mirror that he holds up to his contemporaries: "the more I accuse myself, the more I have a right to judge you" (Camus 1956: 140).

But the result of this clever intellectual maneuver of sidestepping the shadow has been to leave him stagnating in a state of both unresolved and projected guilt. There is no symbolic initiatory death for him, and so also no midlife rebirth and transformation. He mentions how at one point in his crisis "the thought of death burst into my daily life" (Camus 1956: 89); but nothing seems to have come of these thoughts. But his ordeal of self-doubt and depression, which culminated in the eventual abandonment of his successful career and his departure to Amsterdam, at least gave him a certain amount of lucidity about his untransformed self, as when he says that "crime consists less in making others die than in not dying oneself!" (Camus 1956: 113). Although he becomes adept at self-analysis, he remains stuck in his own shadow, unable to cease identifying himself with it; unable to separate himself from it and to integrate some of it into his life. His flight from his own shadow has become, in fact, the main project of his strange existence. Jung wrote that "one cannot avoid the shadow unless one remains neurotic, and as long as one is neurotic one has omitted the shadow" (Jung 1975: 545). And, sure enough, Clamence's endlessly self-accusing and self-justifying monolog winds up being a portrait of one of the most entertaining neurotics in all of literature.

But his case is more serious than mere neurosis. His state of mind is actually perilous, and he seems to be on the verge of a psychotic breakdown. It is unclear from the text whether the young woman's falling into the river or the bursts of laughter behind his back were real events or auditory hallucinations; but Clamence has in Amsterdam a recurring vision that clearly verges on the psychotic: his vision of the doves. He tries to convince his friendly listener of the reality of his delusionary vision:

> Haven't you noticed that the sky of Holland is filled with millions of doves, invisible because of their altitude, which flap their wings, rise or fall in unison, filling the heavenly space with dense multitudes of grayish feathers carried hither and thither by the wind? The doves wait up there all year round. They wheel above the earth, look down, and would like to come down. But there is nothing but the sea and the canals, roofs covered with shop signs, and never a head on which to light.
>
> (Camus 1956: 73)

It is clear that he is not simply creating a poetic metaphor for the cloudy skies of Holland, but rather is close to cherishing an insane delusion that he is an avatar of John the Baptist, whose baptism of Christ was accompanied by the descent of the Holy Spirit in the form of a dove—only this time around, in the modern world, nothing will happen, and the modern John the Baptist will cry in the wilderness in vain: the doves will never come down, since there is no Good News to proclaim. His identification with John the Baptist and even with Christ and the Pope has taken him very close to insanity—and all of this to avoid his own shadow!

By the end of the text Clamence is clearly about to lose his mind. He becomes feverish and agitated, as he reveals to the friendly stranger that he has been harboring in his room a stolen artwork, a painting of inestimable worth, whose theft the police have been investigating for years. It is, he reveals, *The Just Judges*, one of the panels of Van Eyck's altarpiece *The Mystic Lamb*, which had been stolen from the cathedral of Ghent in 1934. (This detail is historically accurate, as is Clamence's claim that the original painting had been replaced by a copy and was never recovered.) This outlandishly criminal act is part of his whole delusional project to escape judgment by being judge and accused in one person. Through his universal condemnation of all human beings ("I am for any theory that refuses to grant man innocence and for any practice that treats him as guilty" [Camus 1956: 131–132]), he imagines that he will escape any meaningful coming to terms with his own individual shadow. This desperate evasion of self-knowledge— his endless self-analysis resulting only in endless self-justification—has brought him to the verge of insanity.

Is this then the end of the strange case of Jean-Baptiste Clamence? Not necessarily. He is manifestly in need of someone who could help him to see himself clearly and empathically, since, as regards the shadow, nobody can see his own back without a mirror. This need for a friendly mirroring presence seems to be becoming conscious with him, as his relationship with his friendly stranger develops into a kind of therapeutic friendship. His midlife transformation process, which seems to have stalled permanently, may still be a work in progress. Perhaps, as regards coming to terms with his shadow, Camus's Mr. Enright has found his Mr. Utterson, that is, someone who does not judge him, and who listens to him with sympathy, understanding and patience, even when he is clearly ranting and on the edge of insanity. The unidentified stranger, although a fellow lawyer, acts much like a therapist for him. In that case, there may still be hope for Jean-Baptiste Clamence.

In both the texts analyzed so far in this chapter, the midlife process of facing and integrating the shadow was shown to be stymied, through overidentification in the one case (Dr. Jekyll believes he is the same person as Mr. Hyde), and in the other through psychological evasion (Clamence weaves an intellectual web of words, whose function is to forestall his coming to terms with his own shadow). In terms of cultural background, Dr. Jekyll is dangerously complacent as the "other Victorian," and yet rigidly moralistic as a typical Victorian gentleman, who believes that evil must be vanquished, not integrated, and who is his own severest judge, who eventually condemns himself to death. Jean-Baptiste Clamence, by contrast, is Camus's satirical portrait of a self-confident and self-important leftist Parisian intellectual, perhaps somewhat modeled on his erstwhile friend Jean-Paul Sartre, who loudly condemns social oppression and injustice, but who also, in the process of consigning the world to the judgment of history and revolution, forgets the moral challenge of his own shadow. Both men are left to live out their lives in a shadow world that they have not been able to escape, although there remains some hope for Camus's character, who has found a therapeutic relationship that may yet pull him out of his midlife morass.

Daryl Sharp has pointed out how Jungian typology can help clarify some aspects of the shadow problem:

> Since the opposite attitude [extroversion or introversion] and the inferior functions [sensation, intuition, feeling, or thinking] are by definition relatively unconscious, they are naturally tied up with the shadow.
>
> (Sharp 1987: 95)

This means that some shadow aspects of a person's typology—the opposite attitude and the inferior function—may suddenly provide the opportunity for further growth at midlife, although, as Sharp notes, the initial mani-festations of this may result in

> infantile fantasies and a variety of personality disturbances. This is what regularly happens in a so-called mid-life crisis, when an individual has neglected aspects of the personality for so long that they finally demand to be recognized.
>
> (Sharp 1987: 23–24)

Thus it would appear that Dr. Jekyll, who could be typed as an introverted intuitive type living by himself and increasingly concerned with original if bizarre experiments in his private home laboratory, develops the "infantile fantasy" of temporarily becoming another person, who will live out for him his desire for a more extroverted and sensation-oriented life prowling the streets of London in search of the physical pleasures he has denied himself after the first flush of youth has passed. Such a regressive midlife *enantio-dromia* can easily lead, Sharp suggests, to a nervous breakdown. But Dr. Jekyll and his supposed double, Mr. Hyde, constitute an extreme case, and one may well take Stevenson's mythic and science fiction tale as an oneiric text representing "a more serious psychotic break," in which Jekyll suffers the delusion of thinking he is actually able to assume a different body and a radically different personality in order to live out his "unlived life." In other words, he experiences in extreme fashion the more normal psychodrama of "the introverted man . . . under the influence of his inferior extroverted shadow," who

> is prone to imagine he is missing something: vivacious women, fast company, excitement. He himself may see these as chimaeras, but his shadow yearns for them. His shadow will lead him into the darkest venues, and then, as often as not, whimsically abandon him. What is left? A lonely introvert yearning for home.
>
> (Sharp 1987: 98)

Or, in Dr. Jekyll's extreme case, what is left is a desperate man, who feels that he must commit suicide in order to escape his shadow.

Jean-Baptiste Clamence represents the opposite move: one from extro-version to a sudden fall into introversion. Amiable and popular, supremely at home in his own physical body, Clamence can probably be typed as an extroverted sensation-feeling type. But his introverted shadow leads him to abandon the extroverted social and professional life as a cheerful Don Juan and successful lawyer he had previously enjoyed without the trace of any self-awareness or self-criticism. The *enantiodromia* is triggered by the laughter that reminds him of how cowardly and unconcerned he had been when he failed to come to the rescue of a young woman he believed had thrown herself into the Seine, and this realization propels him into a life of self-doubt and radical attempts to deny his shadow side. His lonely life in Amsterdam shows how his introverted side has taken him over, and not in a happy way. His life as a near psychotic recluse has allowed his inferior thinking and intuitive functions to trap him in a ludicrous theory of how one can supposedly escape the judgment of one's fellow men by becoming a "judge-penitent." Neither he nor Dr. Jekyll has been able, by the end of their stories, to integrate their shadows or to find some new center of balance in their lives. Each is overwhelmed and swamped by shadow energies, and their fates are tragic, although, as we have seen, there may still be hope for Clamence.

For a clear and succinct case of successful shadow integration, it is, oddly enough, a very ancient myth that provides perhaps the best illustrative oneiric text. It is also a wonderful fairy tale for modern adults! The text of the Sumerian myth of "the Descent of Inanna" was buried in the sands of Mesopotamia (present day Iraq) for over two millennia. It was pieced together slowly from the clay cuneiform tablets from the late nineteenth century onwards, until at last its clear outlines were revealed in the second half of the twentieth. Inanna was a goddess who embodied sensual love and royal authority, and her marriage to the shepherd Dumuzi was celebrated in one of the major rituals of ancient Sumeria. She is both a goddess worshipped at her temple in Uruk, Dumuzi's wife, a queen and the mother of two teenage sons. But it is her midlife transformation that is celebrated in the tale of her *katabasis* to the underworld, where she has gone in order to visit her dark sister the goddess Ereshkigal. Why she undertook this perilous voyage to the land of the dead is a question left unspecified in the text, which simply states in its opening line that "from the Great Above she opened her ear to the Great Below" (Wolkstein and Kramer 1983: 52). She will later claim that she came to attend the funeral rites of her sister's husband, Gugulanna, the Bull of Heaven, but this seems to be a fairly lame attempt on her part to explain to the gatekeepers as to why she is suddenly seeking admittance to the sacred underworld realm of Ereshkigal. In all events, she is clearly aware of the potentially fatal dangers of her midlife initiatory journey, since she has prepared an exit strategy. In case of her failure to return to the land of the living, her faithful woman servant Ninshubur is to go to the god of wisdom, Enki, hoping that he will be able to devise some clever means of obtaining her release from the underworld.

Inanna's first ordeal, as she enters the gates of Ereshkigal's dark realm, is to be stripped of all the attributes of her worldly power—of everything that makes her a powerful queen and a goddess of love: her crown, her beads, her breastplate named alluringly "come man, come," her ring, her surveying rod, and at last her royal robe, at which point "naked and bowed low, Inanna entered the throne room." She is not well received, to say the least. First the judges of the underworld condemn her, and

Then Ereshkigal fastened on Inanna the eye of death.
She spoke against her the word of wrath.
She uttered against her the cry of guilt.
She struck her.
Inanna was turned into a corpse,
A piece of rotting meat,
And was hung from a hook on the wall.
                    (Wolkstein and Kramer 1983: 60)

But after three days had passed and Inanna had not returned from the underworld, her faithful servant Ninshubur began to mourn her with great demonstrations of anguish, and then, after having been angrily refused help by the gods Enlil and Nanna, who felt that their daughter had gotten what she deserved, she beseeched the god of wisdom, Enki, to do something. Enki was in great sorrow at hearing of Inanna's disappearance, and created some magical creatures to get her out of the clutches of Ereshkigal, telling them

Go to the underworld,
Enter the doors like flies,
Ereshkigal, the Queen of the Underworld, is moaning,
With the cries of a woman about to give birth . . .
When she cries, "Oh! Oh! My inside!"
Cry also "Oh! Oh! Your inside!"
When she cries: "Oh! Oh! My outside!"
Cry also "Oh! Oh! Your outside!"
The queen will be pleased.
She will offer you a gift.
Ask her for the corpse that hangs from the hook on the wall.
                    (Wolkstein and Kramer 1987: 64)

The magical little creatures are then able to reclaim and revive the corpse of Inanna.

But the judges of the underworld insist that, if Inanna wishes to return to Uruk, she must provide them with someone to take her place. Accompanied by the galla, the demons of the underworld, Inanna returns to the surface of the earth, where she first finds her faithful servant Ninshubur mourning her in sackcloth and ashes, who throws herself at her feet as soon as she sees her. Inanna clearly cannot give Ninshubur over to the demons. Next she meets her two sons, both of whom are also in mourning for her, and who also throw themselves at her feet as soon as they see her. Clearly she cannot sacrifice their lives either. But, once she catches sight of her husband, Dumuzi, the situation changes dramatically. She finds Dumuzi sitting on her throne, dressed not in sackcloth but in royal robes. He does not even bother to rise from the throne when his wife returns from the dead. It is clearly the usurper Dumuzi who deserves to become the sacrifice she needs, and so

> Inanna fastened on Dumuzi the eye of death.
> She spoke against him the word of wrath.
> She uttered against him the cry of guilt.

And she cries out in anger at his indifference to her, and at his usurping of her throne: "Take him away! Take Dumuzi away!" (Wolkstein and Kramer 1987: 71). And that is what the demons do.

Of course, the words Inanna uses to curse her faithless husband Dumuzi are exactly the same words that were earlier used against her by Ereshkigal. Ereshkigal, although her sister, is in many ways her polar opposite. Ereshkigal has no children, and her barrenness is emphasized by her cries like those of "a woman about to give birth," since nothing can be born in the realm of the dead. Her husband Gugulanna, the Bull of Heaven, has recently died, and so she is, as a childless widow, the opposite of Inanna, married with two sons who adore her. Ereshkigal is violent, whereas Inanna is a goddess of love. But they are sisters, and so the link between them is indissoluble, and one can readily see Ereshkigal playing the role of Inanna's shadow in the myth. Inanna, in appropriating for her own purposes the exact words of Ereshkigal's curse, has integrated some of her shadow/sister's murderous powers, and has used them to regain her throne from her usurping husband and possibly even to save her own life, at the cost, no doubt, of condemning Dumuzi to death.

Fortunately for Dumuzi, his sister Gestinnana intervenes, and he is allowed to return to Inanna. But one imagines that, after Inanna's midlife acquisition of aggressive energy and self-assertive power, their marriage will never be the same. In contacting Ereshkigal, Inanna has risked her life, much as Dr. Jekyll had risked his in creating Mr. Hyde. But for her the final outcome is not tragic—far from it, since Inanna becomes at midlife a woman supremely confident in her newly acquired powers of self-assertion, a protector of her sons and of her faithful servant Ninshubur. She is no longer helpless in the face of the abusive power of her husband, who usurped her throne while she was gone, and showed no joy at her return. Her queenly role has been enhanced and stabilized by her coming to terms with her shadow through her dramatic encounter with her sister, the queen of hell, but so ultimately has her role as wife, since her marriage with Dumuzi was not ultimately destroyed by this midlife *enantiodromia*, and the myth shows that it has become now a marriage of equals.

Unlike the shadow, the contrasexual archetype (the anima in men, and the animus in women) is by no means entirely a creation of personal impressions and repressed impulses. The anima and the animus are both personal and archetypal in nature. As regards their personal side, in the construction of a gender identity an individual normally represses certain contrasexual traits, even when they could become valuable components of the personality. The individual is guided and encouraged in this process of repression by the gender norms of his or her particular society. For instance, a man may repress tenderness, and a woman self-assertive aggressiveness. Memories and impressions of people who attracted them early in life may also add specific traits to their personal contrasexual image. But this is not the whole story. The fascinating and sometimes even overwhelming power of the anima and the animus derive from their archetypal dimension, since each represents the instinctual power of sexual attraction in all its richness and variety, from pure physical desire to the heights of spiritual love. For a man or a woman, the power of the anima and the animus, unconsciously projected onto a significant other, is likely to be experienced most vividly in the romantic adventures of youth. Falling in love is a very special state of mind, and may look ridiculous from the outside, but from the inside it appears to be sheer magic. Falling in love is thus something that one would not wish to miss out on in life, even though one might say of it, as the Japanese say of climbing Mount Fuji, that everyone should climb it once, but only a fool climbs it twice. Of course, good advice from friends and painful experience of the fleeting nature of romantic love have rarely stopped anyone from falling in love again, sometimes even over and over again. The opportunity of experiencing the archetypal power of anima or animus fascination is more than most people can resist.

At midlife, however, the possibility exists for the contrasexual archetype to be experienced more consciously than in youth, that is, not only through unconscious projection (falling in love or in lust), but through increased and incremental knowledge of one's own contrasexual traits. But this new introspective knowledge does not necessarily forestall the romantic infatuations and recouplings so common during the midlife crisis—even at midlife, it is still love that makes the world go round, or, to put it in more Jungian terms, anima and animus fascination continue to put people's minds in a whirl! But, whether the anima and the animus are experienced through unconscious projection or more directly and consciously through introspection and the analysis of dreams, it is as though, for an individual who has achieved the capacity for long-term intimacy in youth, and some success in the world and in establishing a family, the resurgence of anima or animus represents unfinished business at midlife, whether in the sexual, psychological, intellectual or spiritual planes.

In Jung's 1913 vision, the beautiful young girl he called Salome and in the dream he had the same year the white bird that changed into an eight-year-old girl with blond hair, who he later said reminded him of his eldest daughter (Bennet 1985: 59), both represented anima figures who acted as psychopomps in his imminent midlife descent into the archetypal world of the psyche. However, Jung also experienced the power of the contrasexual archetype at midlife in a more ordinarily romantic way. Jung noted in his autobiography that his early childhood impressions of the maid who looked after him while his mother was hospitalized later became a component of his anima:

> I still remember her picking me up and laying my head against her shoulder. She had black hair and an olive complexion, and was quite different from my mother. I can see, even now, her hairline, her throat, with its darkly pigmented skin, and her ear. All this seemed to me very strange and yet strangely familiar. It was as though she belonged not to my family but only to me, as though she were connected in some way with other mysterious things I could not understand. . . . The feeling of strangeness which she conveyed, and yet of having known her always, was a characteristic of that figure which later came to symbolize for me the whole essence of womanhood.
>
> (Jung 1963: 8–9)

During his midlife crisis, Jung began a lifelong love affair with Toni Wolff, who was—guess what?—dark haired and dark complexioned, and in her late twenties while he was in his late thirties. In so doing, not only had Jung succumbed to a romantic infatuation based initially on anima fascination, but he had found in his lover a person who could save his sanity when it was threatened—a good angel, who was also a real woman of flesh and blood.

In Federico Fellini's film *8½* (*Otto e mezzo*, 1963) the film director Guido Anselmi, age forty-three, discovers in a beautiful anima figure (who is also a real person embodied by the actress Claudia Cardinale playing herself near the end of the film) the good angel who will bring to his life and to the film he is making a greatly needed sense of order and harmony. The fact that the anima is to all appearances represented in this film in a thoroughly Jungian fashion is not at all coincidental, for Fellini was in the midst of an enthusiastic discovery of Jungian psychology, under the guidance of his Jungian analyst Dr. Bernhard. Charles Affron has noted, in his edition of the continuity script of the film, that in one of Guido's significant childhood memories the twelve-year-old girl who utters the magic formula ASA NISI MASA that will reveal the location of a treasure (Fellini 1987: 86) is actually speaking in "'la lengua serpentina' (serpentine language), a children's language akin to pig Latin that inserts 'sa' and 'si' syllables into existing words" (Fellini 1987: 13). In this case, the formula she repeats indicates the talismanic word "ANIMA" (A-sa NI-si MA-sa). Guido, who is fumbling around desperately with the idea for a new film that he cannot figure out how to organize meaningfully, remembers this magic formula; its presence in his mind puzzles the telepathic performer, the old woman Maya, who cannot understand what it means or why he is thinking about it. So the film *8½*, with its emphasis on anima dreams and fantasies, is to some degree programmatically Jungian, and deals with a midlife crisis that reflects that of its director, who was at that time under the spell of his recent discovery of analytical psychology and Jung's concept of the anima. This does not lessen the film's value as a masterpiece of oneiric representation; it just means that what one finds in the film in the way of an extraordinarily rich evocation of the anima is there because Fellini deliberately put it there.

Guido's midlife crisis (he is strung out between his wife Luisa and his mistress Carla, and his marriage is on the rocks) coincides with a crisis in creativity (the film he cannot seem to get a creative grip on). Oneiric representations of his anima include the twelve-year-old girl and her magic formula ASA NISI MASA of his childhood memories as well as the maturely elegant "Beautiful Unknown Woman," with whom the director Guido is fascinated at a distance. The latter appears briefly several times in the course of the film, most notably when Guido overhears her saying, tearfully and with deep feeling, in a conversation over the hotel lobby telephone, that "I forgive him everything. Everything. I forgive him everything" (Fellini 1987: 88).

But it is above all the beautiful star Claudia Cardinale who brings to the role of Guido's anima a charm and a fascination that was hers personally. Appearing first as a vision of a young woman giving him a cup of mineral water from the springs of a spa resort (the actual young woman serving him is hot and irritated), she then appears in a major dream sequence as a chamber maid who turns down his bed, looks at the script he has been working on, bursts out laughing, and then murmurs to him just as he is about to wake up "I've come, never to leave again. . . . I want to make order. I want to make things clean" (*far ordine, far pulizia*) (Fellini 1987: 186).

In spite of these significant anima apparitions, Guido continues on the path that seems to be leading him in the direction of a failed career as a filmmaker and a failed marriage. As the crisis in his film and in his marriage come to a head, Claudia Cardinale finally appears as herself, that is, as a friend of the director as well as an actress who has come to play a part in his film. She listens to him sympathetically, and then, as he rambles on about the film that reflects very closely his own midlife crisis, complaining that it has become a project he can't seem to bring to fruition, Claudia says about his main protagonist in the film:

> I've understood almost nothing about the story you told me. Listen, a man like that . . . the way you describe him . . . who doesn't love anybody . . . no one is going to feel very sorry for him, you know. Basically, it's his fault. . . . Because he doesn't know how to love.
> (Fellini: 1987: 176)

She repeats "because he doesn't know how to love" three times, like a magic formula, and this proves ultimately to be the anima's "magic formula" that will lead Guido to discover the "treasure."

Guido is faced with what looks like the necessity of closing down the production set, with its expensive but now useless rocket launching towers, that was intended to be the scene at the end of his film for the departure of a small group of human beings from a nuclear devastated earth. He imagines vividly his own suicide at this point of despair and desperation, but Claudia's sudden and final reappearance suddenly inspires him with the idea of a different ending for his film. In this new ending, all the characters in the film and all the people he cherishes in real life or remembers with fondness come down from the launching platform, join hands and dance in a joyful circle. Guido realizes gratefully that he cannot do without them, that he can accept them all, and that he now knows how to love them all, starting first and foremost with his wife, Luisa, whose hand he takes when he too joins the joyful circle:

> I didn't understand. I didn't know. How right it is to accept you, to love you! And how simple it is! Luisa, I feel as if I've been freed. Everything seems good. Everything is meaningful. Everything is true.
>
> (Fellini 1987: 186)

So it is Claudia Cardinale's inspiring anima influence and advice that have saved Guido from possible suicide and triggered his move into a liberating sense of generativity, in both affective and creative terms. Claudia's role with Guido thus parallels to some degree the mentoring anima role that we have seen was played by Toni Wolff in Jung's own personal life.

Like Fellini's *8½*, Akira Kurosawa's film masterpiece *Ikiru* (1952) represents an aging man responding in a creative and generative way to anima inspirations embodied by an actual young woman. But Watanabe seems prematurely old, well past the age when he should have been through some form of midlife transformation. In addition, he is suffering from incurable stomach cancer, as he finds out at the opening of the film, and so feels that his life is rapidly coming to an end. Yet he still remains stuck in midlife stagnation, doting on his grown up son, who has little affection for him, and working as a bureau chief in city hall, but actually doing little more than pushing paper. Watanabe is a typical postwar Japanese figure caught between an authoritarian tradition and liberal democratic ideals of promoting economic and social progress.

But Watanabe is also a deliberately scripted reincarnation of Goethe's figure of Faust, the description of whose midlife crisis is probably the most richly symbolic in all of Western literature. Faust's midlife transformation is catalyzed by his relationship both with the diabolical shadow figure of Mephistopheles and with the young girl Gretchen, who carries his anima projection. *Ikiru*'s debt to Goethe's *Faust*, both Parts 1 and 2, was first discussed by Barbara Carr, who argued that the similarities between the two works were "remarkable and intriguing, and inescapably intentional," even going so far as to call *Ikiru* "Kurosawa's translation of Goethe's *Faust*" (Carr 1996: 275, 278). But Carr also acknowledges that what Kurosawa does with *Faust* is something quite original, for the Japanese director has eliminated the metaphysical frame of Goethe's tragedy, and with it any possibility of an other-worldly ending. Watanabe, Kurosawa's municipal-bureau-chief Faust figure, will in the end, like Faust, be "saved," in a manner of speaking. However, he will not be saved, as in Goethe's *Faust* Part 2, in an afterlife through the power of cosmic love or through heavenly grace in the form of the Eternal Feminine (of which his young beloved Gretchen is a partial manifestation), but rather through the earthly achievement of what he leaves behind him after he dies: a children's park created by draining a swampy area of a neglected neighborhood in Tokyo, which *yakuza* (gangster) business interests had been eyeing as a good site for a tavern.

But there are two major issues that Carr's article does not explore. First of all, the degree to which Kurosawa has created, in his portrayal of a postwar Japanese Faust, a more positive figure whose sins are sins of omission, not sins of commission. In Goethe's tragedy, Faust's midlife passion destroys Gretchen's life; in Kurosawa's film, Watanabe has no such blood on his hands. Secondly, Kurosawa has sanitized his Japanese Faust's relationship with his Gretchen, without however denying the ethical imperative of making their problematic relationship come out right in the end. Goethe's Faust's anima infatuation with Gretchen leads to the tragedy of her execution for infanticide, a fate from which Faust proves unable to save her. Watanabe, by contrast, ultimately negotiates his relationship with the young Miss Toyo properly, and he will have no seduction of a young and innocent Gretchen on his conscience, for which he must later atone. The sin Watanabe must expiate in the second half of the film is not the seduction and ruin of a young girl, but rather that of his callous bureaucratic neglect of the public interest. For the atonement of this sin, Kurosawa's film allows Watanabe the opportunity of refashioning himself into a model of civic responsibility through generative social activity: his heroic struggle to create a children's playground in spite of stubborn bureaucratic resistance and gangster threats to his life. Watanabe's move into midlife generativity coincides with his awareness of his imminent death (a major initiatory motif, as we have seen), but also with his deployment of the anima energies released by his fascination with Miss Toyo.

As the plot of *Ikiru* begins to unfold, Watanabe, like Faust, is a man on the verge of death—Faust by suicide (barely forestalled at the opening of Goethe's tragedy by the Easter chorus), Watanabe by a diagnosis of incurable stomach cancer that his doctors have been unable to conceal from him.

Both men are trapped in occupations that have ceased to interest them: Faust in his work as a scholar, and Watanabe in his position as a paper-pushing bureau chief of the Citizen's Section of City Hall. (The image of the huge piles and shelves of paperwork and records looming over Watanabe in his office is a clever reminder of the books that presumably loomed over Faust in his study.) The way out of this lifeless stagnation comes in Watanabe's case with his encounter in a tavern with a Bohemian writer of cheap fiction with a black dog (a black dog was the first sign of Mephisto-pheles' appearance in *Faust*), who is drinking himself silly on whisky and crying out for sleeping pills, with which Watanabe spontaneously offers to supply him. As the two men begin to converse, Watanabe reveals that he has incurable stomach cancer, and that, although he wants to spend all the money he has on him on having a good time, he does not know how to proceed. This confession provides the Bohemian writer with the opportunity of stepping into his Mephistophelean role, and he says (making the allusion so clear that one wonders why critics have not made more of the Faustian dimension of the odd couple): "Tonight I'll be your Mephistopheles, but a good one, who won't ask to be paid. Look, we even have a black dog!" (Kurosawa 1968: 34). These lines reveal succinctly just how much Kurosawa is intent on differentiating his Japanese Faust from Goethe's Faust, by making everything for Watanabe come out right in the end, as well as by giving him a *good* Mephistopheles as companion and guide, with no pact with the devil, and with a black dog that gets kicked and yelps immediately after his acceptance of the offer, as if to indicate the exorcism of any diabolical element in their agreement.

The Bohemian writer's philosophy does, however, sound rather Meph-istophelean and Faustian in its praise of experience and self-gratification, as when he says to Watanabe:

> Up until now you've been life's slave but now you're going to be its master. And it is man's duty to enjoy life; it's against nature not to. Man must have a greed for life. We're taught that that's immoral, but it isn't. The greed to live is a virtue.
>
> (Kurosawa 1968: 34)

But the wild time that Goethe's Faust had with Mephistopheles at Auerbach's Tavern and the Witch's Kitchen is recreated in *Ikiru* in a poignant and melodramatic mode. The Bohemian writer of cheap fiction desperately tries to show Watanabe a good time in Tokyo's entertainment district. But, in spite of his best efforts, Watanabe winds up getting every-one depressed ("Tears stream down Watanabe's face. There is silence" [Kurosawa 1968: 34]), as he sings a poignant little song "Life is so short / Fall in love, dear maiden"—a song that he will sing again as he spends his last moments on the swing of the newly opened children's playground he has succeeded in bringing into existence. The sentimental and gently humorous melodrama of Watanabe trying desperately to live it up for once in his life is a sanitized version of Faust's encounters with diabolical revelry, but it turns out to be completely suited to the character: in the end, Faustian greed for unlimited experience is not to be Watanabe's path to midlife transformation.

The same intention to cleanse his Japanese Faust of the taint of perversity and brutality associated with the Goethean original is obvious in the way Kurosawa handles the film's equivalent of the Gretchen episode, that is, Watanabe's sudden romantic infatuation with Miss Toyo, a young woman who once worked in his office, but who quit her job out of boredom shortly after the film began, and took up work in a toy factory. She had been the only woman in an office of male office workers, where her high spirits and sense of humor had contrasted with the stolid seriousness of the other municipal employees. Watanabe runs into her by chance in the street on his return from his night on the town. All this could and does suggest a well-off older man about to begin a midlife affair with a factory girl— nothing too out of the ordinary in terms of traditional Japanese norms of male conduct, but still a bit disreputable, as his son Mitsuo tries to tell him when he returns home:

> You've already spent over fifty thousand yen on her—girls nowadays! . . . The idea—bringing a girl here, and holding hands too. I was terribly embarrassed when the housekeeper told me.
>
> (Kurosawa 1968: 53)

But his father is not deterred. Two weeks later we see him outside the toy factory where Miss Toyo is now working, as she berates him for wanting to go out with her every night. "Let's just stop it," she says. "It's . . . it's unnatural" (Kurosawa 1968: 54). So Watanabe seems to want to be involved in what would appear to Miss Toyo, at least, to be an inappropriate sexual relationship with a girl young enough to be his daughter. (This is what his older brother is later to conclude, although he considers the imagined situation quite indulgently.)

But it turns out that if Miss Toyo is supremely important for Watanabe at this moment of crisis in his life, it is not because he wants to have a romantic sexual relationship with her.

TOYO: You make me nervous. Why do you pay so much attention to me?
WATANABE: It's because . . .
TOYO: Because why?
WATANABE: Well, I just enjoy being with you.
TOYO: I hope it isn't love.

WATANABE: No, it's not . . .
TOYO: Why don't you speak more clearly—say what you mean!
(Kurosawa 1968: 55)

He then bares his heart to her and confesses that he is dying of stomach cancer, and that he has less than a year to live. (Meanwhile the record player in the coffee shop plays Victor Herbert's "March of the Wooden Soldiers," as if to mock the stagnating, mechanical and duty-bound existence he has led up to this point.) This key scene reveals the real nature of Watanabe's attraction to Miss Toyo, who represents anima inspiration rather than sexual opportunity for him, as he tells her, but with such intensity that she instinctively recoils from him:

> You are so full of life and . . . I'm envious of that. If only I could be like you for one day before I die. I won't be able to die unless I can be. Oh, I want to do something. Only you can show me. I don't know what to do. I don't know how to do it. Maybe you don't either, but, please, if you can, show me how to be like you.
>
> (Kurosawa 1968: 56)

But the specific nature of what Watanabe wants to do stays undefined, even as he casts Toyo in the role of his inspirational Muse.

Toyo's initial response to all this is confusion:

TOYO: I don't know.
WATANABE: How can I be like you?
TOYO: But all I do is work and eat—that's all.
WATANABE: Really?
TOYO: Really. That and make toys like this one.

She has a toy rabbit in her pocket. She takes it out, winds it up, puts it on the table in front of them; it hops towards him; she picks it up, starts it over again.

TOYO: That's all I do, but it's fun. I feel as if I were friends with all the children in Japan now. Mr. Watanabe, why don't you do something like that, too?
(Kurosawa 1968: 56)

It is Toyo's suggestion that triggers Watanabe's midlife generative project— to do something that will make him a friend to the children of the neighborhood who need a playground—and it is directly inspired by Toyo's remarks about her own life, and how as a worker in a factory she makes toy wind-up rabbits that delight the children of Japan. By the end of the film, by creating a children's playground, he has become "like her," and, after singing his poignant little song "Life is so short," he dies on a swing in the playground he has created.

Having brought to fruition this anima-inspired generative project deriving from what can be typed as a traditionally feminine concern for small children, Watanabe is able to meet his death cheerfully, and dies happy, as the policeman, who at first thought he was just a harmless drunk, reports at his wake. Thus what Kurosawa has done is to make his modern Japanese version of Faust come out right—unequivocally. He has made his Watanabe, inspired and transformed by his anima connection with Miss Toyo, into a positive hero of generative social concern and civic responsibility, thanks to the anima inspiration for which she has proved to be the catalyst.

In R.K. Narayan's novel *The English Teacher* (1945), written when the Indian author was in his mid-thirties, the creative anima impulse at midlife is memorably described as catalyzed by someone who is identified as the spirit of his dead wife. This second half of the novel is a supernatural tale that contrasts vividly with the gentle realism of the first half, which evokes the early years of marriage of a Hindu schoolteacher in British India. It was only years later that the Indian author revealed in his autobiography *My Days* (1973–4) that the novel was based on his own experiences. Thus not only had Narayan's own wife died under circumstances very similar to those in which the narrator's wife contracted typhoid and died in *The English Teacher*, but the eerie communication with her beyond the grave, Narayan insisted, had also occurred in real life.

In *My Days* R.K. Narayan presents himself as someone who, after his wife's death in June 1939 from typhoid, had "no faith in spiritualism, which seemed to oversimplify the whole problem of life and death with its trappings and lingo" (Narayan 1996: 141). In similar fashion his protagonist Krishna, in *The English Teacher*, initially shows no interest in the occult, and indeed is quite incensed when his mother-in-law arranges for an exorcist to come to her sick daughter's bedside. Nevertheless, both Narayan and his fictional alter ego Krishna subsequently accepted the offer of a medium's attempt to communicate with the spirit of the departed through spiritualistic procedures. The medium allowed his hand to write whatever came into his mind, and these messages were interpreted as attempts on the spirit's part to communicate with her grief-stricken husband. At first the messages were from what was called "your band of helpers":

> The lady wants to assure you that she exists but in a different state, she wants you to lighten your mind too, and not to let gloom weigh you down. She says, now you are told I am here; by and by when you have attuned yourself, you will feel without proof or argument that I am at your side and that will transform your outlook.
>
> (Narayan 1996: 143)

In his autobiography, Narayan describes these words and others as having been written down by Narayan's medium at a rate of twenty-four hundred in thirty minutes (cf. Stevenson's speed in writing *Dr. Jekyll and Mr. Hyde*); in the novel *The English Teacher*, by contrast, there is no such breakneck rush of words, and Krishna observes a thirty-minute limit on writing sessions. There is no point, however, in comparing the two narratives in detail, since Narayan is quite right in affirming in *My Days* that they both tell essentially the same story:

> More than any other book [of mine], *The English Teacher* is autobiographical in content, very little part of it being fiction. The "English teacher" of the novel, Krishna, is a fictional character in the fictional city of Malgudi; but he goes through the same experience I had gone through, and he calls his wife Susila [instead of Rajam], and the child is Leela instead of Hema.
>
> (Narayan 1996: 135)

But what is worth further comment is what Narayan wrote about the reactions of his readers to the supernatural, occult dimension of the second half of the novel:

> That book falls into two parts: one is domestic and the other half is "spiritual." Many readers have gone through the first half with interest and the second half with bewilderment and even resentment, perhaps feeling that they have been baited with the domestic picture into tragedy, death, and nebulous, impossible speculations. The dedication of the book to the memory of my wife [Dedicated to my wife RAJAM] should to some extent give the reader a clue that the book may not be all fiction; still, most readers resist, naturally, as one always does, the transition from life to death and beyond.
>
> (Narayan 1996: 135)

"I am at your side and that will transform your outlook": these words of the wife's spirit taken down at breakneck speed by Raghunatha Rao, a rich lawyer friend of one of Narayan's cousins, mark the onset of the theme of midlife transformation in *My Days*:

> All the factual side seemed to me immaterial. Even if Rao had had his own sources of enquiry and was dashing off the information at the sitting, even if Rao caught telepathically whatever went on in my or anyone else's mind, it did not matter to me. Even if the whole thing was a grand fraud, it would not matter. What was important was the sensing of the presence in that room [the presence of his wife's spirit], which transformed my outlook.
>
> (Narayan 1996: 144)

Throughout his autobiography, R.K. Narayan, even when he alludes to such apparently irrefutable evidence as his wife's spirit's reference to a box of jewelry of which his conscious mind was totally unaware, maintains that the value of the experience lay not in demonstrating the reality of life after death, but rather this: "what really mattered to me ultimately was the specific directions she gave step by step in order to help me attain clarity of mind and receptivity" (Narayan 1996: 145). Following this initial contact with his wife through the medium's writings, later sittings at a distance were able to work through thought transference alone; eventually, as in the novel, "even that amount of dependence on the medium became unnecessary . . . psychic experience seemed to have become a part of my normal life and thought" (Narayan 1996: 146). After becoming adept at this type of unmediated thought communication with his wife, and after having practiced establishing psychic contacts "for some years, almost every night," "gradually," writes Narayan, "the interest diminished when I began to feel satisfied that I had attained an understanding of life and death" (Narayan 1996: 145).

Although Narayan's technique of conversing with the spirit of his dead wife presents, as we will see, an eerie resemblance with Jung's advocacy of "conversations with the anima," there is no evidence that Jung had any discernible influence on Narayan. Rather, it was Paul Brunton, an English friend and mystic, whom he credits for inspiring him to write a book about the personal tragedy that had overtaken him, and for teaching him procedures for abstracting himself from the body, and entering into communication with the world of the spirits. In *The Wisdom of the Overself* (published in 1943, one year before the publication of *The English Teacher*), Brunton, no doubt inspired to some degree by the recent psychic experiences of his friend R.K. Narayan, evoked the possibility of establishing communication with the spirit world. In most cases, however, wrote Brunton,

> both sitter and medium are usually ignorant of the workings of the deeper layers of their own minds, an ignorance which often leads them to ascribe to a spirit words and visions which emanate from themselves alone.
>
> (Brunton 1983: 137)

But Brunton is willing to admit that there are exceptions, in which "by the force of great love genuine communication is sometimes effected through a medium and does bring great comfort to a bereaved person." Still, a better procedure, he maintains, is to do without the services of a medium altogether. Brunton writes that "it is also the only satisfying method, because it involves one's own personal experience, not something got at second hand." Brunton's evocation of this direct communication encapsulates the experiences of R.K. Narayan in *My Days* as well as those of his fictional alter ego Krishna in *The English Teacher*:

> Truly a deep noble affection between two persons conquers the chasm set up by death and brings . . . loving thoughts from the spirit to the receptive consciousness of the living person . . . [and] a sense of its personal presence to a sensitive mind.
>
> (Brunton 1983: 137–138)

Yet the reader may well feel entitled to remain incredulous. We have seen that even Narayan did not completely discount the possibility of the medium's "telepathic competence" being the source of what were presented as communications with his wife's spirit, even though he seems to interpret these messages and conversations as being cases of literal thought-communication with his dead wife. But Jung's theory of the anima provides a more plausible way of making psychological sense out of the spiritualist adventure of the second half of the novel, which, for some one hundred pages or so, is oriented around these spirit conversations and their transformative effect on the narrator's life.

In his essay entitled "The Relations Between the Ego and the Unconscious" (published in Switzerland in 1945, the year after the publication of *The English Teacher*), Jung discussed a technique for psychological development that bears much resemblance to what the grieving widower Krishna attempts to do in his conversations with the spirit of his dear departed wife. Jung advocated in this particular essay the technique of holding actual conversations with this figure of the psychological imagination. Such conversations would involve two things: first, the objectification of the anima (treating her as a real figure separate from one's own mind); and then the establishment of a kind of personal relationship with her by asking her questions and engaging in a dialog with her. Jung was aware of the fairly outlandish nature of the endeavor: "to anyone accustomed to proceed purely intellectually and rationally, this [procedure] may seem altogether ridiculous" (Jung 1956: 212).

Jung proposed this odd procedure as "an actual technique" of "allowing our invisible opponent to make herself heard, by putting the mechanism of expression momentarily at her disposal." These "conversations with the anima" thus constituted a technique worth pursuing with all seriousness: "statement and answer must follow one another until a satisfactory end to the discussion is reached" (Jung 1956: 213–214). However, wrote Jung, this was not a technique suitable for everyone:

> I would expressly point out that I am not recommending the above technique as either necessary or even useful, to any person not driven to it by necessity . . . . I can imagine someone using this technique out

of a kind of holy inquisitiveness, some youth, perhaps, who would like to set wings to his feet, not because of lameness, but because he yearns for the sun.

(Jung 1956: 214)

But for a man or woman at midlife, driven to desperation by the ordeal of midlife crisis, it may be all the more necessary to establish a conscious inner relationship with the anima or the animus, and such "conversations" may be one way to begin.

At such a moment of midlife despair and disorientation, this is, in Narayan's novel, what Krishna was driven to, when he, against his better judgment, submitted to the process of entering into communication with what he took to be the spirit of his dead wife, Susila, who becomes for him a mentoring female presence in a way she had never been while she was alive. "At stated hours sit for psychic development," she tells him, in order "to enable me to get in touch with you directly without the intervention of the medium" (Narayan 2001: 177). These first steps are quite hard for him, even for the mere ten-minute sessions she has prescribed. But Krishna makes heroic efforts to concentrate his mind on her, and, in so doing, he Krishna naturally assumes that Susila is asking him to practice some variety of Indian yoga involving one-pointed concentration, with the mental image of his wife serving as the focus of his unwavering attention. But that is not it at all, she says. She is adamant in asserting that one-pointed meditative concentration on her image is the opposite of what she is asking of him:

> Your mind may now be compared to the body of a yogi who sits motionless. This is not what you seek to achieve, do you? . . . What is still required is that you should be able to receive my thoughts. It can be done only if you do not make a stone image of me. I want you to behave just as you would if I were conversing with you. You would pay attention. Now it borders on worship.
>
> (Narayan 2001: 182–183)

In fact, the procedure she urges on him is much more a psychological than a meditative exercise. The specific points of similarity between Krishna's post mortem conversations with Susila and Jung's "conversations with the anima" can be summarized briefly under the three following headings: (1) both involve, not mental concentration, but psychic relaxation and receptivity; (2) both use actual questions as part of a systematic attempt to engage the "feminine side" in an intrapsychic dialogue; and (3) both lead to a transformation of the man's psychological outlook and being. As regards this last point, the narrator leaves off his description of the conversations with Susila just when the reader begins to wonder exactly what effect conversations with this figure, who is both his wife and yet more than his wife, will have on his life. "Ever since these communications began," he tells the reader, "I felt, now and then, that she showed a greater wisdom than I had known her to possess" (Narayan 2001: 148). But he tells the reader little about the content of this supposed "wisdom." In fact, Narayan is far more interested in demonstrating the emotional and spiritual effect of the psychic presence of his wife's spirit on the narrator's life than in specifying the "greater wisdom" she allegedly communicates. But what *was* the effect of these conversations on Krishna? How did such conversations transform him?

The theme of midlife transformation does indeed eventually achieve prominence by the end of the novel. Krishna finally quits his work as a schoolteacher in the pay of the British Empire; he begins to take good care of his little daughter; and soon he assumes responsibility for fostering and managing a progressive school for children run along authentically Indian lines. His former English language students at the Albert Mission College now see him as a patriot working for the cause of "national regeneration." But Krishna modestly sees himself as mainly continuing the introverted work of psychological development and inner harmony that had begun with his conversations with his wife's spirit: "I'm seeking a great inner peace" (Narayan 2001: 211). But in fact his new work at an experimental Indian school for young children, which promotes an original and creative vision of education, is a highly generative project. It can be seen as having been inspired, more indirectly than directly, by his many "conversations with the anima," since in the course of these long conversations the unconscious feminine side of his psyche has became more activated and then partly integrated into his conscious life and activities. This integration of his anima has enabled him to undertake work that is more feminine and maternal in nature than the reluctant and resentful stuffing of teenage boys' minds with British literature that had been his earlier occupation.

The English Teacher ends most dramatically with Krishna's actual waking vision of his wife. At this magical moment, the reader can feel that, beyond the literal description of such an unusual psychic phenomenon, it is the integration of his feminine side, of his anima, that is symbolized by the poetic evocation of this final reunion of husband and wife:

> We stood at the window, gazing on a slender red streak over the eastern rim of the earth. A cool breeze lapped our faces. The boundaries of our personalities suddenly dissolved. It was a moment of rare, immutable joy, a moment for which one feels grateful to Life and Death.
>
> (Narayan 2001: 213)

As Narayan writes in his autobiography, what the "psychic contacts" with his wife's spirit gave him was simply "an understanding of life and death" (Narayan 1996: 147)—the wisdom that accompanies an initiatory close encounter with death leading to midlife transformation. On the purely practical side, the effect of Narayan's new wisdom, vaguely articulated as it may have been, was to enable him to pick up his career as a novelist, which had been interrupted during several years of grief-stricken liminality, by writing his novel *The English Teacher*. But the writing of the novel constituted a generative act that enabled him to share with his readers a sense of that "rare, immutable joy" that had entered his life through contact with what, seen from a Jungian perspective, was the psychic reality of the anima.

The dramatic resurgence of the anima or the animus at midlife can also prove to be catastrophic rather than beneficial. The French director Louis Malle's English language film *Damage* (1992) provides a stunning example of this. The middle-aged and slightly graying Stephen Barton (played by Jeremy Irons), who has become a successful British politician, falls desperately in love with his son's fiancée Anna (played by Juliette Binoche), and they begin a passionate affair that continues after her marriage. By the end of the film his son is dead, having fallen off the interior balcony of the apartment building after he has just discovered his father and Anna making love. Stephen's wife becomes almost mad with anger and grief. Nothing works out right for anyone in this midlife tragedy that Louis Malle drew from a novel of the same title by Josephine Hart (1991). But, in his director's interview on the DVD, Malle is more than a little disingenuous in failing to name another significant subtext for his film, which is surely Racine's *Phaedra*, a classic tragedy well known to any educated Frenchman. No doubt, Malle has changed Racine's plot significantly, for in Racine's tragedy it is the older wife who falls in love with her young stepson, the relationship between the father Theseus and the fiancée remaining free of any sexual innuendoes. But, just as in Malle's film, the son dies dramatically, in this latter case in a chariot accident in which he is mangled beyond recognition by his panicked horses.

In *Damage*, it is hard to see in the anima-induced passionate relationship between father and daughter-in-law any glimmer of insight or transformation; the anima has made sacrificial victims of Stephen and of everyone else in the twisted familial love imbroglio. But in Racine's tragedy, as we will now see, there is reason to conclude that Phaedra's tragic love for her stepson Hippolytus has, in the end, transformed her in a positive way, although the transformation is too late to save her and him from death.

Phaedra is one of the great tragic roles in classical French theater. Her fate as a woman and a mother bedeviled at midlife with passionate desires she cannot control would have spoken directly to the hearts of the many middle-aged French aristocratic ladies, whose critical opinions could make or break a play's reputation. In its representation of the power of passion induced by animus infatuation, the play has no equal. I would like to focus briefly on just two aspects of the tragic animus infatuation that is so magnificently portrayed in it.

It is clear at the opening of the play that Phaedra has lost her mind through love, and that nothing she can do can help her regain her psychological footing. She enters on stage in the middle of an erotic fantasy that places her in the company of her stepson, the entrancing young Hippolytus, as he hunts in the forest or competes in a chariot race:

> Oh why am I not sitting in the shade
> Of forests? When may I follow with my eyes
> That racing chariot flying down the course
> Through glorious dust? . . .
> Where am I? Mad?
> What have I said? Where, where have I let stray
> My longings and my self-control?
>
>   (Racine 1961: 41)

This erotic daydream verges on the frighteningly delusional. It is also threatening to Phaedra's life and happiness, since it has as its passionate object Phaedra's own stepson, Hippolytus. Hippolytus is presented as an honest and upright young man, if somewhat inexperienced and naive, who had been dedicated to living a chaste life until the moment when he fell in love with the young princess Aricia, the last surviving member of a family that had rivaled with his father Theseus for the throne of Athens. For both these reasons, he is a tragically dangerous choice as an object of Phaedra's passion. But Phaedra is beyond recall, and the only thing that stops her love madness is when it temporarily turns to hate, once she discovers that the seemingly chaste Hippolytus is actually in love with Aricia. At this point the tragic knots are tightened. Phaedra's husband Theseus has been deliberately lied to by Phaedra's companion Oenone, who has tried to shift the blame for the quasi-incestuous passion to Hippolytus, whom she has accused of trying to rape Phaedra. Hippolytus has been too embarrassed by the whole affair to tell his father the true facts, and so is about to get on his way into exile, cursed by his father who is incensed with what he presumes is his son's criminal attempt at rape. At this juncture Phaedra comes to Theseus, determined at last to tell him the truth before it is too late, but she suddenly changes her mind when she learns about Hippolytus' love for Aricia. Overcome by a murderous rush of jealousy, Phaedra decides to leave Hippolytus and Aricia to their fate, and so Hippolytus' exile proceeds unimpeded and he perishes in the dramatic chariot overturn when trampled by his frightened horses.

At this point in Racine's tragedy Phaedra does something extraordinary and, one could say, strikingly out of character. Having been intensely passionate, then jealous and then vindictive, at the end of the last scene she suddenly becomes courageously honest. Having swallowed a slow-acting fatal poison, she appears before Theseus:

> No, Theseus, I must break this unjust silence:
> Must restore your son's lost innocence.
> He was not guilty.
>
> (Racine 1961: 167)

Through this belated confession—too late to save Hippolytus' life, as he has been attacked by a monstrous bull from the sea and mangled by his own frightened horses—she has brought down Theseus' full hatred and fury upon herself; her brave confession has apparently done no good at all. Or has it? In fact, her confession changes the situation radically at the end of the tragedy. It does not bring Hippolytus back to life, but it has redeemed his memory in the eyes of his father, and it has, in deflecting Theseus' fury onto herself, saved Aricia, whom he now adopts as his daughter. Her generous-minded honesty has proved to be generative for others, however fatal it has proved to be for her.

The motivation for Phaedra's unexpected confession is never made explicit, but a psychological perspective on her animus infatuation with Hippolytus does suggest one possibility. Hippolytus is a young man most notable for his innocence, his honesty, his generous-mindedness and his sense of personal honor. Thus he will not accuse Phaedra to his father, and he prefers exile to having to be the involuntary cause of his father's disgrace. What Phaedra has done by the end of the play is to have integrated, under intense pressure, some of Hippolytus' best qualities, and this leads her to save Hippolytus' honor through an honest confession. By the end of the tragedy she is thus a woman transformed, and it is possible to admire her for her newfound honesty and integrity, acquired under the most difficult of circumstances, and for which she pays the ultimate price.

Racine's *Phaedra* is no doubt a most complex play from the standpoint of psychology, and no one interpretation will satisfy anyone completely. But what is satisfying, from a Jungian standpoint, is to see how Phaedra is able to integrate some of the characteristics of a positive animus—Hippolytus' honesty and sense of honor—and to manifest new energies as a woman transformed at midlife. Such generous and generative honesty is the last thing one would have expected from the passionate, selfish and devious Phaedra who is portrayed throughout most of the play, but this is exactly the virtue she is able to manifest in the end.

Jane Campion's film *The Piano* (1993) provides a less ambiguous example of the positive effects of animus integration. The film was made when the director was in her late thirties. It was partly inspired, she has said (Campion 1999: 125), by Emily Brontë's *Wuthering Heights*, which many Jungians admire for its masterful portrayal of the animus fascination associated with the near mythic character of Heathcliffe, who inspires poor Catherine with a passion from which she can only free herself in death, in spite of her attempts to make a satisfactory married life with the honest if somewhat boring Linton. But Jane Campion, in keeping with the post-modernist tendency to brighten up romantic and tragic themes, provides a happy ending for her heroine's struggle between marital duty and passion, while at the same time giving the theme of animus fascination and integration a subtle and convincing drama in which to play itself out. But the film is not without its tragic side, and has a seriousness that only really lightens at the very end.

The film's heroine Ada McGrath has been mute since the age of six for reasons that are not made explicit. However, since Campion had made an earlier film on the topic of the sexual abuse of children, it is possible to infer that Ada may have been rendered mute by such a traumatic experience, especially since Maya Angelou had already famously described such a situation in her autobiographical narrative *I Know Why the Caged Bird Sings* (1969). Ada's midlife story begins after she and her young daughter Flora have arrived in New Zealand, where Ada has been contracted to marry the rather bashful and immature Stewart, one of the early British settlers who had established themselves in New Zealand in the early nineteenth century. Their marriage, like that of Catherine to Linton in *Wuthering Heights*, is not passionately fulfilling for Ada, and it is Baines, a friend of Stewart's, who has gone native to a certain degree, and sports Maori tattoos on his face and body, who gradually awakens her passionate interests.

As an animus figure to put next to Brontë's Heathcliff, Baines is both similar and different. With his Maori aspects, he is exotically primitivist, just like the dark complexioned Heathcliff, who is said to be an abandoned gypsy child. But he has none of Heathcliff's emotional brutality, and it is clear that Campion has endeavored—quite successfully—to improve on the Heathcliff model, in terms of creating a positive animus figure who will lead the heroine not to death but to a new life. Their love is curiously associated with Ada's piano, which has been a kind of friend and confidant for her in her lonely years as an unmarried mother. This piano has also been for the mute Ada a voice through which she could express herself richly, and it now provides the link between Baines and her, since, after he bought the piano from Stewart, she has been seduced into regaining her instrument key by key through the granting of increasingly intimate sexual favors.

The piano is thus a highly eroticized object. Although inanimate, it rightly gives the film its title, for it has a spooky life of its own, and is twice the occasion for near tragedy. On the first occasion, one of its keys, sent by Ada to Baines as a kind of love token through the intermediary of her daughter Flora, is given to Stewart instead, who becomes wildly jealous, and, in a scene of shocking brutality, takes an axe and cuts off one of his wife's fingers, thus damaging her ability to play the piano. This brutal act spells the end of their marriage, and Ada and Baines set sail together for Nelson, where they hope to build a life together.

At this point Campion does something unexpected and quite remarkable. The piano, which has been a looming presence throughout the film, generally of a positive nature, now becomes a malevolent embodiment of the negative animus that pulls Ada towards death, as Heathcliffe ultimately had done with Catherine. The ambiguous animus figure represented in Brontë's novel by Heathcliff—fascinating but also malevolent—is split in two, with Baines as the positive side, and the piano eventually as the malevolent one. The piano as animus figure? This may seem to be a strange and risky move on the director's part, but the scene where Ada demands that the piano be thrown overboard into the sea is powerful and suggestive. As the ropes holding the piano slither overboard, it is clear—if the spectator watches carefully—that Ada has deliberately entangled her foot in them, and so has impulsively decided to follow the piano into the watery depths, willing herself to replicate Catherine's tragic fate in *Wuthering Heights*. As the camera follows their descent under water, it seems that Ada has been willing her own death, until at the very last minute she struggles to free her foot from the shoe entangled in the ropes binding her to the piano, and floats quickly up to the surface, released from the clutches of the now monstrous piano.

At that point the film segues into a happy ending and shows Ada happily at home with Baines in the city of Nelson, where she gives piano lessons, a silver artificial finger having replaced the one she lost, with which she is seen tapping on the keyboard of a new piano. She has also recovered her voice, and one senses that her adventure in the muddy backwoods of nineteenth-century New Zealand has been an ordeal through which she has achieved at last a happy and harmonious relationship with the masculine. Ada has integrated some of the power of the animus, and this has brought her regeneration, midlife transformation and a new life.

Chapter 3

Oedipus, mentors and male midlife transformation

The myth of Oedipus is arguably the key myth of Freudian psychology, where it expresses the dramatic tensions of a crucial developmental stage in a boy's life and its regressive neurotic effects on a man's later years. Thus it may come as a surprise to revision Oedipus as a Jungian hero of a rich male midlife passage as represented symbolically in Sophocles' tragedy *Oedipus the King*. The erstwhile youthful hero who had famously delivered the people of Thebes from the predations of the Sphinx and had married their queen Jocasta becomes, in the course of the action of this exemplary oneiric drama, an increasingly enigmatic figure, as he sheds his social persona as king, father and husband and reluctantly yields to a process of anguished midlife transformation. Oedipus, like Jung, found himself at midlife floundering in a nightmare come to life, and, again like Jung, was barely able to keep his head above water. His relative success in surviving the experience of the deeper reaches of the archetypal unconscious makes him paradigmatic as regards the analysis of two key elements of men's journey into midlife: the possibility of a radical midlife transformation in depth, and a problematic relationship with a midlife mentor.

In his book *Oedipus* Thomas Van Nortwick has shown how Sophocles' play anatomizes a midlife transition in terms of the discovery of a new identity for Oedipus: "the hero blinds himself as a way of turning inward toward the darkness inside himself, to face those aspects of his identity that have been kept from his conscious attention" (Van Nortwick 1998: 80). In particular he locates the significance of Oedipus' involuntary incest as something that "can symbolize . . . a tension between young and old" (Van Nortwick 1998: 82), thus marking the beginning of the liminal state at the onset of middle age. Van Nortwick's analysis draws on Jungian perspectives on midlife, but also on Daniel J. Levinson's pioneering study *The Seasons of a Man's Life* (1978). My own analysis of Sophocles' tragedy will stress the hermeneutic value of Jung's account of his own near psychotic breakdown at midlife in *Memories, Dreams, Reflections* (1963), an oneiric text that provides a key to what is a potentially puzzling and disconcerting text for the modern mind already saturated with Freudian ideas concerning the Oedipus complex. The problem the reader faces is this: if all Oedipus did was to discover his own Oedipus complex, he would hardly deserve the exceptional status Sophocles seems to want to grant him at the end of the play, where he is precisely *not* represented as an Everyman discovering his painfully regressive and neurotic tendencies concerning parricide and maternal incest, but rather as a mysterious figure who has assumed the burden of an exceptional fate. There is, no doubt, a regressive (and Oedipal) side to Sophocles' Oedipus, but there is much more to him than neurotic petulance and bluster. What, then, is the nature of Oedipus' midlife transformation, if it is not limited to taking on at the end of the tragedy the stigmatized identity of a despised outcast who has violated some basic human laws? In fact, Sophocles dramatizes the Oedipus myth in a way that undermines what might have been its original significance, that is, a hero finally punished for acts of parricide and maternal incest committed years before, but accidentally and unknowingly.

Oedipus not only provided Freud with a name for the complex, but also provided René Girard with an important example for his provocatively original analysis of the scapegoating process. Girard's theory posited the ultimate innocence of all scapegoats—at least, as regards the crimes they are charged with having committed—as well as the ultimate injustice and brutality of their accusers. The scapegoat's accusers are caught up in a collective frenzy, and "know not what they do," as Christ (for Girard the exemplary scapegoat, whose story reveals the monstrous injustice of the process) said of his own accusers. Girard's defense of Oedipus, and of all scapegoats in history and mythology, is thus a vindication of an innocent person, usually a foreigner or member of a stigmatized group, falsely accused of crimes he did not commit. Since scapegoating myths, asserts Girard, take the side of the accusers, Oedipus in the end is condemned without appeal. In a recent interview Girard has said that "I call mythical every text imprisoned in a system of representation structured by a hidden scapegoat" (Golsan 2002: 133). Thus for Girard the Oedipus myth is hardly unique as regards its "deep-seated complicity" with the lynch mob and the whole long sorry history of representations of scapegoating throughout the ages. For Girard, "scapegoat representation is subjacent to all [mythological] texts" (Golsan 2002: 133), and all myths affirm over and over again the guilt of the scapegoat and justify the mob violence that characterizes the scapegoating frenzy. All mythic texts for Girard take the standpoint of the persecutors, with the signal exception of the account in the Gospels of the scapegoating process leading to the Passion of Christ, where the divine Victim is exceptionally represented as totally innocent of all the charges laid against him. Thus Girard sees an enormous difference between the Christ story and the Oedipus story. The Gospel narratives insist on Christ's innocence, whereas the Oedipus myth, like all other scapegoat myths, is told from the standpoint of the accusers, and so insists on Oedipus' guilt.[1]

According to Girard, Sophocles' tragedy *Oedipus the King* demonstrates that "Oedipus is really guilty, really responsible for the plague" and that "the Thebans are perfectly right to expel him" (Girard and Anspach 2004: 67). Frederick Ahl, no doubt, has made a valiant attempt to demonstrate that things are not so simple in *Oedipus the King*, and that the various accusations against him, which ultimately rely on the oracle of Delphi and Apollo for their authority, may in fact constitute pernicious attempts to implicate Oedipus in crimes he has not committed. But there is no need to go as far as Frederick Ahl has recently gone in seeing in Oedipus the hapless victim of trumped up charges and the classical equivalent of a malevolent disinformation campaign.[2] In my opinion, Oedipus does not require such a brilliantly clever and subtle defense to prove his innocence, because Sophocles' play itself resists Girard's interpretation in much more obvious ways.

For one thing, it is not the Thebans who expel Oedipus from Thebes at the end of the play, but rather Oedipus who expels himself. The burden of proving Oedipus' guilt has shifted in the course of the play from his accusers onto Oedipus himself as his own self-accuser. What happens in the course of the play is thus the unexpected *internalization* of the scapegoating process that Oedipus himself had initiated at the behest of the Delphic oracle, when he decided to send his brother-in-law Creon to Delphi to inquire on ways to end the terrible plague that was decimating Thebes. The oracle's answer—in essence, "the murderer of the old king Laius has gone unpunished, and, since this is what has caused the plague, you must find the murderer and punish him"—might seem to be a perfect example of pure Girardian scapegoating, because Oedipus is eventually revealed to be the one responsible for the death of Laius, and so punishing Oedipus should make the plague disappear—end of story. But in Sophocles' tragedy the accusation and the condemnation of the scapegoat morph into the self-accusation and self-conviction of the scapegoat himself, as the drama develops according to its own peculiar internal logic. What is initially a clear-cut drama of social scapegoating turns into something much more complicated: a complex psychological drama that involves Oedipus in a radical reassessment of what kind of man he really is. For Oedipus' dramatic midlife change in self-identity, as Van Nortwick has stressed, is primarily psychological in reference, not social. It is not how Oedipus is judged by others but how he judges himself that becomes the main theme of the play; it is not how others punish him, but rather how he punishes himself that becomes the primary focus.

So Oedipus becomes a scapegoat *in his own eyes*, and this makes for an entirely different kind of scapegoat drama in several significant ways. Once the truth of his situation has been revealed, it turns out that Oedipus is *not*, like Girard's typical scapegoat, a foreigner or resident alien: he is revealed to be a native Theban and furthermore to be the son of the former king.

Next, the "lynching mob" that Girard sees at work behind this as well as all other nonbiblical myths, is not what Girard takes to be the "generative force" of the scapegoating process (Girard and Anspach 2004: 101); rather, the generative force is the investigating mind of Oedipus himself. And there is no question of what Girard believes is revealed to be his "malevolence" (Girard and Anspach 2004: 101), because his parricide and incest were clearly unintended, which is why Oedipus may be said to be *responsible* but *not guilty*. Aristotle wrestled with this problem of the tragic hero not entirely deserving of his fate, with special reference to *Oedipus the King* (which he tended in his *Poetics* to view as the paradigmatic tragedy), and resolved it, at least to his own satisfaction, with his theory of *hamartia*, according to which the tragic hero, a figure somewhat larger than life but neither entirely good nor entirely bad, meets his fate through a terrible miscalculation or tragic mistake, that leads him to take an action whose unintended result is tragic. In this case, Oedipus perseveres in his tragic mistake of continuing to investigate the murder of King Laius, hoping, as the hero who had once saved Thebes from the murderous Sphinx, that he may once again become its savior by uncovering and punishing the regicide, no doubt with the initial expectation that in the process he will also clear himself of any suspicions that have begun to point in his direction. But his very dogged persistence in pursuing the truth, admirable as it may well be, produces the opposite result of what he intended, since it culminates in the revelation that he is the one whose crime has been the cause of the plague that threatens his people with destruction.

It is thus Oedipus' gradual discovery of his own unwitting responsibility for the death of Laius that slowly leads us away from the scapegoat drama that Girard would have us see in *Oedipus the King*, however present it may be in the opening scenes. The clearest indication of this shift in perception lies in the way everyone by the end of the play tends to forget about the murder that the oracle had declared to be the cause of the plague, in order to focus instead on the one thing that is totally irrelevant to the initial premises of this specific scapegoating process, which is maternal incest. Maternal incest was precisely *not* what the oracle of Delphi mentioned, when questioned about how to eliminate the plague; rather, it directed attention only to the necessity of finding and punishing the murderer of King Laius. The issue of maternal incest is something that raises its ugly head only as part of the message of the old prophet Teiresias, who, with great reluctance, and after being goaded into responding, tries to get Oedipus to deal with the possibility that he himself was the problem: a problem for his people, and a problem for himself. Thus the primary internalized problem *of* Oedipus *for* Oedipus was the revelation of his marriage with his mother—not the murder of the old king, and not even the discovery that the old king was his father. One of the dramatic ironies of the play is that his wife (and soon to be revealed mother) Jocasta may well have glimpsed the truth before Oedipus does, but seems prepared to live with it as far as she herself is concerned. However, since Jocasta seems to think that Oedipus will be incapable of facing it, and will even be destroyed by the revelation, she tries to divert him from the truth, when she argues that anxiety about maternal incest is nothing but the stuff of dreams:

> How many men, in dreams, have lain with their mothers!
> No reasonable man is troubled by such things.
>   (Sophocles 1977: 51)

Thus what started out as a scapegoat drama in which Oedipus is the chosen victim has turned into something radically different, as Oedipus' nightmare gradually comes to life with each appearance of a significant piece of evidence. What new kind of drama is it, then? It is, I would argue, the dramatization of a powerful oneiric text, in which Oedipus ultimately condemns himself to bearing the heavy burden of a *fate*, not the burden of guilt for a *crime*.

But what in the case of Oedipus is the specific nature of this tragic fate? Whatever its symbolic nature, it is embodied in the pairing of the involuntary crimes of parricide and incest, and it is necessary at this point to look well beyond Freud's theory of the Oedipus complex as well as Girard's theory of the scapegoat. The exceptional character of Oedipus—his larger-than-life dimension, his mythic grandeur—does not fit well into a Freudian interpretation that would reduce him to an all too common example of how the Oedipus complex can cast its shadow on the whole of a man's life. Of course, a side of the personality of Oedipus *is* quite typically Oedipal: his blustering rages, his almost paranoiac suspicion of others, and his midlife rigidity and unwillingness to compromise, are shadow qualities that he shares with many men at midlife. But what in Oedipus' tragic burden of fate is exceptional and unusual? A Jungian approach would see the heavy burden Oedipus carries as not only personal in nature but also as archetypal, and viewing it this way changes the picture completely. Inasmuch as the motif of the pairing of parricide and incest is symbolically charged with a meaning that is hyperdetermined (i.e., capable of symbolizing any number of things; e.g., Van Nortwick's "tension between young and old"), it is necessary to seek first the general import of the pairing of parricide and incest, and then its possible specific meaning in the case of Sophocles' Oedipus.

As regards the first point, I would propose that Sophocles' Oedipus has stumbled inadvertently onto a domain of archetypal psychological experience that few men in ancient Greece would have had the courage or the capacity to experience directly or to deal with successfully. As his oneiric drama unfolds, it is no longer a question for Oedipus of dealing with mere fantasy and dream (to which Jocasta would like him to attribute his anxiety regarding incest), nor even with the accumulation of evidence pointing to him as the murderer of Laius; it is rather the dawning realization that both incest and parricide have become for him *psychic realities* that define who he is now as much as—or more than—they define what he has done in the past. Given the emotional intensity of the response they evoke in him, for Oedipus they constitute a terrible and frightening experience of the *numinous*—a *mysterium tremendum*—of the sort that nearly caused Jung to lose his mind in a psychotic breakdown, when he confronted for the first time unmediated archetypal material from the collective unconscious. Jung's later assessment of the dangers of such direct unmediated experience of the archetypal unconscious was eminently tragic:

> There is no point in wishing to *know* more of the collective unconscious than one gets through dreams and intuition. The more you know of it, the greater and heavier becomes your moral burden, because the unconscious contents transform themselves into your individual tasks and duties as soon as they begin to become conscious. Do you want to increase loneliness and misunderstanding? Do you want to find more and more complications and increasing responsibilities? You get enough of it.
>
> (Jung 1975: II, 172)

Oedipus through his stubborn determination to *know* has brought himself to just such a point of extreme loneliness and isolation. The new identity that his midlife transformation has bestowed upon him at the end of the tragedy is that of a solitary wanderer, rather like a wandering Indian holy man or *sannyasi*—rather like, as many have pointed out, the blind Teiresias, whose loss of physical sight is compensated by his capacity for inner sight: for insight and wisdom. Having resisted the prophet Teiresias and having treated him with savage rage at the opening of the tragedy, the irony is that by the end of the play the self-blinded Oedipus has *become* Teiresias, so to speak. His duties and responsibilities are now defined in terms of this new identity as lonely wanderer, accompanied by a sense that eventually there will be some great fulfillment ahead of him, some fate whose full nature will only become clear in some kind of transfiguration at the time of his death:

> And yet I know
> Death will not ever come to me through sickness
> Or in any natural way: I have been preserved
> For some unthinkable fate.
>
> (Sophocles 1977: 77)[3]

That "unthinkable fate" is all for the future, of course; for now, Oedipus' self-defined duty is to exile himself from the city.

But the ostensible reason for his exile—the need to save the city from the plague through the expulsion of a scapegoat—is, most curiously, never mentioned at the end of the play—not by Oedipus, not by Creon (who has now become king), and not even by the members of the chorus, who represent the plague ridden people of Thebes. Even if one could claim that the spectators would automatically have assumed that Oedipus' departure would stop the plague, one would still expect some mention to be made of this at the end of the play, at least by a properly grateful chorus. But the chorus says nothing about the plague or the effect on it of Oedipus' exile. By the end of the play Oedipus has clearly stepped outside the parameters of the scapegoat drama imagined by Girard, and consequently the audience is no longer expected to exit rejoicing at the punishing of the guilty scapegoat, but rather to leave the theater in awe of a man who has brought ruin on himself, but through this symbolic death has been reborn at midlife as a new incarnation of a prophet and sage, who, like Teiresias, has seen what others could not have dared to see.

His new identity as prophet and sage has thus displaced his former identity as the hero, who had once saved the city of Thebes from the monstrous Sphinx. However, there is a potential problem even with this earlier part of his mythic identity, as Jean-Joseph Goux has argued, in his book *Oedipus, Philosopher* (1993). However much he may brag of having become the heroic savior of Thebes by answering the riddle of the Sphinx and killing that strange half-woman half-lion monster, Oedipus in his youth was in fact a flawed hero, whose defects are apparent when one compares his myth to that of other Greek heroes. Unlike them, his great heroic feat of dealing with the Sphinx was not assigned to him by any "dispatcher king," as they were for example in the case of the labors of Heracles, assigned to him by King Erystheus. Goux thus concludes that the myth of Oedipus is "a myth of the absence of the trial-imposing king" (Goux 1993: 35). Thus there is something already suspect and anomalous in the self-proclaimed heroic stature of this self-declared self-made man.

Goux also argues that Oedipus' youthful heroic deed—dealing success-fully with the Sphinx and her famous riddle—had not been fully heroic. It suffered from being the result of intellectual cleverness, and did not manifest the union of body and mind that characterizes the true heroic act, typically the killing of a monster, and often a female monster. He writes that

> In the struggle against the frightful beast, dragon or Medusa, the hero develops his masculinity; he mobilizes inner forces that transform his infantile dependence into a concentrated and combative manhood. That is why, in the paradigmatic myth of the hero, it is the force of arms and not merely shrewdness that determines the victory over the female monster. In the case of Oedipus, it appears clearly that his full

manhood has not been mobilized, that it is the intelligence of the head
and not the courage of the chest . . . that make success possible.

(Goux 1993: 37)

This acute observation leads Goux to conclude that "the myth of Oedipus
the king is a myth of avoidance of initiation" (Goux 1993: 18).

We may agree with Goux as regards the uninitiated quality of the
younger Oedipus, who, at the opening of *Oedipus the King*, still manifests
regressively some of the characteristics of the young uninitiated male, who
rages against any perceived affront to his grandiosity. This type of arrogant
conduct characterized the stereotypical tyrant figure in democratic
Athenian theater, a figure that allied the bullying of youth with the rigid
authoritism of midlife in a way that catered to the democratic Athenian
audience's visceral hatred of tyranny in general. Up to this point, at least,
Oedipus is rather typical of the figure of the youthful tyrant grown older
but not wiser, whose arrogance and bullying indicate that already in his
youth he had not been properly socialized through submission to the higher
power of the dispatching king, a partial image of the initiating mentor. But,
as did Girard, Goux tends to focus on the myth of Oedipus' heroic youth
instead of on the Sophoclean tragedy, in which he is presented as a
successful king and the middle-aged father of several children. Sophocles'
Oedipus the King is very much a drama of initiation, yet not of delayed
youthful initiation, but rather of *midlife* initiation. Even if Oedipus, as
Goux has argued, was only partially and inadequately initiated in his
youth, he would not however escape the challenge of initiation at midlife—
in fact, his midlife initiation would be dramatically spectacular. If incest
and parricide occupy almost the totality of its symbolic field, it is precisely
because they have something crucial to add in the way of symbolic significance, as we will see.

The process that has led Oedipus to his august fate at midlife has its own
peculiar characteristics, and now it is possible for us to attempt to assign
some specific meaning to the symbolically overloaded terms of "parricide"
and "incest" as they relate to Oedipus' exceptional midlife transformation.
For Oedipus' burden of guilt as well as for his burden of fate, "parricide" is
a loaded term. It applies most directly to his rage-filled killing of King Laius,
an old man, who was himself acting abusively and arrogantly when he struck
at the young man, actually his own son unbeknownst to him, in order to
force him to make way for his chariot at a lonely crossroads. In Sophocles'
tragedy—so years later—the theme of parricide is latently present in
Oedipus' raging against another father figure who is, unbeknownst to him,
in fact his maternal uncle, that is, his brother-in-law Creon. In his treatment
of Creon, Oedipus verges on paranoia, threatening him with execution for
his alleged treasonous plotting against his throne. Such quasi-parricidal
raging is also present in the scene with the old prophet Teiresias, who

attempts unsuccessfully to play a mentoring role in his life, and again in the scene with the old shepherd, whom Oedipus threatens to torture, in spite of the fact that he had saved the life of the infant Oedipus, after he had been exposed on a mountainside to die. All of these father figures prove vulnerable, one after the other, to Oedipus' Oedipal rages against older men.

The irony of these attempts at symbolic parricide is that, in two of the instances, the "father" Oedipus rages against turns out to be a potential midlife mentor. In Teiresias the audience would have recognized the sage who had famously counseled Odysseus in Hades in Homer's *Odyssey*. While in *Oedipus the King* he is presented as irascible and impulsive (in that respect resembling Oedipus' actual father Laius), Teiresias' wisdom, however angrily presented to Oedipus, could have been crucial in helping him engage with his fate more quickly and effectively. If he had listened to Teiresias, he might have decided not to pursue his inquiry concerning the murder of Laius, for example, or he might have accepted the burden of his fate more gracefully, and have avoided causing misery and suffering for those around him who wished him well. Teiresias' midlife mentoring message consisted essentially in turning Oedipus' gaze inward, and in having him see himself as the source of a problem he is stubbornly insisting he has nothing to do with. His wife Jocasta tries to dissuade Oedipus from listening to Teiresias:

> Set your mind at rest.
> If it is a question of soothsayers, I tell you
> That you will find no man whose craft gives knowledge
> Of the unknowable.
>
> (Sophocles 1977: 35)

But everything revealed or hinted at by Teiresias will eventually be corroborated by an increasing weight of evidence and testimony. Oedipus' quasi-parricidal rage against Teiresias thus stems from his resistance to midlife transformation, and his resistance to Teiresias proves to be ultimately futile, since, by the end of the tragedy, he in his turn will be transformed into a blind man tapping the ground with his staff, just like the prophet Teiresias.

Oedipus' brother-in-law Creon turns out—paradoxically and unexpectedly—to be his second midlife mentor. The role of Creon has the second greatest number of lines in the play, but it is strange how little attention has been paid to him in commentaries and criticism. Although Creon, Jocasta's brother, is presented in the play only as Oedipus' brother-in-law, by the end of the play the spectator discovers that he is also Oedipus' maternal uncle. (Although this new relationship is never mentioned explicitly in the text, it is clear from the context.) In many archaic societies, it would have been normal for a man to act as mentor for his sister's son, and this is what Creon winds up doing. After Teiresias has been driven from the stage, it is

Creon who is left to guide Oedipus. Their final exchange is full of subtle suggestions that point to a change in the nature of their relationship. When Oedipus wishes to be the one to order his own exile, Creon demurs; when Oedipus quotes the oracle of Apollo, Creon urges restraint and taking time to reflect:

(Creon) And what is that you would have me do?
(Oedipus) Drive me out of the country as quickly as may be
To a place where no human voice can ever greet me.
(Creon) I should have done that before now—only,
God's will had not been wholly revealed to me.
(Oedipus) But his command is plain: the parricide
Must be destroyed. I am that evil man.
(Creon) That is the sense of it, yes; but as things are,
We had best discover clearly what is to be done.
(Oedipus) You would learn more about a man like me?
(Creon) You are ready now to listen to the god.
(Oedipus) I will listen. But it is to you
That I must turn for help.

(Sophocles 1997: 80)

Throughout this dialog Creon speaks very carefully, always with a concern for not claiming to know more than he really knows of the will of the gods. Given the horrible irony of the results of Oedipus' attempt to know everything no matter what the cost, it seems appropriate that Creon considers his faith in his own powers of insight to be limited by his sense that it is the gods, and most specifically Apollo and his oracle at Delphi, that have the ultimate knowledge. When he says to Oedipus, who insists on being sent away from Thebes, that he should ask this of Apollo, not of him, one senses in Creon a humility and an unwillingness to speak for the gods, that is, to speak beyond his own limited knowledge. Creon provides an example of how human wisdom needs to acknowledge all that it does not know of the hidden depths—the archetypal depths—of divine wisdom, and to remain humble and uninflated in the face of it.

By the end of the play Creon has been accused by Oedipus of sedition and menaced with death, and his sister Jocasta has hanged herself because of the disgrace her husband/son has brought upon her and the family. Under these dreadful circumstances, it must be acknowledged that Creon treats Oedipus with the care, generosity and kindness worthy of a midlife mentoring figure. In the last scene Oedipus is shown once more trying to have things his own way and clinging to his daughters desperately as potential companions in his exile—a regressively Oedipal situation in the making! Yet Creon's brief words to him have the resonance of healing wisdom for a man who had succumbed to the rigid and dystonic authoritism of middle age, until fate at last opened up his mind to the presence of an abyss within:

> Think no longer
> That you are in command here, but rather think
> How, when you were, you served your own destruction.
>
> (Sophocles 1997: 80)

The abyss within—the archetypal contents constellated in the course of Oedipus' midlife crisis—consists above all of the symbolic field of maternal incest, which had an especially strong mythological resonance in the context of the patriarchal culture of ancient Greece. Oedipus had lived out literally a myth that would have been for other men, according to his wife Jocasta, only a disturbing dream. But maternal incest also has an archetypal dimension in the play. It represents an unholy but archetypal union of mother and son, and so it is the power of this mythic mother–son conjunction that needs to be analyzed in terms of its specifically Greek cultural context. Greek mythology rejected or obfuscated to a large degree the son–lover relationship celebrated openly in the mythology of the Mediterranean Great Mother. But it survived in veiled form in such myths as the story of Aphrodite and Adonis, or of disastrous amorous meetings between mortal men and female divinities. The imbalance in Greek hypermasculine patriarchal culture, with its celebration of male energies and dominance, would have been expressed in its most frightening form by horrendous images of the repressed feminine, as at the end of Book 11 of the *Odyssey*, where Odysseus is shown to panic at the very thought of a Gorgon figure, a symbolic image of frightening female power. Actual mother–son incest literalizes this mythic and symbolic image, and gives it an unmediated impact. It is as though Oedipus had unwittingly stumbled into an archetypal domain with which he and his culture were ill prepared to come to terms. Like Odysseus in Hades, terrified by the mere thought of a Gorgon's head, Oedipus bears the heavy burden of a cultural imbalance, which can only react with utter horror at the thought of mother–son incest, not only because of the social taboo, but also because of the panic fear of the archetypal power of the Mother in a hypermasculine patriarchal and warrior culture. Oedipus' incest with his mother involves more than breaking a social taboo: it is an act willed by the gods, that is, it is incest in its sacred and archetypal dimension. Oedipus, by assuming this archetypal burden and by suffering the consequences of living out the dreaded myth, becomes at the end of his midlife crisis a kind of culture hero, in that it is from the paralyzing fear of this myth as much as from the plague that he saves Thebes.

Thus Oedipus' self-imposed and undeserved sufferings present him not only as an innocent victim and a scapegoat, but also as a man whose midlife wisdom is earned though agony and ordeal. The wisdom he learned through suffering is this: that a culture can face its own worst demons, if the way is shown by a superior man who can face them alone without flinching, and who can demonstrate in his own life that the apparently unbearable insight can be borne by the true psychological hero that he proves himself to be. Oedipus has thus become truly generative at midlife, not only by accepting to be himself the willing scapegoat who sacrifices himself for the welfare of the community, but even more by facing what his culture fears most, that is, the archetypal power represented by the myth of mother–son incest. However initially resistant he was to the process— however reluctantly he listened to his midlife mentors—Oedipus by the end of the play has shown himself to be capable of shouldering an archetypal burden that even Teiresias doubted he could bear. It is no wonder that Creon and the Theban people treat him with both compassion and awe as he prepares to exit the stage. Later Sophocles was to write a tragedy, *Oedipus at Colonus*, in which Oedipus' almost divine status as heroic seer is celebrated in a mysterious death scene that is described as strangely numinous. But already at the end of *Oedipus the King*, the spectator can sense dimly that Oedipus is in the process of becoming a seer like Teiresias—someone who sees deeply into the archetypal nature of things, and whose hard-won wisdom can help the community face and come to terms with its own cultural demons.

Jung felt that the initiation process was "engraved on the unconscious as a primordial image," and that it was "almost an instinctive mechanism" (Jung 1989b: 40–41). The psychic hunger and thirst for a mentor is as old as initiation itself, for one cannot imagine one without the other. Initiation cannot proceed successfully without the mentor. But mentors can be unreliable, and their messages can be mixed messages. For that reason, among others, mentors and their messages may be hard to trust. And there are excellent reasons why modern men, like Oedipus, have developed a distrust of mentors and mentoring. The history of the last one hundred years provides a depressing spectacle of a variety of political idols with feet of clay, who have been instigators of death trips that have resulted in the betrayal of young men in uniform by older men in suits. And even at midlife it is certainly hard to trust older men as mentors in the highly competitive world of corporate culture, where a friendly handshake may be followed by a stab in the back.

But even a bit of genuine mentoring can be valuable, and it can happen quite unexpectedly, as I once experienced personally. I was sitting in the back of a large auditorium with five hundred or so other New Yorkers, listening to the Jungian writer James Hillman give a paper on *Oedipus at Colonus*, Sophocles' play about the approaching death of an exiled king, now old and wise but still enough of his old patriarchal Oedipal self to curse his sons cruelly and to lean heavily on his daughters for support. In the discussion that followed the lecture, I asked Hillman a question from the back of the auditorium (I could barely see him, and hearing him wasn't easy either), to which he replied "[somethingsomethingsomething] . . . submission without castration." I don't remember what my question was, and I did not catch his complete answer, but I felt that I had really been spoken to. Those three words "submission without castration" have stuck with me for years. Looking back on this moment, I feel that those three words probably spoke to my need at midlife to put Oedipal fears and resentments behind me, and to freely and willingly "submit to a higher power" in a way that, as a self-assertive young hero, I once would have found distasteful. This is, I think, what Oedipus did in *Oedipus the King*, when he submitted to the authority of the Delphic oracle, accepted however reluctantly the authority of Creon, and finally assumed the terrible burden of the fate the gods had assigned to him, and that Teiresias had correctly predicted.

Once again, *Oedipus the King* is an excellent text to turn to for a symbolic representation of issues concerning midlife mentoring and initiation, although in so doing I may seem at times to contradict what I said about Oedipus earlier, at least to the extent that I failed to insist that Oedipus' tragic disregard for his midlife mentors was an ultimately fortunate mistake, since it brought to a head the process of working through his own distrust of anyone who reminded him unconsciously of his abusive father. Oedipus thus found his own Oedipus complex to be a good place to start his initiation process, and that is, of course, what Freudian therapists have been urging on men for generations. However, it is clearly no easy task, not for them and not, as we have seen, for Oedipus. In fact, shortly after the play opens, Oedipus does not seem to be working through his Oedipus complex at all; rather, he appears to be thoroughly mired in it, ranting and raving about a plot to unseat him from his throne, which he mainly accuses his brother-in-law Creon of fomenting. After rudely dismissing the old prophet Teiresias' attempts to help him, Oedipus subjects Creon, who has been nothing if not generous minded in trying to assist Oedipus in finding out why his people were dying of the plague, to intolerable abuse and threats to his life. What will we say is the unconscious psychological reason for this lack of trust—that Oedipus' fear of symbolic castration prevents him from submitting to any higher authority or mentor? Oedipus the King, full of grandiosity, will submit to no one; he resists seeing himself as anything other than the once and future savior of his people, in the past through the killing of the Sphinx, and now through his attempt to uncover the cause of the plague and save his people from it. When the truth comes out, namely that he himself, through the murder of his father King Laius, is the actual cause of the plague, Oedipus has a lot to lose, and when he finally loses it, he does not do so gracefully.

As we have seen, the Freudian interpretation of Oedipus' tragedy stands at the origin of modern psychoanalytical thinking, but it has focused too exclusively on the regressive pull of unresolved childhood conflicts, at the expense of dealing with problems that owe their existence to actions taken in the present. What is needed now for the twenty-first-century adult male, in the context of what has been an ongoing revisioning of masculinities and the recreation of helpful bonding between men and midlife mentors, is a distancing from the image of Oedipus as the victim of past abuses and accidents, and the re-imaging of Oedipus as someone who, although he found it hard to trust the mentor's voice as it spoke to him through his maternal uncle Creon, ultimately accepted his guidance and his wisdom. This relationship of trust with Creon as a midlife mentor enabled Oedipus to take his fate into his own hands, and to bear its heavy burden. Seen in this light, the tragedy of Oedipus is the tragedy of a man who needed a midlife mentor badly, but who, almost up until the end, feared and rejected anyone who reminded him of his father's patriarchal abusive power.

The early history of modern psychoanalysis illustrates how a mentoring relationship can famously go wrong. A series of letters between Sigmund Freud (who was old enough to be Jung's "maternal uncle") and Carl Gustav Jung reveals in some detail what the problem seems to have been.[4] The letters reveal the growing estrangement of Jung from Freud, the mentor of his younger years, starting in 1911, when Jung was about thirty-six, until January 1913, when a break occurred that was never to be healed. Could this tragic break arguably based on unresolved Oedipal fear and rivalry have been avoided? This is impossible to say with certainty, but I feel that things might have gone better between them if Freud had acted less like a patriarchal tyrant defending his throne, and Jung had followed the spirit of James Hillman's later advice to me about "submission without castration."

But this is not what happened. No doubt, Jung's wife, Emma, had tried to mediate their growing estrangement, occasioned in the first instance by Jung's preparation for publication of his trailblazing book *Transformation and Symbolism of the Libido*, which he feared—correctly—would not be to Freud's liking. In a secret letter to Freud (November 6, 1911), Emma Jung reminded Freud of what he himself had called his own "streak of pater-nalism," and urged him "not to think of Carl with a father's feeling . . . but rather as one human being thinks of another, who, like you, has his own law to fulfill." She also analyzed her husband Carl's anxieties as the partial result of his unconsciously envisaging his relationship with Freud as a father–son relationship (McGuire 1989: 203–204). When Jung the next week wrote to Freud that "you are a dangerous rival" (McGuire 1979: 205), Freud immediately fired back with "the trouble with you younger men seems to be a lack of understanding in dealing with your father-complexes" (McGuire 1977: 213). When Freud failed to visit Jung during a brief trip to Switzerland, Jung wrote bitterly that "your . . . gesture has dealt me a lasting wound." He also noted resentfully that, regarding his respect for

Freud as the leader of the psychoanalytical movement, "I can only assure you that there is no resistance on my side, unless it be my refusal to be treated like a fool riddled with complexes" (McGuire 1977: 238).

By the end of November 1912, after various conflicts and reconciliations between them, Jung was able to write to Freud that he realized "how different I am from you" (McGuire 1977: 243). At the beginning of December, he began to be more frank about his ambivalent feelings towards his mentor, and urged Freud to "stop playing the father" (McGuire 1977: 253). Freud apparently found all this Oedipal rage more than he could take, and ended their friendship and their correspondence on January 3, 1913. The hidden hand of Oedipal rivalry, operating unconsciously but very effectively, had ruined the creative mentoring relationship between Freud and Jung, and the consequences of their break are with us a century later, with Freudians and Jungians still not on the best of speaking terms.

Looking back to ancient texts such as *Oedipus the King* helps reveal the age-old nature of the problem of mentors and mentoring, especially as regards the negative influence of the patriarchal attitudes that modern culture is struggling to disengage itself from today. The Men's Movement of the 1980s and 90s, much maligned then and now somewhat forgotten, nevertheless did much to highlight the realization that patriarchy can be not only defined as the rule of the fathers (in the positive, generative sense of the term), but also as the rule of uninitiated grown-up boys, schoolyard bullies grown older but not wiser—ageing Oedipal sons, who are still seeking revenge against their father and anyone else who reminds them unconsciously of their father for the unhealed wounds of their childhood.

A bit of speculative history on my part (or better: myth-making, of the sort that Freud excelled in[5]) may help clarify the issue. In ages past (*in illo tempore*), "father" would have been a positive term, and a father's "power" would have designated the means he had available to give expression to his love and generative concern for his children. But under patriarchy the power of the father was increasingly contaminated by its association with the power of the tyrant. This excessive power of the father made it difficult for the son to come into his own as a man (as one who "has his own law to fulfill," as Emma Jung put it), since any act of independence could be taken as posing a threat to the absolute power of the father. The problem of initiating the son into manhood and independence was thus made into something highly problematic and fraught with anxiety; at one extreme, initiation might require the son to kill the father in order to take his place, as in the myth of Oedipus he literally did; at the other extreme, the uninitiated son might find himself incapable of ever taking his father's place, and thus would be bossed around by one father figure or another for the rest of his life. This patriarchal dilemma must have seemed at one point in time to be well nigh unsolvable. Then the mentor stepped in as the solution to this patriarchal dilemma. Whether as maternal uncle, tribal elder or guru, the mentor could sponsor and encourage a man's maturation process and independence from his father's potentially abusive control, without the mentor feeling personally threatened by it himself. Not so much father as "godfather," the mentor was not directly implicated in the Oedipal competition between father and son, and so could stand outside the dysfunctional patriarchal initiation system and provide a solution to its dilemma.

But, even in the best of circumstances, Oedipal rivalry risked contaminating the mentoring relationship, as it did between Creon and Oedipus, or between Freud and Jung. The symbolic solution that classic patriarchy found for this particular dilemma was a brilliant one: to symbolically kill the father figure as abusive tyrant in one form, in order to bond with him as compassionate mentor in another. In other words, to establish a relationship of trust with the mentor, it was necessary to free the mentor from the hostile Oedipal projections that were inevitable under patriarchy: in order to establish a relationship of trust with the Good Mentor. An inherently resentful and rage-filled relationship with the Bad Father had to be sacrificed: the Bad Father as Oedipal rival had to be symbolically killed. This peculiar sacrifice is the key to the patriarchal solution to the problem of mentoring, whether in youth or at midlife.

So a man at midlife, just like a young man, needs to find another father, but a godfather this time, that is, a mentor. But the mentor does not necessarily have to be one in flesh and blood. Jung, for example, once he had made his painful break with Freud, began to have mental conversations with a Wise Old Man figure he called Philemon. As a mentor for Jung in his midlife transition period, Philemon took up where Freud left off. He seemed, wrote Jung, to be "quite real, as if he were a living personality." They would converse together, as Jung went "walking up and down the garden with him," and Jung would later claim that in Philemon he had found "what the Indians call a guru" (Jung 1963: 183), or, more precisely, a "ghostly guru" or disembodied spirit for a teacher—a bit of Hindu lore Jung was to find "both illuminating and reassuring" (Jung 1963: 184).

A true midlife mentor is not a father, even though a man, disoriented and overwhelmed by regressive yearnings, may initially mistake him for one. The desire to worship some supremely wise and powerful being and to give up control of one's decision-making process to a man older and wiser than oneself is the patriarchal legacy of centuries of excessive vesting of power in the father. This excessive power mistakenly invested in the mentor inevitably becomes abusive ("power corrupts, and absolute power corrupts absolutely"), and paves the way for everything that has given patriarchy a bad name in the first place. Thus Freud increasingly acted, at least in Jung's eyes, as an abusive patriarch; Philemon, by contrast, was a transformative archetypal image of the wise and compassionate mentor, and was a figure fashioned out of Jung's deepest yearnings for someone who would respect his freedom, dignity and integrity. For a man's midlife mentor is only worthy of trust when he does not tamper with the freedom of the adult man he mentors. And, even if he proves worthy of trust, he is still not to be taken as all knowing. The mentor's message may need to be decoded, and even then it may be incomplete. It may well turn out to be a mixed message, that is, a mixture of direct and indirect statements whose relevance to one's own life needs to be uncovered gradually through a long process of questioning and testing against experience.

Homer's *Odyssey* offers a good illustration of the range and the limitations of midlife mentoring. The whole point of Odysseus' journey to the Land of the Dead in Book 11 is to meet and converse with the spirit of the prophet Teiresias. Unlike Oedipus, Odysseus is quite willing to accept advice from this Wise Old Man, and Teiresias does give Odysseus some excellent counsel, some of which he proves capable of following eventually. Teiresias urges Odysseus to do two things: to keep good control of his men, and to restrain his *thymos*, the latter word being a nearly untranslatable Greek term designating the emotional energy, especially of an aggressive nature, lodged in what the Greeks imagined was the liver; we might simply translate the advice as "to restrain your heroic fighting spirit." In other words, "stop being a mindlessly self-assertive young man; let the young hero in yourself give place to another sort of hero whose actions are based on patience, endurance and generative intention." In fact, this is exactly what Odysseus will have to do when he arrives home disguised as an old beggar and waits for the proper moment to strike the deadly blow that will win him back his kingdom, and so save his family and his people from the tyrannical oppression of Penelope's bullying young suitors.

The first part of Teiresias' advice (to keep good control of his men) is also good advice. Unfortunately, in this case Odysseus will be unable to follow it, and will suffer accordingly; his men will all die, and, as Teiresias predicted, Odysseus will return home alone after many long years of exile. But it was not all Odysseus' fault. The reader of the *Odyssey* already knows that Teiresias' message to him was startlingly incomplete. What this wise but somewhat unreliable mentor either failed to see, or failed to tell, was what was going to happen to Odysseus after all his men had perished: the eight long years he would be forced to spend on the island of the nymph Kalypso, the *belle dame sans merci* who would keep him in thrall as her love slave until the gods finally intervened to send him home. Perhaps Teiresias, patriarchal seer that he was, could not have foreseen to what degree the power of the feminine could derail the course of a man's life, even that of a great hero like Odysseus.

If classical literature provides us with a rich fund of images and stories of mentors and mentoring under the problematic aegis of the patriarchal dilemma, by contrast modern literature and film seems to shy away from the topic almost completely, at least until fairly recently. It is as though, in seeing through patriarchy and its dirty secrets, the postpatriarchal imagination had thrown out the mentor with the bath water.

Take, for instance, Joseph Conrad's novel *Heart of Darkness* (1902), possibly the most commented upon piece of fiction in the English language after James Joyce's *Ulysses* (1922). The novel consists mainly of a tale, told by the somewhat longwinded seaman Marlow (and as reported by an unidentified acquaintance), of a modern descent to Hades, something like Odysseus' journey to the Land of the Dead. Only this time the descent or *katabasis* takes the form of an oneiric narrative of an expedition up the Congo River during the early years of the European colonial exploitation of Africa. The purpose of Marlow's expedition was the rescue of Kurtz, a colonial ivory trader whom Marlow remembers afterwards as a "remarkable man" (Conrad 1993: 88), but also as a "soul satiated with primitive emotions, avid of lying fame, of sham distinction, of all the appearances of success and power" (Conrad 1993: 97). Throughout the tale Marlow is clearly obsessed with Kurtz; he literally cannot stop talking about him. Behind Marlow's garrulous verbal screen lies an emotional intensity that is the key to his devotion to the memory of the now dead Kurtz—an emotional intensity rooted in his desperate yearning to find a mentor and to talk with him. One can gauge the power of Marlow's yearning for a mentor of archetypal proportions when he suddenly falls silent, in what is the only extended interruption in the text of his relentless yarn spinning. Marlow's sudden silence signals the presence in him of feelings too deep for words, and follows directly upon the emotional muddle of his halting attempt to communicate to his listener some of his feelings for Kurtz, even before he had met the man: "Do you see him? Do you see the story? Do you see anything? It seems to me I am trying to tell you a dream" (Conrad 1993: 37). During the pause that Marlow's silence provides for reflection, the reader may begin to gauge how much Marlow is attached to an oneiric image of Kurtz, onto whom he has projected all the desperate longing for a mentor of which a man at midlife is capable. Later, when he is informed (erroneously, it turns out) of Kurtz's death, he admits that he felt

> a sense of extreme disappointment, as though I had found out that I had been striving after something altogether without a substance. I couldn't have been more disgusted if I had travelled all this way for the sole purpose of talking with Mr. Kurtz. Talking with . . .

He then realizes that such was indeed the case: "that was exactly what I had been looking forward to—a talk with Kurtz" (Conrad 1993: 65–66).

Unfortunately for Marlow, that is all there will be to Kurtz: just talk—talk that cannot conceal a deep inner darkness. Even so, the rumor of Kurtz's death leaves Marlow with a "sorrow" that had a startling extravagance of emotion . . . I couldn't have felt more of lonely desolation somehow, had I been robbed of a belief or had missed my destiny in life.

(Conrad 1993: 66)

And, after Kurtz's actual death, it is clear that Marlow's meeting this strange man had indeed been the greatest event of his life.

Conrad's *Heart of Darkness* leaves the reader aghast, however, at the degree to which Marlow has transformed Kurtz, in reality little more than a morbidly greedy agent of colonialist piracy, into the ideal mentor of his dreams. As Marlow puts it half ironically later on, "it was written that I should be loyal to the nightmare of my choice" (Conrad 1993: 91). For Marlow is not blind to Kurtz's shortcomings; he savagely criticizes him and, in one dramatic scene, even threatens to kill him (Conrad 1993: 93). At the same time desperately loyal to Kurtz and aggressively hostile to him, Marlow, in his peculiar relationship to the mentor of his dreams, is entangled in the complicated network of adulation and contempt that characterizes the patriarchal dilemma in the area of mentoring. In other words, Marlow vents on Kurtz the anger he feels for the Bad Father, even as he sets Kurtz up in his imagination as the ideal mentor, to whom he remains desperately loyal. But the reader is unable to share Marlow's desperate enthusiasm, and this, I think, is precisely Conrad's ironic point: that a truly enlightened and disillusioned modern man (the reader, not Marlow) must be willing to do without a mentor, if the only mentor available is someone like Kurtz. As an agent of savage European imperialism in Africa, Kurtz can only be a parody of a mentor—a pseudomentor from the ironic perspective of the text, on whom Marlow has naively projected the image of the archetypal mentor.

Another notable modernist masterpiece, D.H. Lawrence's *Kangaroo* (1923), also took as its theme the unmasking of the unworthy mentor, and foresaw with some acuity how the period of fascist and communist revolutions was also to be the age of the pseudomentor (Hitler, Mussolini, Stalin, and the lot).[6] Lawrence's protagonist, Richard Somers, is initially a representation of someone seized by morbid fascination with a kind of pseudomentoring that tends to fill the vacuum left by the absence of real mentoring—the vacuum that Kurtz filled for Marlow, as we have seen. But Somers, unlike Marlow, rejects this pseudomentoring in no uncertain terms by the end of the novel. Politically, Lawrence has Somers make the right choice in rejecting the seductive allure of Kangaroo, who wishes to install a paramilitary dictatorship in post-World War I Australia. Psychologically, Somers is also right in refusing to trust a mentor who has not disengaged himself from the abusive power of the father. The hidden hand of the patriarchal dilemma can be glimpsed in Kangaroo's insistence that man

needs to be relieved of this terrible responsibility of governing himself
when he doesn't know what he wants, and has no aim towards which to
govern himself. Man again needs a father . . .

(Lawrence 1992: 126–127)

To Kangaroo's doctrine of seemingly benign patriarchal love, Somers finds
immediate objections, and resists vigorously: "Damn his love. He wants to
force me" (Lawrence 1992: 240).

The next to last chapter, "Kangaroo Is Killed," in which the fascist
leader is fatally wounded during a riot he himself has provoked, has
Kangaroo on his deathbed whispering perversely to Somers: "You've killed
me" (Lawrence 1992: 392). Although this is not literally true, one might
expect that, in accordance with the scenario established by the patriarchal
dilemma, the killing of the father/mentor in one form is followed by
the bonding with the father/mentor in another. However, Somers's symbolic murder of the Bad Father leads to no such meeting with the Good
Mentor, for Lawrence has represented in Somers the thoroughly modern
man, who may yearn for a mentor, but can do without, if a proper one
is not available—tough it out on his own, if necessary, however great the
disappointment.

In the last pages of *Kangaroo*, the Australian bush becomes for Somers a
symbolic refuge from his disappointed expectations of finding a mentor of
real substance rather than a mere master of words. The bush becomes for
him a place in which to enjoy his isolated and unmentored individuality, a
consoling image for him of a world without lying words:

the vast continent is really void of speech. Only man makes noises to
man, from habit. Richard found that he never wanted to talk to
anybody, never wanted to be with anybody. He had fallen apart out of
the human association.

(Lawrence 1992: 403)

Of course, there is one small irony: Richard has not quite "fallen out of
association" with his wife, who "loathed Australia, with wet, dark repulsion" (Lawrence 1992: 410). *Kangaroo* ends, in spite of a lengthy and lyrical
evocation of the Australian bush in spring, with the couple's departure for
America. The thoroughly modern man may do without a mentor, but he is
not about to do without a wife. I am not positive that Lawrence intended
the delicious irony of this ending consciously. But I suspect that he did.

Recent film culture has frequently perpetuated an antiquated but ever
appealing Hollywood vision of a man's quest for fulfillment in life, which is
both Oedipal and quasi-patriarchal. Plotwise, the bad guy (read: Bad
Father) must be killed, and the girl (read: Good Mother) must be rescued
and won. It is always High Noon somewhere on the silver screen, with all

problems solved, as soon as the hero gets the love of a good woman. There is usually little room in the film's plot for viable mentor figures, either because they are too weak to be anything other than sidekicks, or because, as potential mentors, they tend to fall into the category of the Bad Father, whose abusive power the hero must either resist or flee, as in Lawrence's *Kangaroo*. But there are exceptions, certainly in the wake of George Lucas's *Star Wars* films (from 1977 onwards), which used the work of Joseph Campbell to reinstate compelling and complex images of mentors and mentoring at the stage of the passage from adolescence to young adulthood. Especially since the 1980s or so, it is possible to detect a slight change in popular cinematic culture's attitudes towards mentors and mentoring, some of which may be due to the direct impact of the Men's Movement on film writers and directors. Since films are carefully crafted in view of immediate audience appeal, some recent films provide evidence that at least part of their audience is increasingly willing to imagine mentoring relationships that are neither patriarchally abusive nor evasively trivialized.

Take, for example, a film whose classic cult status is now firmly established: Wes Craven's horror film and primitivist fantasy *The Serpent and the Rainbow* (1988). In it a Harvard graduate student in anthropology is initiated by an Amazonian shaman, and receives in a vision the jaguar as his power animal. This shamanic initiation enables him at a later date to defeat the spirit power of the head of the Tonton Macoutes, to save the girl, and to be a hero in the Haitian revolution against the Duvalier regime. The film is primarily an Oedipal political fantasy: defeat Bad Father, save Mom and live happily ever after. The head of the Tonton Macoutes who almost—by a hair—castrates the hero, is himself punished by actual castration at the end, in a vivid if somewhat silly phantasmagorical finale. But the impressive figure of the Amazonian shaman—exotic with his paint and feathers, but friendly, tricksterish, dignified and tough—gives at least a glimpse of a postpatriarchal, non-Oedipal vision of the mentor. *The Serpent and the Rainbow* may be a primitivist fantasy, but it is a good one.

Mike Nichols's thriller *Wolf* (1994) has the Jack Nicholson character on the verge of a total midlife metamorphosis into the ruthless animal the publishing industry seems to require in the nineties; his identification with shadow energies is almost complete. But the intervention of a retired Indian scholar (played by Om Puri) saves the day. The elderly scholar is modest in his claims to be a mentor ("You should be visiting a shaman: he will tell you the rules; I can tell you only the theory"), but he gives him an amulet that his native tradition values as an apotropaic charm against turning into a wolf after being bitten by a demon wolf ("I have no idea if any of it is true, but it is yours"). The Indian mentor is also appreciative of the value for himself of this encounter with a man at midlife in need of an older man's help: "it has been a privilege—I've never met one like you"—no Oedipal rivalry here! Such a figure of a positive mentor also gives an otherwise fairly sensational film a welcome bit of worthwhile psychological contextualizing. The mentor's message, while mixed and incomplete, suggests the Jungian paradigm of the potentially beneficial integration of potentially beneficial shadow impulses at midlife: "it feels good to be a wolf: power without guilt, love without doubt." The Jack Nicholson character, an old-fashioned senior editor who, before the wolf's providential bite, is too naive—too "civilized"—for his own good, winds up benefiting from an infusion of wolfish self-assertiveness, as long as it does not go too far. Of course, it eventually does go too far, when he discards the amulet in order to save Michelle Pfeiffer from a sex-crazed wolf of a junior editor, who has no civilized instincts left at all. The promise of a midlife Oedipal romance (older man, younger woman, of course), founded this time on the symbolic murder of the Bad Son (the junior editor), ultimately takes precedence over the representation of any meaningful psychological change. But this is a Hollywood film, after all, and its audience was perhaps not yet ready to let the hero walk off (or lope away) without the rescued girl on his arm, even if it means accepting the rather dizzying proposition that the increasingly lupine Michelle Pfeiffer is going to join Jack Nicholson in the woods as a woman who runs with the wolves.

A laudable failure to adhere to the stereotypical Hollywood Oedipal romantic plot characterizes Michael Tolkin's notable film *The New Age* (1995). Its somewhat scandalously innovative plot is centered on the recently jobless—and increasingly suicidal—advertising executive Peter, who moves at midlife into the circle of an ambiguously charming older New Age guru, a French-speaking Belgian "spiritual teacher" by the name of Jean Lévy, whose wisdom seems to be embodied in his cryptic dictum "Live with the question." For Peter, caught in an anguished fall from economic grace, death rather than life seems to offer a more palatable answer to the question of unemployment. But his wife Katherine's decision to divorce him, as well as his father's refusal to provide financial backing, give him a salutary shock, and bring him to a point where he has to discover his own way of living out the practical implications of his mentor's cryptic advice.

Still, as regards its representation of a man in midlife transition, *The New Age* is clearly ambivalent. On the negative side, Peter's father, who himself is desperately trying to be young again through affairs with younger women, is too weak and self-involved for Peter to need or even to want to kill symbolically. Peter's New Age mentor Lévy, whose head is usually in the clouds, leaves him pretty much to his own devices with spiritual advice empty of any practical considerations, until it is too late. On the positive side, however, *The New Age* does represent postpatriarchal midlife mentoring of a sort, in which the theme of the recognition of Peter's freedom and integrity has replaced the more traditional theme of escape from patriarchal domination and control. At least it is mentoring that helps Peter find a new life and a new identity.

The end of *The New Age* is hardly upbeat. Peter is divorced, and is scrambling desperately to make a living. But it is clear at least that he has been initiated into a "new age," and can begin to confront a harsh economic situation in his own way, helped along by a thoroughly practical African-American man who trains people in the techniques of telemarketing, who thus provides Peter with the practical mentoring Jean Lévy was too much up in the clouds to give him. "Did you know," Peter queries the telephone sales trainees for whom he is now responsible, "in Chinese the word for crisis is the same as the word for opportunity—did you know that?" Peter knows it, because he is repeating one of the wise sayings he has heard from Lévy. His mentor's contribution to this seriocomic outcome is also stressed in the final shot, where Jean Lévy, alone and facing the audience, intones portentously, for the third and last time in the film, "Live with the question." It is a kind of life-enhancing wisdom that the once discouraged and suicidal Peter seems to have absorbed.

The New Age represents the best attempt I know of in fairly recent American cinema to represent a modern postpatriarchal midlife mentoring relationship between men. But for me the most satisfying cinematic images of noncoercive and friendly midlife mentoring occur in two films by eminent French directors relatively unaffected by Hollywood norms: Alain Resnais's *My American Uncle* (*Mon oncle d'Amérique*, 1980) and Louis Malle's *My Dinner with André* (1981). Interestingly enough, in both films the actor playing the mentor figure (the scientist and philosopher Henri Laborit, and the experimental theater director André Gregory) does not play a fictional role, but rather plays himself.[7]

My American Uncle is a tribute to the director Alain Resnais's own fascination with the eminent scientist (he discovered the first tranquillizer) and popular philosopher Henri Laborit, whose neo-Kantian scientism may be said to boil down to a sociobiological theme and variations on Kant's idea that "freedom consists in the recognition of necessity." This tough-minded philosophy, vividly illustrated by interspersed images from both the human and the animal realms (which sometimes overlap, as when an experiment with white rats leads to a scene with actors playing their roles wearing white rat masks), is stated and restated in the course of the film by Laborit himself. While Laborit in his published writings shows no sign of being acquainted with Jung's psychology, his sense of the determining role played by basic instincts in human life is close in its way to the spirit of Jung's psychology, where archetypes play an analogous role, predisposing human beings to act in certain ways, whether they are aware of the powers shaping their ends or not. Laborit and Jung thus share a kind of fatalistic determinism as regards human affairs, although not without recognition of the human capacity to change fate to some degree through the conscious recognition of the effect of archetypal or instinctual impulses.

Born in 1915, Henri Laborit was about sixty-five at the time of the filming, while the two midlife male characters in the film would have been young enough to take him as an older mentor. In the film, Laborit gives a devastating critique of the pretences of human reason to total lucidity and control, and foregrounds the unconscious biological determinants of human beings' tragic misbehavior with one another. Without the recognition of the power of these primordial biological patterns, says Laborit, human beings will continue to act and interact with one another irrationally like instinct-driven animals. For Laborit, to become a mature human being is to become conscious of the biologically programmed nature of human behavior, and then to search for creative and consciously chosen alternatives. Laborit's tone throughout the film is insistent but not hectoring. The director, Resnais, clearly intends Laborit's backstage presence to provide a direct philosophical and psychological perspective on the characters' troubled lives. But the perspective is one of which they themselves will remain tragically unconscious, since Laborit does not intervene in the characters' lives, nor does he speak to any one of them directly, but only to the viewers of the film. His role as a mentor is thus directed only at the audience, for whom the muddled and sometimes tragic lives of the characters provide cautionary examples of what the absence of proper guidance at midlife can lead to: job loss and attempted suicide, for starters. The characters in the film, since they never get to hear his message, are left unenlightened and unmentored.

The case is quite otherwise (message given, message received) in Louis Malle's film *My Dinner with André* (1981) in which the representation of a one-on-one midlife mentoring relationship is grounded in the real-life collaborative creative partnership between the two screenwriters André Gregory and Wallace Shawn. In his preface to the film script, Wallace Shawn presents himself as already a hero-worshipper of his older colleague: "if André agreed to be the hero, then how could it [the film] fail? (Shawn and Gregory 1981: 14). The film itself presents a subtler version of this theme of trust in a mentor—a trust that is preceded, it must be said, by a fair amount of suspicion and misgivings on the younger Wally's part.

But it all works out in the end. André Gregory invites the younger screenwriter Wally to dinner, although it is not clear at first whether it is to give help or to ask for help. Wally is thirty-six years old and on the verge of a midlife crisis, which he experiences primarily in terms of an increasing dissatisfaction with his struggling career that verges on depression. André Gregory, however, is already famous as an avant-garde director, who had left the American theater scene to spend some time with the genial dramatist Jerzy Grotowski in Poland. Now returned to New York, he is, at age forty-five, at the other end of his midlife initiation transformation, which he describes in vivid detail, course after course, at a fancy but very old-fashioned

New York restaurant. (Their silent but attentive waiter is a seventy-year-old man, thus completing the picture of three generations of men.)

If ever there were a model of a postpatriarchal representation of a long talk with a midlife mentor that can set a man back on track and give him a renewed faith in life, *My Dinner with André* must be it. If the idea of a film consisting almost entirely of a dinner conversation seems boring, the actual film is anything but. The film's dramatic momentum is carried along by the archetypal emotional resonance of a mentoring situation that seems to come into being spontaneously, and that develops with a great sense of naturalness and ease. André does most of the talking, but he is not overbearing—well, he is not *too* overbearing, and when he is, it is always in a friendly and compassionate manner. He does not give Wally advice, so much as share his own experience; he does not pretend to tell Wally how to live his life or how to build his career. Nevertheless, the effect of his midlife mentoring is substantial. Although there is no indication at the end of the film that Wally is about to change his life or make new decisions, the groundwork has apparently been laid for his midlife transition. As Wally returns to his apartment (he has exceptionally treated himself to a taxi), he is smiling to himself and clearly in a very different mood from the anxious and depressed state he was in before André began his wild tale of midnight ceremonies in Poland and symbolic burials on Long Island. These tales added a note of exotic mystery to André's account of his own midlife initiation, but the point of his telling them was not to push Wally into any such extravagant gestures (something the down-to-earth nature of Wally would probably not have accepted), but rather to communicate enthusiasm and trust in life to the younger man at a moment when he was discouraged in his professional situation and perhaps on the way to being dangerously depressed.

Initiatory transformative images of the sort we have highlighted may prove helpful to men who are trying to overcome centuries of suspicion and distrust of midlife mentoring. My sense is that modern men are now becoming more willing to own up to their need for an older man's mentoring affection and assistance. It is interesting, by way of conclusion, to note that Albert Camus's last (and unfinished) novel *The First Man* (*Le premier homme*), was published only in 1994, years after Camus's death in 1960, and thus had to wait over a generation to reach its readers.[8] One might speculate that its posthumous publication was a synchronistic event, since it is only recently that men have begun to distinguish the role of the postpatriarchal mentor from the more traditional role of the patriarchal father. Whatever the reason, Camus's last novel has revealed to a modern set of readers the lifelong affection and mutual respect that linked the author and his onetime schoolteacher Monsieur Bernard. Their relationship seems to have been a model of postpatriarchal mentoring.

The First Man is the story, loosely autobiographical, of a man who seeks information about his father killed in World War I shortly after the author's birth. Unfortunately, he discovers little or nothing about him, and his link with his father turns out to have been irretrievably broken by the war in which his father was killed. However, instead of an unhappy tale of a failed quest for a father, *The First Man* winds up being a celebration of a mentoring relationship that lasted in one form or another a whole life. Monsieur Bernard, the schoolteacher who had given the boy Camus the encouragement he needed when he most needed it, was to remain his mentor and friend throughout his life. (Some of their moving correspondence is published at the back of the French edition.) The novel's tone is emotionally warm and quite unlike that of the cool irony of some of Camus's other writings, including *The Fall*. It is as though Camus in his mid forties felt a powerful need to give a vivid verbal representation of his beloved mentoring figure before it was too late. The manuscript was with him in the car crash that took his life.

Notes

1 Girard, as a staunch Catholic, draws conclusions that may seem tendentious, since he is committed to establishing the ultimate superiority (and even uniqueness) of the Christian *mythos* over all other present and past religions and mythologies, because for him the Christian myth, unlike all others, is *true*. This leads him in the end to a fascinating but, in my opinion, unconvincing presentation of the scapegoat myth's presence in Sophocles' *Oedipus the King*. However, his reading of the play is a "strong misreading," which I am happy to use as a foil to my own reading of the play as a drama transcending its initial scapegoating premise.

2 Frederick Ahl's reading of the tragedy in *Sophocles' Oedipus* (1991), however original and nuanced it is, seems ultimately too subtle to apply to a text designed for public performance, that is, to a script that had to be, at least as regards its basic plot, clear and unambiguous for the purposes of stage performance.

3 Oedipus' almost mystical transfiguration is described enigmatically near the end of Sophocles' *Oedipus at Colonus*, written years later.

4 Eventually published after Jung's death as *The Freud/Jung Letters*, edited by William McGuire.

5 See especially *Totem and Taboo* and *Moses and Monotheism* as examples of Freud's extraordinary mythopoetic imagination.

6 Lawrence's fictional fascist leader was probably inspired by Sir Charles Rosenthal, one of the first fascist leaders to emerge in the wake of World War I, who was the head of a paramilitary organization, the King and Empire Alliance. See Darroch 1981.

7 The same could be said for another notable representation of a postpatriarchal midlife mentor, Peter Falk, who plays himself in Wim Wenders' 1987 film *Wings of Desire/Der Himmel über Berlin*.

8 It was almost immediately translated into English by David Hapgood (New York: Knopf, 1995).

Chapter 4

Ariadne, abandonment and female midlife initiation

Based on the analysis of the texts highlighted in this chapter, Erikson's theory of the stages of life and Jung's theory of midlife *enantiodromia* would seem to apply as readily to texts concerning women as to those concerning men. For women, too, the youthful search for intimacy, whether it has been totally successful or not, is displaced by the midlife quest to become generative beyond the immediate family and circle of intimates, and to forge new values that support this quest. This may, as with men, be a fairly unconscious process, and it may stay that way if no obstacles force the individual into a greater conscious awareness of the activation of a new inner process supporting midlife transformation. No doubt, the specific results of the midlife transformation may vary in content, from individual to individual, and from culture to culture. But the general result will be this: that, whatever may have been the specific values and strengths that flourished during the period of youth, it can be guaranteed that they will be altered significantly, or even change into their opposites.

However, I will venture the hypothesis that there is a substantial difference between male and female midlife transition as regards the specific transformational images involved in the process. The slaying of Siegfried as the archetypal representation of the youthful male hero had provided a transformational image for Jung's midlife rejection of Freud and of himself as Freud's crown prince and of the change in the direction of his psychic energies, but there is no reason why this specific archetypal paradigm—represented by the death of the mythic youthful hero—would necessarily apply to women as well as to men. How then might female midlife initiation and transformation proceed? Are there potentially major differences between them and the male versions I have suggested as templates? I will try to make the case that, as an archetypal process, the female midlife transition is activated by the mythic theme of "tragic abandonment," and not of "the death of the young hero." In addition, although the phenomenon of the emergence of the shadow as a problem to be dealt with more thoroughly at midlife may be generally the same for men and for women, the typical shadow contents may differ, to the extent that the early socialization of women encouraged the repression of different character traits in the interests of social gender definition and formation—once again, and as always, with individual and cultural variations. Finally, the coming into greater consciousness of the contrasexual archetype of the animus may encourage in women the development of more masculine energies just as in men the emergence of the anima may sponsor greater activation and integration of feminine traits. But, in each case, the energies and traits will be different in nature, at least to some degree. All in all, the hypothesis that male and female midlife transformation processes may have somewhat different gestalts seems defensible.

Our investigation of the nature of a specifically female midlife archetypal transformation pattern takes as its point of departure Linda Fierz-David's book *Dreaming in Red* (2005). Fierz-David, a Swiss therapist and docent at the C.G. Jung Institute in Zurich, undertook, before her death in 1955, a detailed Jungian interpretation of the famous frescoes of the Villa of Mysteries in Pompeii. These had been discovered only in 1910 during ongoing excavations of that ancient Roman city, which had been covered by lava during the eruption of Mt. Vesuvius in AD 79. The results of her study, initially available only in German in mimeographed form for limited circulation in Jungian circles, were finally published in English translation in 1988. She interpreted the frescoes as the depiction, in both realistic and symbolic imagery, of an esoteric midlife initiation ritual designed for educated upper-class Roman women around the time of Augustus. Fierz-David's book is equally valuable, whether one takes it as a scholarly interpretation of some intriguing but hermetic classical Roman transformational images or as a psychological meditation on the problems of modern women's midlife transition using the ancient frescoes as a basis for reflection. Although Fierz-David does not label the initiation a specifically *midlife* initiation—she does not even use the term "midlife" in her treatise—it is clear that in her interpretations the woman initiate arguably depicted on the frescoes is past her first youth and is a "matron" undergoing a transition to a stage of life made emblematic by the statue of Augustus' wife Livia prominently sited in the entrance hallway—a stage of life thus characterized by the authority in the wider social world symbolized by Livia, a woman of great capacity and energy, and the power behind the imperial throne.[1]

The frescoes gracing the walls of the inner chamber of the house—for Fierz-David, the initiation chamber itself—constituted for her a visual oneiric text of extraordinary significance:

> these pictures have something so unusually lively and original—they so clearly represent the experience from a beginning stage to a goal—that I asked myself whether one might not regard them from a psychological standpoint, like a dream series, for example.
>
> (Fierz-David 2005: 23)

For our purposes, the pictures provide an opportunity to set up a hypo-thetical paradigm for a specifically female form of midlife initiation, although how completely this paradigm might apply to modern women is a question to which we will have to return later.

The key transformative image in the Pompeian frescoes is that of the god Dionysos reclining against his bride Ariadne enthroned behind him, in a posture that suggests the peaceful and confident nature of Ariadne's conjugal love for him, after her tragic abandonment by the hero Theseus, to whom she was initially betrothed. Dionysos can be taken as the god of initiatory transformation, in that his divine birth was the result of an unusual *rebirth*. His mother Semele, having slept with Zeus, conceived a divine child. But when she wished to see her lover in his godlike glory, Zeus appeared to her as lightning, and this bolt from the blue incinerated her. Zeus, however, was able to save the child Dionysos by enclosing him in his thigh (a male womb, so to speak), thus guaranteeing a second birth for the infant god. The rebirth motif in the myth of Dionysos was later repeated when he was torn apart and dismembered by the Titans, but, unlike Humpty-Dumpty, was put back together again. Rebirth and transforma-tion are thus inscribed in his myth from the start. In addition, his various metamorphoses—as a bull, as wine and as symbolized by the empty dra-matic mask of Greek theater—highlight his role as the god of transforma-tion. His androgynous appearance sets him apart to some degree from the fixed gender identities of the other Olympians, and his powerful sway over the Maenads or Bacchantes, the women who danced wildly and ecstatically in his honor, signal his special cult appeal to women.

As for Ariadne, daughter of King Minos of Crete, her myth was even-tually entwined with his. After having saved the hero Theseus' life by giving him a simple spool of thread that he could unroll behind him as he made his way into the labyrinth in order to kill the Minotaur (perhaps only a woman might have thought of this simple device, so emblematic of women's household activities), she set sail with him for Athens, where she fully expected to become his wife. But Theseus callously abandoned her on the island of Naxos. Ready to take her own life, she was in a state of the greatest despair, when suddenly the god Dionysos appeared to her and claimed her as his bride. The abandoned Ariadne is thus transformed into the happy and glorious bride of the god Dionysos, and a new identity is made possible for her by the god's miraculous intervention in her life at its moment of deepest tragedy, and at an initiatory moment of imminent death. Writes Fierz-David, "her forlorn condition shows that she is threat-ened by *spiritual death*," adding that "this feeling of death, this situation of isolation is terrible, but it is also healing: it is the pressure that can lead to transformation" (Fierz-David 2005: 33). It is possible, speculates Fierz-David, that the first step of this Roman midlife initiation was preceded by a period of isolation for the initiate, "such an isolation" being typical not only of "many older initiations" but also "of the beginning of the way of individuation" (Fierz-David 2005: 41). If such was the latent archetypal content of the frescoes, in the myth of Ariadne abandoned by her intended spouse the initiate would have found much to ponder sadly, and in her subsequent marriage to Dionysos much to hope for as well.

This iconic image of Dionysos and Ariadne is notable for the fact that the other figures of the series of frescoes do not seem to notice them or to interact with them directly; as Fierz-David says, it is as though Dionysos and Ariadne

> are represented as *being there invisibly*. They personify the central symbol that is removed from human eyes, that unites the ancient opposites of the masculine and the feminine in the conjunction. Psychologically expressed, this means that in this room Dionysos-Ariadne is the symbol of the Self.
>
> (Fierz-David 2005: 24)

For Fierz-David, "Ariadne's way is a mythical representation of the transformation process that we today call the individuation process" (Fierz-David 2005: 33). I will argue, however, that it is more specifically the midlife transformation process that is symbolically represented in the frescoes. The myth of the abandoned Ariadne is a powerful transformative image, not only because it addresses directly a woman's fear of abandonment at midlife by her faithless spouse (a topic Fellini will address in his film *Juliet of the Spirits*, as we will see), but above all because it addresses her need to move beyond the intimate bonds of youth, and especially of marriage and family, into the generative world of midlife. Ariadne is enthroned not as the bride of a mortal man—hers is not a marriage in a human social sense—but rather as a goddess figure sitting in splendor, holding the god Dionysos protectively as he leans against her lap; her power within the relationship is almost maternal. By contrast, but also by extension, the statue of Livia, to which Fierz-David gives such importance, can be taken as an iconic image of a woman standing alone, serenely confident in her own power. But behind the initiated woman's serenity and new-found confidence in her power would lie her earlier marriage with Dionysos and the initiatory ordeal that led up to it. It is this inner marriage—this connection with the archetypal forces represented by the god—that enables her to put behind her the tragic abandonment that ended her relationship with Theseus. Once again, some contact with the divine and the spiritual seems to be one of the keys to a successful negotiation of the midlife passage.

Fierz-David's analysis of the sequence of frescoes in the Villa of Mysteries in Pompeii is rich and challenging in its detail and subtlety of interpretation. To my mind, however, she sometimes errs in her overuse of the term "individuation" and in her emphasis on the purely spiritual dimension of the initiation represented both realistically and symbolically in the frescoes, as though the result of the initiation were something definitive, a mystical culmination of sorts, and not, as I would say, a midlife transformation whose results, like those of all transformations, are not definitive and fixed, anymore than life itself is. So I will only mention a few of the major points that she makes as she shows the initiation paradigm in the process of unfolding, especially as regards what I interpret to be the female midlife experience of transformation.

First of all, as Fierz-David notes, "everywhere in the world, a *teaching* belonged to every initiation, which consisted of the ritual telling of sacred myths" (Fierz-David 2005: 42). The boy reading out loud from a book in the first scene, under the direction of the priestess, is arguably recounting the myth of the horrible death and rebirth of Dionysos. The message of this myth would be that the way of transformation lies through the Dionysian experience of the death of one's former self, and that the process of rebirth itself can be accompanied by anguish and despair—the pains of death leading to rebirth. Thus, in the fourth image, the initiate (the so-called "terrified woman") covers her head; "perhaps her terror," notes Fierz-David, "reflects a presentiment of the coming torture" (Fierz-David 2005: 73). She also notes that "covering the head during a mystery initiation signified the *death* of the initiate" (Fierz-David 2005: 79)—the symbolic death that precedes rebirth and transformation.

Any process of initiation involves at some point a mentoring figure or set of figures, and on the frescoes the first midlife mentor seems to be the mythological figure of Silenus, one of the chief associates of Dionysos. He is represented as a fat and rather androgynous figure playing on a lyre in a pastoral landscape. A strange figure, perhaps, for a midlife mentor! But, as a symbol of the peaceful and harmonious blending of male and female characteristics, Silenus is a powerful transformative image, which encourages the woman being initiated to leave behind her purely feminine definition of self, and to move into the realm of midlife androgyny. Silenus is thus both a "mother-father" and "a wise teacher" (Fierz-David 2005: 71). But, through his close association with the god Dionysos, Silenus is also a figure of archetypal Dionysian sexuality, and thus his presence at the opening of the sequence heralds the latent theme of sex as "an experience of depth" (Fierz-David 2005: 74).

In the next scene, Silenus appears as a psychopomp who frightens the terrified woman of the fourth and fifth scenes with a vision of a grimacing satyr-mask reflected in a silver receptacle, a mask that Fierz-David interprets as "the terrible mask which belongs to Dionysos as ruler of the underworld" (Fierz-David 2005: 74). In a later scene, another woman initiate is being tortured through flagellation, and much of Fierz-David's interpretation emphasizes the physical and psychological ordeal of this phase of the initiation—the flagellation, the despair, the terrors of the *katabasis*. However, the woman manages to return from her descent into hell with a newly established connection with Dionysos, bringing back a basket containing the ritual phallus representing the newborn god. But her ordeal is not yet over: she is rebuked by a dark angel who, according to Fierz-David, prevents her from uncovering the phallus and rashly taking possession of it, usurping something divine for her own purposes. The ritual phallus of Dionysos is not to be confused with an instrument of sexual pleasure or as human phallic energy, but as an archetypal image that should be treated with awe and caution. Thus the initiate's saving virtue at this point, writes Fierz-David, is the feeling of *modesty*. Modesty is what prevents the initiate from attempting a sacrilegious personal appropriation of the ritual phallus, and it also brings her back from an inflated state in which she has identified herself with the divine—back into her humble and deflated state of humanity and womanhood. This deflation, however, is painful. Through the experience of tragic despair and terror she has been reduced to the status of an abject human victim of divine forces. She remains for a while in this state of relinquishment and destitution, after having almost succumbed to a dangerous state of inflation with Dionysian energy, in which she would have identified herself completely with the power of the god, and having been saved from this peril only by the feeling of modesty forced on her by the power of the dark angel.

Fierz-David places great emphasis on the salutary effect for modern women as well, of this feeling of modesty, which is for her a key, if somewhat unacknowledged, feminine virtue:

> That such a sense of modesty could and must exist for them, most modern women little realize—as little as the Orphic initiate represented in the Pompeian frescoes. Modern women, too, just in the decisive phase of their psychic-spiritual development, can be driven by an unconscious, compulsive eroticism to throw themselves away on the divine-demonic figure of the *animus* in holy-unholy shamelessness, like a Babylonian *hierodule* (holy slave). The insight that the virtue of modesty is necessary for women in regard to the archetypal figure of the spirit can be granted only by an act of grace from the pneuma, if she cannot be reached by the moderating counsel of well-wishing friends.
> (Fierz-David 2005: 121)

In our own time, this may sound a bit like old-fashioned 1950s moralistic preaching: if a woman today wishes to abandon herself to "compulsive eroticism," isn't that her right? However, Fierz-David's point is not moral but psychological: being inflated with Dionysian energies from the unconscious may be a necessary first step (Jung believed that in the process of experiencing archetypal contents one inevitably becomes inflated with them for a while), but the next step must involve a return to a sense of one's ordinary humanity, and a corresponding disidentification (deflation) is imperative. Recognizing the numinous power of these archetypal energies, but not becoming their inflated victim, is thus the key, and for this recognition a feeling of modesty is a saving grace.

In the eighth scene of the frescoes, the initiate's head lies on the lap of the priestess, who "has laid her left hand in motherly protection upon the disheveled hair of the initiate, and with the right she pushes the drapery over her back a little so that the angel may really strike her" (Fierz-David 2005: 125). This ritual flagellation marks the end of the initiate's ordeal. She is now presumably ready, having "died to everything in which she as a woman had been entangled", to assume the new identity of a transformed self. For Fierz-David the "archetypal image" which is of the "deepest significance for just this femininity resting entirely upon itself" is the forsaken Ariadne, who is at first "entirely alone in the divine seclusion of the island" of Naxos, but who then becomes "the mother-bride of the divine father-bridegroom" (Fierz-David 2005: 129).

In the last two frescoes it is possible to see two striking images of the newborn self that is now the initiate's new identity. The first is the image of a serenely relaxed lady whose hair is being dressed by a female attendant; the latter is looking into a mirror held up to her by a Cupid figure. The lady appears composed and dignified, and gazes directly at the spectator (for Fierz-David, she "gazes thoughtfully into the distance" [Fierz-David 2005: 144]). Her quiet dignity and self-possession stand in stark contrast to the emotional upheavals of the scenes of the ordeal through which she has passed. The second and final image in the tenth fresco is commonly called the Domina: an aristocratic matron sitting on an elegant chair, leaning on a cushion with her right hand against her chin and gazing to her right at the sequence of events in the preceding frescoes. Fierz-David identifies her as possibly an allegorical figure of Mnemosyne or Remembrance, but I prefer a simpler interpretation: she is the image of the transformed woman who has come into her own at midlife. She has no one with her: no attendant, no mythological figure, no priestess, and no man. She is completely by herself, relaxed and thoughtful.

If the initiation sequence of the Villa of Mysteries as interpreted by Linda Fierz-David can be said to provide a possible template for the archetypal pattern of women's initiation at midlife, several major differences from the male process are worth noting. First of all, there is the importance of Dionysian sexuality as an experience of depth. No longer restrained or as much restrained by the pressure of society and family, the initiate must come to terms with a flood of sexual energy represented by the appearance of the ritual phallus of Dionysus. At this crucial juncture, where Dionysian energies risk overwhelming the initiate, Fierz-David finds her *feeling of modesty* to be the saving grace, in that it forestalls her inflation with the frenzy that accompanies Dionysian ecstasy, while enabling her to integrate it more consciously. The initiate does not have to do this all on her own, however. Her experience of the Dionysian is mentored by the figure of the godling Silenus, who, like his master Dionysus, embodies both male and female characteristics.

The initiate must then go on to manifest (as Inanna did) heroic energies in undertaking a *katabasis* that will take her to the very edge of despair and death. At the end of her *katabasis*—of her descent to the archetypal world of the unconscious—a priestess, a Wise Old Woman, also serves a mentoring function for her, and together Silenus and the priestess represent a dual midlife mentoring that combines ecstatic (Silenus with his lyre) and maternally protective roles (the priestess on whose lap she lays her head). The painful and terrifying ordeal she has undergone has cast her upon the shore of her own personal island of Naxos, where the abandoned Ariadne serves as the mythic model for her plight. Since the arrival of Dionysos would be her salvation but also would entail her destruction as a human individual, the "dark angel" who threatens her and presumably flagellates her may represent an image of the spiritual animus who "whips her into shape," so to speak, and so enables her to disengage herself from the Dionysian terrors and frenzy associated with the myth of the dismembered god, whose archetypal force could tear her apart.

Saved from what could be described (as in Jung's own case) as a near psychotic breakdown at midlife, the initiate comes into her own as a mature and thoughtful woman, who is now grounded in her own sense of individuality, and who is able to function generatively in the wider world beyond the immediate family. As we have seen, the ideal of the generative woman reborn at midlife is represented in the statue of Livia located at the heart of the house, and visible from many perspectives within it. As the wife of the emperor Augustus, and by all accounts not only a power behind the throne but a woman with enormous influence and power over the affairs of the empire, she was noted for exercising a generative function in many different areas. She also stood as an iconic example of the traditional virtues of the Roman matrons of old, in sharp contrast with Augustus' daughter Julia, who succumbed to what Fierz-David calls "Titanic greed," that is, to Dionysian excess unbridled by any feeling of modesty. Livia's freestanding statue prominently placed in the Villa of Mysteries thus had not only a conventional political meaning (loyalty to the emperor and his wife) but also and above all an iconic status as the ideal result of the midlife initiation ceremonies celebrated within the Villa of Mysteries: to be a woman like Livia, calm and confident in her power, and able to stand alone.

Much of Fierz-David's interpretation is admittedly designed as much to enlighten modern women at midlife as it is to reconstruct imaginatively the mentality of aristocratic women in ancient Rome. But there may be a problem in taking an esoteric rite from Roman times and assuming that the midlife needs of aristocratic slave-owning Roman matrons would coincide exactly with those of modern educated women. For example, the dominant status of the Roman matrons within the society whose apex they occupied resulted in a set of social prejudices and attitudes (arrogance, indifference to suffering, haughtiness) that no doubt needed to be challenged and chastened through ritual humiliation, even through ritual flagellation. Flagellation (whipping) was usually reserved for slaves; aristocratic Roman women would have frequently ordered it for their own slaves. Their class consciousness and their arrogant pride in their high social standing, which would have been obstacles to the success of the initiatory process, which involves a breaking down of the social persona and indeed a Dionysian dismembering of the personality as a prelude to rebirth, needed to be chastened. Fierz-David sees the Roman initiate near the end of her ordeal as "unreservedly surrendering to her own abasement" (Fierz-David 2005: 124). Although this ritual abasement may have served as a valuable compensation for the fiercely dominant status of the aristocratic Roman woman within her own household, that is, as a social corrective as well as a psychological shock, one may question whether this ritual "abasement" would be as valuable—or valuable at all—for an educated modern woman. If not, we might expect to find the motif of ritual flagellation missing in the symbolic representations of modern women's midlife transformation in the texts that will concern us now, beginning with Federico Fellini's 1965 film *Juliet of the Spirits*.

Fresh from the extraordinary success of his previous film *8½*, with its portrayal of man's midlife crisis and transformation, Fellini now tried to represent with a great wealth of fantasy imagery and mythic color the midlife initiation of a woman, played memorably by his own wife Giulietta Masina. But this anatomy of a modern woman's midlife crisis by a male director might be considered problematic at best, and at worst of dubious value. How can a man understand from the inside what a woman goes through at midlife? During an interview with the director, Tullio Kezich, by way of opening up a discussion of Fellini's recent film *Juliet of the Spirits*, read to him a passage from Jung's 1927 lecture "The Woman in Europe," in which Jung, who was by that time one of Fellini's great culture heroes, had asked, "Can a man be capable of writing about a woman, his opposite? I mean writing something true and fair, beyond every sexual concept or resentment, beyond any illusion or theory." He answered his own question, "I really don't know who could assume such a superiority." To which Fellini responded in turn, "That seems to me to be very true. To speak calmly and clearly about a woman is almost impossible for a man." That said, Fellini insisted on the right of the storyteller "to speak about everything, regardless of his inadequacy" (Fellini 1965: 54). With these remarks in mind, we can proceed to an examination of *Juliet of the Spirits* as an oneiric film text concerning a woman's midlife transformation, even if only seen through a glass darkly, that is, through the prism of a male imagination. Of course, just as the director Guido in *8½* can be taken at least partially as a self-portrait of Fellini, so in *Juliet of the Spirits* the role of Giulietta, played by his wife, seems to indicate some possible biographical tie-in with his life partner. Whether this suggests the possibility of Fellini being arguably capable in this instance of a reasonably accurate and fair-minded portrayal of a woman at midlife is of course debatable. But given the closeness of their marital relationship, and the successful quality of their artistic collaboration on this film ("a number of times I just asked Giulietta what she would say, what she would do, and I accepted her solutions without the slightest change" [Fellini 1965: 54]), I would be inclined to answer in the affirmative.

It is also quite possible that Linda Fierz-David's interpretations of the frescoes of the Villa of Mysteries provided a catalyst for *Juliet of the Spirits* through the intermediary of Dr. Ernst Bernhard. Born in Berlin in 1896, eventually a student of Jung's in Zurich, Dr. Bernhard had been instrumental in establishing Jungian analytical psychology in Italy in the 1930s. He was later to become Fellini's therapist during the time when he was making *8½* and *Juliet of the Spirits*, and they saw each other several times a week on a regular basis for about four years. Dr. Bernhard was more than a therapist, however; he was a genuine midlife mentor for the director. Aldo Carotenuto, in the course of an account of a long conversation he had with Fellini in August of 1976, evokes Bernhard and Fellini's first meeting and their later close association, writing that

> their relationship remained one of the most important elements in Fellini's life. Bernhard was like a father to him, in the true sense of the word, without changing anything—leaving intact Fellini's protracted adolescence, his playful sense—which allowed him to become detached, to see himself, without rejecting anything. And this is a great and miraculous thing.
>
> (Carotenuto 1977: online)

Dr. Bernhard introduced Fellini to Jung's writings *in extenso*, and in an interview published in 1972, Fellini affirmed that

> I have complete faith in Jung and total admiration for him. . . . My admiration for him is the sort felt for an elder brother, for someone who knows more than you do and teaches it to you. It is the admiration we owe to one of the great traveling companions of this century: the prophet-scientist.
>
> (Fellini 1996: 147)

It is more than likely that the German-speaking Dr. Bernhard was familiar via their transcription with the lectures Linda Fierz-David gave in German on the Villa of Mysteries before her death in 1955. These lectures on ancient Roman frescoes at Pompeii would certainly have been of special interest to Fellini, whose fascination with life in Roman times was to result a few years later in a film (*Satyricon*, 1969) set entirely in pagan Roman antiquity. One imagines readily that Fierz-David's lectures might well have been the topic of conversations between Bernhard and Fellini. Mimeographed transcripts of the Fierz-David's course of German language lectures—including copies of Gladys Phelan's English translation made in 1957—were available for private circulation in Jungian circles. Whether Fellini knew anything about them in detail or not (it seems likely to me that he did, given the precise parallels that I will highlight between the text and his film), *Juliet of the Spirits* is a film that can be paired with Fierz-David's interpretations of the frescoes of the Villa of Mysteries as a modern attempt to imagine a woman at midlife undergoing an initiatory ordeal that leads to her transformation.

At the opening of *Juliet of the Spirits*, Giorgio, Giulietta's fortyish husband and the great love of her youth, comes home having totally forgotten about celebrating their fifteenth wedding anniversary. She soon discovers that he is about to leave her for a younger woman. Their beautiful beach house at Fregene on the Mediterranean coast near Rome, will soon become her island of Naxos, a site of painful abandonment. Her ordeal will go on until the end of the film. At first, nobody can help her in her misery and anxiety—not her husband, who treats her with benign neglect; not her servant girls, who have their own lives and love affairs; not her two sisters, who are preoccupied with children or career; and not her still beautiful mother, who maintains an attitude of thinly veiled contempt for the ugly duckling of the family. But suffering and pain will take her more deeply into her own depths in a *katabasis* from which she will ultimately emerge transformed, but not after many strange and frightening experiences and even serious thoughts of suicide will have forced themselves upon her.

During a spirit rapping seance held in her home, a friendly spirit who identifies herself as Iris (the female messenger of the gods in Roman mythology) gives the message *Amore per tutti* (Love for everyone), but almost immediately she is interrupted by another spirit with a message for Giulietta's ears only that cruelly contradicts the first: "You're of no importance to anyone . . . to anyone. You're a derelict (*derelito*)." Overcome by her sense of worthlessness, Giulietta faints and collapses on the floor. The spirit who utters these discouraging words had identified himself as "Olaf," and, for a Jungian artist such as Fellini, this harshly critical male voice would be identifiable as the voice of the negative animus, and is the first sign that Giulietta's midlife *katabasis* has begun with the resurgence of the contrasexual archetype.

Giulietta is no ordinary woman. Like the director Fellini in real life, she is subject to hallucinatory visions that are sometimes bizarre and frightening, and that set her apart from the superficial social world around her—

hence her cognomen "Giulietta degli Spiriti." Various "spirits" will thus appear to her in the course of the film, which in many ways is structured around these supernatural appearances. For instance, early in the film, she suddenly sees a vision of an old man coming out of the sea pulling a rope, which he hands over to her to pull: "now it concerns you." As she pulls the rope, it brings near to shore a barge with people in it, and a raft on which there are three horses, one of which is dead.[2] For Giulietta this bizarre vision prepares her for coming to terms with what is dead in her past (the dead horse), and what is still alive (the two live horses). The two live horses are powerful images of animal vitality—energies that Giulietta, who seems rather passive and mousey in the opening scenes of the film, needs to acknowledge and reclaim in herself. A second raft is full of vaguely threatening men, some of whom seem to be like barbarian invaders. In this image her negative animus has presented himself to her again, this time in multiple forms.

The following night she is introduced to Bhisma, an androgynous Silenus-like Hindu teacher with closely cropped white hair, "a man-woman" who "knows the secrets of both sexes." A curiously ambiguous mentor figure, Bhisma is presented with outrageous histrionic overemphasis as a grotesque mixture of genuine wisdom and pure charlatanism. Giulietta—and the spectator—is being prepared to deal with him and other mentoring figures she will meet in the course of the film with discrimination, mixing a willingness to learn with a healthy skepticism. In Bhisma's case, she is presented with the challenge of also knowing "the secrets of both sexes," that is, of integrating some masculinity into her overly feminine and somewhat childish personality. Bhisma's advice to her consists of random quotations from the *Kama Sutra*, after which he urges her to learn to please her husband better in bed, to do her "job" better. Giulietta takes offence at this "whoring" he is urging her to engage in. Bhisma suddenly tells "Olaf" not to interfere, and then begins speaking about "sangria" in a voice no one can recognize, but which is later revealed to be that of José, a positive animus figure, who appears a bit later in the film.

Meanwhile, Bhisma's evocation of the art of sexual love brings her back to a very significant memory of her childhood: her grandfather's suddenly running off with a sexy circus performer, and losing his job as a teacher in the process. This scene is, on one level, Fellini's salute to Josef von Sternberg's 1930 film *The Blue Angel*, in which a teacher runs off with a loose woman and ruins his life, but with the difference that her grandfather returns two years later as happy as ever. But, after this scandalous escapade, Giulietta's mother forbids him to continue living at their home, so he becomes a secret mentor of the little Giulietta, whom she sees on rare but precious occasions, especially at Christmas. Her grandfather plays in Giulietta's inner theater of the mind the role of a helpful and positive spirit; he is a vital and anticlerical figure, who countered the influence of her

Catholic education. Once in a school dramatic production she played the role of a Christian martyr, who ascended to heaven on a burning brazier; her grandfather had indignantly interrupted the performance, and had untied the bonds that attached her to her flaming martyr's bed. But Giulietta remains torn between the appealing image of herself as a young martyr and that of a little girl who loved her rascal of a grandfather, who, as a Wise Old Man or a Wise Old Fool, represented for her a kind of devil-may-care nonconformism. But he cannot help her now. By the end of the film she will imagine that it is she who is untying her child self from the bonds attaching her to the flaming martyr's bed. But at present she is badly in need of assistance—of mentoring—in her midlife crisis of abandonment.

Giulietta returns home after dark to discover a mysterious and handsome stranger in her garden, who talks with her as if he always had known her. He prepares sangria, and offers it to her in a glass as a precious and magic concoction in a ritualized gesture of communion. His face up to this point is completely in the shadow, but eventually it turns out that he is José, a Spanish friend of her husband, whom Fellini endows with the gentle charm, mystery and concern of a positive spiritual animus figure, rather than with the dangerous seductive passion of a demon lover. With a certain campy romanticism that emphasizes the unreal but psychic dimension of the figure, José fascinates Giulietta with his talk about bullfighting, which he demonstrates with her red shawl, telling her that with "a calculated spontaneity", "pure thoughts" and "clarity", the bull—the "monster"—can be defeated. It is at this point that the camera pans to her husband, Giorgio, sitting at the table by himself, and slumped over in a slightly menacing way, who then gets up and pretends he is the bull. Giorgio thus represents the "monster" that she will be able to defeat. José, the mysterious stranger, with his foreign accent, his exotic toreador dimension and his tender love is able to give Giulietta inspiration for imagining a life without Giorgio. He is a quietly inspiring positive animus figure represented in clearly Jungian terms as partly real, with an actual personal relationship with Giulietta, and as partly mythological, and hence as archetypal as an intrapsychic mentoring figure.

More mentoring is also on the way for Giulietta in the form of Suzy, her beautiful and sensual next-door neighbor. Earlier, in the scene on the beach, Suzy had sent over to her a basket of luscious fruits right after Giulietta had had the disturbing vision of the old man emerging from the sea. She later visits Suzy in her house and gets to know her better. Suzy embodies a clear-sighted Dionysian acceptance of sexuality and ecstasy, as well as a kind of sensual greed and excess: "I fulfill my desires—I don't deny myself anything," she says of herself. Up to a point, Suzy may be said to embody Fierz-David's vision of a woman given over to "compulsive eroticism," but with the difference that she seems completely aware of what she is doing. Later at Suzy's house, a spirit voice (identified as that of Iris, the messenger of the gods) issuing from a bouquet of violets addresses

Giulietta directly: "Suzy is your teacher (*maestra*). Listen to her; follow her." Just as Fellini had given the lovely actress Claudia Cardinale the role of Guido's midlife mentor in *8½* (with her message "you don't know how to love"), so he gives Giulietta a midlife mentor with a different kind of message: "fulfill your desires—don't deny yourself anything." Suzy loves fighting, she says about herself, and here her message coincides partially with Bhisma's: love is a battle, and Giulietta needs to integrate some aggressiveness into her personality.

In Fierz-David's terms, Suzy's teaching is necessary Dionysian wisdom—necessary to shake Giulietta out of her Catholic martyr complex—but one that, if followed unthinkingly by her, could lead her to disaster. What is the right path for Suzy may not be the right one for her. But she is tempted, and when Suzy invites two young men, who had followed them on motor scooters, to join with the two of them in an orgy in her tree-house boudoir, Giulietta declines the invitation and goes home. Near the end of the film, she is invited to a social gathering that turns into a kind of orgy. She is sure by this time that Giorgio is leaving her for the beautiful young model Gabriella, since the private detective she had hired to gather information has already submitted his report. Dressed all in red, she seems about to succumb on Suzy's own bed to the charms of Suzy's dark skinned "god child," a seductive Krishna-like figure, who, as a Dionysian lover, can promise her sexual pleasure and temporary relief from her anguished sense of abandonment. But something stops her at the last minute—not only her inhibiting martyr complex (the vision of her child self as a Christian martyr appears again at this juncture), but also, it seems clear from the scene, something close to Fierz-David's "feeling of modesty." And so she steps back from the brink. At this juncture, it is clear that Suzy's Dionysian teaching and personal example have taken Giulietta as far as they can; she now needs a different kind of mentoring. But the world is full of contra-dictory advice, everyone telling her to do something different. "My life is full of people talking, talking, talking," she says to herself bitterly.

Once again, it is José, her spiritual animus figure, who provides a bridge to the resolution of her problems. "Don't be afraid of the truth," he tells her in her garden.

> The truth sets us free. After all, who cares about other people's opinion? In my country there's a saying: "I am my own roof, window and hearth. I feed on my words and drink from my thoughts. Therefore I am happy."

Intrigued but baffled by the mysterious psychic dimension of the figure of José, who hardly ever looks at her directly, as though speaking from his own inner realm, she asks him, "Are you real? Yes or no." (Fellini's portrayal of inner psychological reality as opposed to external reality as it pertains to José is masterful, and yet to some degree programmatic; it is a "portrait of an animus" deliberately composed along Jungian lines, much as his anima figure of Claudia in *8½* was of direct Jungian inspiration.) For her, José's message, although expressed in beautiful poetic terms, is all the same a bit up in the air, in that it does not address directly the pain and anguish of her experience of abandonment, and so leaves her hanging betwixt and between conflict and resolution. When she asks him what advice he can give her, all he can reply is that he wants her to live happily. She thus remains unsatisfied by such ambiguous animus wisdom, and needs someone else to help her deal more directly with her situation as an abandoned Ariadne.

This more focused mentoring is provided (not surprisingly, given Fellini's close relationship with his analyst Dr. Bernhard) by the psychoanalyst Dr. Miller, a middle-aged woman with gray hair who speaks Italian with an American accent. She has a new message for Giulietta, which she enunciates near the very end of the film, as the two of them walk underneath beautiful high trees. Dr. Miller shocks Giulietta by telling her that, in her heart, she actually wants her husband to leave her: "you want to be left alone . . . Without Giorgio you start to breathe and become yourself again." The trees themselves provide a living symbolic image of psychological individuation, she tells her. "We must learn to fulfill ourselves spontaneously, avoiding passions and desires," Dr. Miller thus provides her with a wonderful transformative image:

> Tall old trees are the most impressive symbol of this way of life, deeply rooted in the earth, branches stretched out into the sky, opening in all directions. Theirs is a spontaneous growth. This is the great and simple mystery we must learn.

At the end of the film Giorgio finally backs his bags and leaves Giulietta. At this worst moment of her ordeal, when she realizes that her marriage is truly over, a series of frightening and troubling visions plagues her, and she is clearly (like Jung at midlife) on the edge of a psychotic breakdown. She has thoughts of suicide, and this crucial initiatory symbolic element of death is associated especially with her poignant teenage memories of Laura (ironically, the name of the poet Petrarch's beloved), who, at age fifteen, drowned herself because of an unhappy love; Giulietta comes very close now to following her example. But suddenly a terrible vision of her mother appears, to whom she pleads for help. Her mother sternly forbids her to open the little backlit door, behind which she hears someone crying. But Julia now has the courage to disobey her ("I am not afraid of you any longer") and finds behind the door her child self roped to a martyr's flaming bed. She rushes over to her, and with great effort manages to untie her. At that very moment, the phantasmagoria of visions retreats and disappears. Her beloved grandfather comes down from the sky in his biplane accompanied by his circus performer lover in order to be with her while she waves goodbye to the retreating procession of visions. He then affectionately bids her farewell in turn: "I am also one of your inventions. You don't need me any more."

Freed from the visions that have almost driven her insane, Giulietta steps outside of her garden gate, and hears little child voices, like the flower voices earlier in the film, who tell her in eager tones that they can stay with her now, if she wishes. Giulietta looks happy and composed for the first time in a long while, as the camera follows her walking under huge beautiful parasol pines, which embody the numinous vision of the archetypal trees evoked by Dr. Miller. Giulietta is a transformed figure, who walks beneath the trees by herself, confident and self-possessed.

Part of the problem in dealing with this rich cinematic attempt to show the inner as well as the outer dimensions of a woman's midlife transformation is, as we have already warned, that Fellini, as a male director, may not have gotten everything right—may not, as he stated in the later interview, have been completely able to "speak calmly and clearly about a woman," even a woman portrayed by his own wife. One wonders, for example, just where Giulietta's life will be going now: in a generative direction, like that of the director Guido, perhaps? But the film gives no indication. In addition, there is a problem, as we have seen, with the film being overly programmatic, in that it takes its inspiration from Fellini's recent discovery of Jungian psychology, and to some degree seems deliberately scripted along Jungian lines.

That is why Nina Paley's animated feature *Sita Sings the Blues* (2008) is doubly valuable at this juncture as a cinematic evocation of a woman's midlife transformation: first, in that it is by a woman director, and second, in that the director, unlike Fellini, shows no sign of having been influenced by Jungian theories. But in this film, too, the autobiographical back story is important. Nina Paley was left by her husband in 2002 when she was thirty-four; in one of the sequences of the film his brutally short e-mail reads "Dear Nina, don't come back. Love, Dave." *Sita Sings the Blues* is thus directly inspired by Paley's personal experience of the anguish of abandonment at midlife. The film is the product, one could say, of generative energies released by her own midlife crisis and transformation, resulting in an animated feature that has won prizes at numerous international film festivals.

Two things had happened synchronistically to Paley at this time of life trauma that became catalysts for the making of her film. The first event, (Paley 2009) as she describes it in her director's commentary for the DVD was that, at the time when she was being "dumped by e-mail by [her] husband," she happened to be "in the midst of reading various *Ramayanas.*" (There exist many versions of the story of Rama and Sita, beginning with Valmiki's classical Sanskrit epic, which inspired directly or indirectly a variety of texts in India and in Southeast Asia.) At the same time she discovered the torch songs recorded by Annette Hanshaw, the most famous white jazz singer of the 1920s. Hanshaw's songs became an obsession with her; she played them over and over again for the next three months of anguished abandonment. One can see why: both the story of the *Ramayana* and the blues songs of Annette Hanshaw deal with the theme of a woman's love for a man who treats her badly and then abandons her. There was for Paley "something really touching me and moving me" in both the jazz songs and the ancient Indian epic text, and "the film came out of that." The startling originality of putting these thematically related but culturally completely unrelated texts together as a basis for her film was thus an artistic inspiration based on a psychological prompting from the unconscious during a period of midlife ordeal. There was obviously a process of esthetic sublimation at work, and projecting her midlife anguish onto a mythic screen depersonalized it and presumably helped her to gradually move beyond it.

At the end of the 1980s the *Ramayana* had been the subject of an immensely popular TV series directed by Ramanand Sagar on Doordarshan, the state TV station of India. It was the latest in a long series of the retellings and reworkings of the story of Rama and Sita that have fascinated Indian audiences for many centuries. Paley's personal fascination with the story of Sita's several tragic repudiations by Rama coincided, as we have seen, with the tragic break up of her own marriage, as it is evoked in parallel sequences in the film, the anime narrative switching back repeatedly between Nina's story and Sita's story. Nina Paley's husband, Dave, had gotten a job with an animation company in Trivandrum, in the south of India. Paley joined him there for a short stay, during which time things do not seem to have gone well between them. After her return to San Francisco, she intended to go back to Trivandrum and rejoin Dave, but the trip was forestalled by his cruelly brief e-mail. Paley would later say (in the DVD director's commentary) that the painful process of coming to terms with being abandoned by her husband involved "accepting who she was, including her inner Sita." She would also say that "everyone has an inner Sita," thus emphasizing how powerful she feels the myth of Sita can be for anyone involved in the anguish of abandonment by a beloved. She also says that she received many "touching responses" to her film from women going through break ups. The myth of Sita thus plays for her and for women in similar circumstances a role that would be analogous to the effect of the myth of the abandoned Ariadne on the ancient Roman matrons of the Villa of Mysteries, in that it projects onto the archetypal screen of myth the personal anguish of a woman at midlife. Such a mythological paradigm of abandonment can provide a woman with a way of understanding her personal plight in archetypal terms, that is, of seeing in it a pattern of human development and an aspect of the general human condition, rather than what otherwise might be experienced only in terms of personal pain and suffering. In Ariadne and in Sita a woman might find a powerful image of suffering that is both transformative and consoling.

The Sanskrit *Ramayana* of Valmiki, the model for all later retellings of the story of Sita, presents Rama as the model king, but his marriage with Sita is presented as a model marriage only up to a point. As an originally secular epic, Valmiki's *Ramayana* can allow for a flawed hero, however much it leans towards presenting Rama as a godlike man possessing all the virtues, a project furthered by later and more overtly devotional religious retellings. When the demon king Ravana abducted Sita, she was held captive in his palace in Sri Lanka for a while, so that, when Rama finally rescued her with the aid of the army of the monkey king Hanuman, he insisted that she undergo a trial by fire (*agni pariksha*) in order to prove her purity, since staying captive so long in another man's house had made her the object of suspicion on the part of Rama's people. She passed this gruesome trial successfully, and so was set to live with Rama happily ever after in his kingdom of Ayodhya.

The story of Rama and Sita might have ended here, and indeed many scholars feel that it did end that way originally. But in *Sita Sings the Blues* Paley follows the storyline found in the last section of the *Ramayana*, the *Uttara Kanda*, which constitutes an inspired instance of the epic's own critical reflection on its attempt to glorify Rama as the perfect man and king. The *Uttara Kanda* recounts how, after Rama's return to Ayodhya, the people gradually began to mutter among themselves, suspecting that Sita's purity might not have been as guaranteed by the *agni pariksha* as they had been told. Sita by this time was pregnant with Rama's sons, the twins Lava and Kusha, but, in spite of this fact (in Paley's retelling, Rama suspects that the unborn offspring may actually be Ravana's), Rama orders his brother Laxman to take her into the wilderness and to abandon her. There she was given shelter, unbeknownst to Rama, by the sage Valmiki, who helped educate the two boys to whom she had given birth. When Rama appears again after many years, he recognizes his teenage sons and decides to bring them back home as well as to reinstate Sita as his queen, but only if she will consent to another trial that will prove her purity. All this Paley follows in her film, as we have seen. And the ending is quite extraordinary.

For the myth of Sita, like the myth of Ariadne, not only provides a compelling and consoling image of suffering writ large on the screen of myth; it also provides a *compensatory* dimension. For Ariadne was not just abandoned by her fiancé Theseus; she also became the bride of the god Dionysos, which more than compensated for her abandonment by a mere mortal man. The case with Paley's Sita is similar, in that abandonment leads eventually to a compensatory experience of the divine, and to a radical transformation at midlife. Having lived as a single mother in the forest for many years, and now subjected once again to Rama's insistence that she prove her purity, Sita has had enough of Rama's suspicions. In the *Uttara Kanda* of Valmiki's *Ramayana*,[3] as in Paley's animated film, Sita refuses Rama's final call for her to prove her purity through another *agni pariksha*; instead, she initiates her own test of purity, calling upon Mother Earth (Bhumi Devi, who in Sita's myth was also her own mother) to receive her back into her womb, if she has always been pure and faithful to her husband. Mother Earth confirms her assertion, and rises out of the ground as a gigantic luminous figure, a transformative image of mythological proportions. Sita runs towards her, with her husband, sons and a whole crowd in hot pursuit, and throws herself into her womb. The final Annette Hanshaw song "I'm fallin'" shows her reviewing the events of her life with Rama, but in a detached mode; at one point Sita is shown as a gigantic figure, with Rama as a little blue figure she holds in the palm of her hand (a momentary state of inflation in which Sita identifies herself with the Divine Mother). With the final singing of the refrain "I've got a feeling that I'm fallin' for you and how—fallin' for nobody else but you" it is not clear who she means she is in love with, Rama or Mother Earth—more likely Mother Earth, who is sinking into the ground, with Sita inside her. In this specific visual context, the refrain can be taken as a kind of modern *a lo divino* devotional hymn by Sita to Bhumi Devi.[4] As the luminous figure of Mother Earth disappears into the ground, taking Sita with her, Rama stares at her, and then . . . one single tear falls from his eye. All is not well with the most perfect of kings.

Paley lets this part of the myth speak for itself, and so the spectator can be puzzled as to whether this is really a happy ending for Sita or not. On the one hand, Sita is shown to be happy reposing within Mother Earth, swimming through the air as though in the amniotic fluid of the womb. On the other hand, her entry into the womb of Mother Earth can be seen as a form of suicide. Paley's DVD director's commentary preserves the sense of the ambiguity: Sita "is detaching, and so she no longer needs to live." But, one way or another, what is clear is that, by the end of the film, Sita is no longer the ill-treated wife of her earlier years, but now a figure blessed with intimate association with Bhumi Devi—a daughter of the Divine Mother. Through her oneiric return to her divine mother's womb, Sita has established a relationship with the archetypal, just as Ariadne had done through her marriage to Dionysos. This adds a new spiritual dimension to her life, which allows her purely personal concerns to be placed in a new archetypal framework. This *transformed* Sita is a new person, confident in her new relation to the divine as well as to her own past, from whose anguish she is now detached and which she can review and remember with equanimity.

The scene then shifts to New York, for the short final scene of the film. At first Nina is seen working at her computer, and then she is shown in bed with her new cat—a black one (a sign of her new witchly power?)—reading a translation of the *Ramayana*, with several other translations and commentaries on the bookshelf above her. The final image is thus that of Nina no longer as a repudiated wife, but rather as a generative creative artist at work gathering ideas and inspiration for her film *Sita Sings the Blues*; when she puts the book back on the shelf, it is as though the creative and generative process has definitely been set in motion. Just as the credits begin to roll, the spectator is treated to a humorous reversal of gender roles among the gods, as Vishnu (of whom Rama is considered in the Hindu tradition to be an avatar) massages the calves of Lakshmi (his four-armed goddess consort, of whom Sita is often considered to be an avatar), whereas, at the opening of the film, it was Lakshmi who was shown massaging her husband, as would be the traditional role for her as his wife. Then Lakshmi gives the spectators a big wink, highlighting the gender role reversal, which had also characterized Sita's final ordeal, in that it was she who this time repudiated Rama, and not vice versa as before. Sita chooses her fate this time, rather than submitting to it.

In her article "Rejecting Sita," Linda Hess has documented how in modern India

> today more than ever Sita is a site of contestation. The Sita who clung to the dharma of worshiping her husband and bowing to his will, even when he repeatedly and cruelly rejected her, is still embraced as the ideal woman by many Hindus of both sexes. But others, increasingly, are describing that ideal as concocted by and serving the interests of dominant males from ancient times to the present.
>
> (Hess 2004: 53)

For many today the traditional story of Rama and Sita, viewed from a modern social and ethical standpoint, is a highly problematic text, and Paley, for all the extraordinary artistic originality of her film, follows in the wake of much recent concern with the contradiction between Rama's traditional status as the perfect king and his seemingly abusive treatment of Sita. So fraught with the potential for controversy is the scene of the *agni pariksha* that Ramanand Sagar's popular seventy-eight-episode TV version (*Ramayan*, 1986) strayed from the mainstream version and made a bodily double (a *chaya Sita*) of the real Sita the victim of Ravana's abduction and of her subsequent trial by fire, while Rama had the actual Sita kept safe and sound back in his palace at Ayodhya. This version of the story may have forestalled controversy, but it also proved confusing for many TV viewers unfamiliar with this curious narrative twist to be found in Tulsidas's sixteenth-century Hindi version of the *Ramayana*. Paley, although she was familiar with the TV series, avoids this narrative subterfuge, and presents Rama mainly as the conceited and abusive patriarchal husband who is the shadow side of the perfect king of the tradition—a "mean" man, who is "the kind of man who needs the kind of woman like me," in the masochistic words of one of Annette Hanshaw's songs.

Paley's somewhat simplistic depiction of Rama allows her to focus on a complex and rich presentation of Sita as Nina's "inner Sita'—as the woman transformed at midlife through an ordeal of abandonment, anguish and isolation. She remains generally faithful to the story of Sita in the *Ramayana*, who exemplifies, like Odysseus' wife Penélopê in Homer's *Odyssey*, the unfolding of an archetypal initiatory predisposition, which enables a woman to endure the midlife ordeal of isolation and abandonment, and eventually to come into her own as a new woman no longer requiring the presence of a man in her life to validate her existence. Paley's Sita's ordeal includes thoughts of suicide, as when she says, "I must have committed a terrible sin in a previous life to deserve such suffering. Were I not carrying Rama's sons, I would throw myself into the river." Symbolic death as a motif accompanying radical transformation constitutes a necessary part of her initiatory process, and will occur again when Sita prays for the earth to open up and take her in at the end of the film.

Listening to the psychological resonances of the mythological tale of Rama and Sita brings new life and relevance to a classical epic narrative. In the first instance, considering that what took Sita away from a life contained within Rama's protection and presence was her abduction by Ravana, it becomes clear that the multiheaded (interesting: an animus whose *heads* are multiple!) and ferocious character of Ravana represents symbolically (like Penélopê's suitors in the *Odyssey*) the resurgence of the animus at midlife, in terms of an animus attack and abduction. First of all, Ravana is literally a demon lover, and Sita's time away from Rama is thus spent fending off animus attacks of a demonic sort; Sita cannot ignore him and is forced to come to terms with him. The psychological dimension of their relationship is highlighted by the fact that Ravana never becomes her actual lover; in other words, the anticipated narrative consequences of the "abduction" are never realized, and instead Sita is under constant pressure to divert her attention from her husband onto something else. Her eventual integration of Ravana-like animus characteristics may be seen in the scenes inspired by the *Uttara Kanda*, the last book of the *Ramayana*. Here, as she shows herself capable of resisting Rama's insistence on another trial of her purity, and then in determining the nature of the trial, which can only result in the dissolution of their marriage, she becomes, like Ravana earlier had become, "the one who takes Sita away from Rama" through a kind of self-abduction and a removal of herself from the marital bonds that have proved to have such a tragic stranglehold on her. The energy that enables her to resist Rama may be seen as deriving from the animus energy she has integrated thanks to her experience of Rama's great enemy, Ravana, the one who is defined in the epic as "the one who resists Rama." By resisting Rama in turn, Sita becomes her own woman, but not in terms of lonely isolation but rather through a close archetypal relationship with Bhumi Devi. She is now the daughter of the Divine Mother, and not only Rama's faithful wife, as she was during her captivity on the island of Lanka. In that sense, then, Ravana does not only play a negative role in her life as abductor and threat to her purity as a wife but also, as several voice-over commentators (intriguingly represented as shadow puppet figures) within the film point out, a positive one. Ravana is "an incredibly learned man" and a good musician (he plays the veena for the god Shiva). He does not force himself on her sexually while she is living in his palace, and treats Sita like a gentleman, which is more than can be said of Rama in the film. In fact, says one of the shadow puppet commentators, "the only bad thing he seems to have done is to kidnap Sita." On the psychological plane, Ravana is for Sita both a threat and a friend, and may be said to represent symbolically the highly significant if ambiguous role of the animus in a woman's life, especially during her midlife crisis.

In the Hindu tradition Sita is seen as all good, but a psychological take on her as a rounded character would sense the presence in her of a shadow, which is suggested in the film by the relentless way Rama and the people suspect that she is not as entirely pure as she maintains she is. These accusations of faithlessness are projections she must deal with, but they also suggest something of her own unacted-out shadow side. The ideal of a woman who would never think of any man other than her husband is literally impossible to realize, since any woman, no matter how dedicated and faithful she may be to her husband, has an unconscious fantasy life and a shadow that is unfaithful to her husband and sexually attracted to other men. In a way, the story obliges Sita, faced with extreme demands to affirm her total purity, to protest too much, and hence to deny shadow suspicions about her—accusations of impure thoughts that, in a less extreme situation, she could have dismissed as having no damaging effect on her essential faithfulness as a wife. But in the film these suspicions surface again and again to cast aspersions on her reputation. Thus we can say that "Sita's shadow" is made up of what the people, and even Rama himself, suspect about her: that she is not as pure as she maintains she is. This image of an "unfaithful Sita," that through the people's suspicions bedevils Sita at midlife, represents a resurgence of the shadow with which she must come to terms. Is it that she is actually unfaithful? No—but she has the shadow potential.

In *Sita Sings the Blues*, the animated character Nina's story largely parallels that of Valmiki's epic heroine, who plays the role, as the director has said, of her "inner Sita." In particular, Nina's separation from her husband Dave leads to a new relationship with the generative maternal principle, which is imaged by her relationship to her new cat, with whom she forms a maternal dyad, the black cat being depicted in the very last scene as lying in the crook of her left arm like a baby as Nina reads the

Ramayana in bed. The earlier cat, Lexi, was a pet she shared with her husband—the light-colored animal companion of their marital happiness. The new cat is black, suggesting a witch's familiar, and is the sole companion of Nina in the film after she has become an artist as opposed to an abandoned wife. The shadow side that Nina Paley herself presumably came to terms with is mentioned briefly in the director's DVD commentary, when she says (à propos of the scene where Nina calls Dave in India and begs to be taken back) that "there was this whole aspect of my personality that I couldn't accept"; that "I had so much self-loathing about the way I was reacting to this breakup," adding that "I must say that I've left out my terrible, terrible behavior" from the film, refusing to say more, even when pressed by her interlocutor to be more specific. So at least in the director's life, if not in the depiction of her animated character Nina, there were shadow elements that she was aware of as they surfaced during her midlife transformation.

A richly layered novel like Toni Morrison's *Beloved* 2004 [1987] presents a multitude of possibilities of signification, but among them some pertain to the novel inasmuch as it is an oneiric text dealing with the theme of a woman's transformation at midlife. To give a bit of back story: by the year 1873 the ex-slave Sethe has been living for a number of years in a black community near Cincinnati in her own house with her teenage daughter Denver. She has been shunned by her neighbors ever since she murdered her infant daughter Beloved in 1855, in order to prevent her from falling into the hands of a slave catcher, who would have returned the whole family to Kentucky and the misery of slavery. After her death at the hands of her mother, who cut her throat with a handsaw, Beloved eventually returns to the house as a ghostly disturbing presence. Her house is now a haunted house, and Sethe's friends and neighbors soon abandon her, "for they would not visit her while the baby ghost filled the house" (Morrison 2004: 112). These years of isolation and loneliness ("twelve years of no visitors" [Morrison 2004: 14]) constituted for Sethe a liminal period preparing the ground for later growth and midlife transformation.

The situation both changes and intensifies when Paul D, who was once a slave on the same Kentucky farm as Sethe, suddenly and unexpectedly shows up at the house. Paul D becomes a special man for Sethe, not only because he reintroduces her to sexual love, but also because

> not even trying, he had become the kind of man who could walk into a house and make the women cry. Because with him, in his presence, they could. There was something blessed in his manner.
>
> (Morrison 2004: 20)

Paul D embodies to some degree aspects of a positive animus figure, in that his appearance begins the process of Sethe's healing. He can give her sympathy and compassion, at least up to a point, and provides a male presence that she badly needs. He may remind the reader of Alice Walker's lyrical portrait of "the Quiet Man" in her dedicatory prose poem in *Good Night, Willie Lee, I'll See You in the Morning* (1975), a book of poems published several years before *Beloved*, with which Toni Morrison might well have been familiar.[5] If so, Walker may have had a role in inspiring her positive portrait of Paul D, a black man whom black women could trust and to whom they could reveal their deepest sufferings. Walker endows her "quiet man," who is described more as a figure of the psyche than as a real person ("a memory of someone she had never known, a high standard") with positive animus traits: he "loved women not just to lie with but he would stand up with them when no one else would. . . . A woman could speak in his company" (A. Walker 1975: vi).

Paul D also takes the momentous step of chasing away the ghost of Beloved that has been creating such a disturbance in Sethe's house: "it took a man, Paul D, to shout it off, beat it off and take its place for himself" (Morrison 2004: 123). But his action winds up complicating matters even more, for Beloved, chased away as a ghost, now returns in the flesh as an eighteen-year-old girl, who eventually seduces Paul D and thus forces Sethe to come to terms with her, not as the memory of a helpless infant or as a ghost, but as the disturbing presence of a willful and seductive teenager.

Sethe then insists that Paul D sleep only in the upstairs room with her, and it looks for a while as though the two will even have children together. But the shadow of Sethe's past now comes between her and Paul D, who cannot bear to stay with her any longer, once he finds out that she had years before tried to murder all her children one after the other. Sethe tries to explain to Paul D that she did this in order to keep them safe ("I took and put my babies where they's be safe" [Morrison 2004: 193])—that is, to save them from a life of slavery. But she succeeded in this project only with Beloved, whose infant throat she managed to slit with a handsaw before she was restrained. For Paul D,

> this here Sethe was new. . . . This here new Sethe talked about safety with a handsaw. This here new Sethe didn't know where the world stopped and she began. . . . more important than what Sethe had done was what she claimed. It scared him.
>
> (Morrison 2004: 193)

This is for Paul D a shocking revelation of Sethe's shadow side—a side she had tried stubbornly to excuse to herself through various rationalizations: excess of mother love, good intentions (to save her children from returning to slavery in Kentucky), and lack of better alternatives. But its evil dimension cannot be seen only as the result of good intentions or love for her babies. There is something horribly frightening in this resurgence of

Sethe's murderous shadow at midlife. There is something in it that calls on her for attention and justification, although past a point it does not yield its secret to rational justification. Now that Paul D knows her secret, she is forced to listen to the way he sees her shadow side as something animalistic, as nonhuman:

> "What you did was wrong, Sethe."
> "I should have gone on back there? Taken my babies back there?"
> "There could have been a way. Some other way."
> "What way?"
> "You got two feet, Sethe, not four," he said, and right then a forest sprang up between them; trackless and quiet.
>
> (Morrison 2004: 194)

For Paul D, Sethe's shadow is "four-legged," that is, animalistic. But that makes it also archetypal to a degree, to the extent that it represents animal energy unintegrated into a human ethical consciousness, and so not quite human; it is the monstrous Mr. Hyde side of Sethe, and so inexplicable in purely human terms. Dazed and frightened by this revelation, Paul D leaves her, because her shadow is more than he can take, his love for her having seemingly reached its limits. Without Paul D, Sethe is on her own again, and her real ordeal is about to begin.

Without Paul D's presence in the house, Beloved begins to take over completely. But who is Beloved exactly? Is she only the ghost of Sethe's murdered infant daughter come back to life? Toni Morrison lets a kind of uncertainty play over what seems at first like a standard plot for a supernatural tale about a haunting and—what is a bit more unusual—a permanent materialization of the ghost. But the phenomenon of Beloved grows more and more mysterious as she takes over the household. At first Beloved is a welcome stimulus for Sethe to relive her most problematic memories, and to free herself from the stigmatized identity that had been hers ever since the momentous occasion when she asserted her maternal rights over the slaveholder's right to reclaim his property. The joy of having her daughter Beloved back with her enables her for a while to justify herself and her past, both to herself and to her long-lost daughter:

> Beloved, she my daughter. She mine. See. She come back to me of her own free will and I don't have to explain a thing. I didn't have time to explain before because it had to be done quick. Quick. She had to be safe and I put her where she would be. But my love was tough and she back now. . . . I won't ever let her go. I'll explain to her, even though I don't have to. Why I did it. How if I hadn't killed her she would have died and that is something I could not bear to happen to her. When I explain it she'll understand, because she understands everything already.
>
> (Morrison 2004: 236)

But it turns out that Beloved is more for Sethe than a cherished partner in a magically reconstituted Mother–Daughter dyad. Soon she becomes a menacing figure who is gradually obsessing Sethe, taking her over completely, monopolizing her attention, making exorbitant demands on her mother for pretty clothes they cannot afford, leading her eventually to neglect basic survival needs, and bringing her to the point of death. For Sethe soon leaves her job at the restaurant, and soon the family is close to starvation. Her other daughter, Denver, senses mortal danger in the way the situation in the house is starting to develop: "she saw themselves beribboned, decked-out, limp and starving but locked in a love that wore everybody out. Now it was obvious that her mother could die and leave them both" (Morrison 2004: 286). The mother–daughter relationship has turned toxic, and the appearance of the initiatory motif of death signals that Sethe is undergoing an ordeal that may cost her her life.

With Beloved now pregnant with Paul D's child, and Sethe close to a psychotic breakdown, Denver goes out of the house to seek a job, in order to save the family from starvation. She is able to confide in Janey, the maid of the Bodwins, a brother and sister pair of abolitionists who had years before helped Sethe escape the gallows. As far as Janey is concerned, "from what Denver told her it seemed the woman had lost her mind. That wasn't the Sethe she remembered. This Sethe had lost her wits" (Morrison 2004: 299). Ella, a wise old woman in the black community, who has had no problem dealing with ghosts and hauntings, is also taken into her confidence:

> As long as the ghost showed out from its ghostly place—shaking stuff, crying, smashing and such—Ella respected it. But if it took flesh and came in her world, well, the shoe was on the other foot. She didn't mind a little communication between the two worlds, but this was an invasion.
>
> (Morrison 2004: 302)

So Ella decides that Sethe must be rescued from the "demon-child" who is plaguing her and driving her insane.

The rescue scene makes clear that there is something fearsome, awesome and supernatural about Beloved—something that represents a frightening yet beautiful aspect of the archetypal Mother. Thirty women arrive at Sethe's house to rescue her, and then see Beloved and Sethe holding hands at the door:

> The devil child was clever, they thought. And beautiful. It had taken the shape of a pregnant woman, naked and smiling in the heat of the afternoon sun. Thunderblack and glistening, she stood on long straight legs, her belly big and tight. Vines of hair twisted all over her. Jesus. Her smile was dazzling.
>
> (Morrison 2004: 308)

Toni Morrison has said in an interview (Plath 1998: 32–33) that the figure of Beloved is complex, both as the spirit of a daughter returned from the dead and as a return in bodily form of a mother who had managed to survive the terrible Middle Passage. For Sethe, Beloved is both the murdered daughter and the dominating mother, as Denver had seen earlier:

> Beloved bending over Sethe looked the mother, Sethe the teething child, for other than those times when Beloved needed her, Sethe confined herself to a corner chair. The bigger Beloved got, the smaller Sethe became; the brighter Beloved's eyes, the more those eyes that used never to look away became slits of sleeplessness. Sethe no longer combed her hair or splashed her face with water. She sat in the chair licking her lips like a chastened child while Beloved ate up her life, took it, swelled up with it, grew taller on it. And the older woman yielded it up without a murmur.
>
> (Morrison 2004: 294–295)

It is clear that the figure of Beloved has a mythic quality, and that, as part of an "invasion" of archetypal forces from the unconscious, she has pulled Sethe down into the archetypal world of the Mother–Daughter dyad, in which Sethe's sense of ordinary human reality is rapidly being lost, and in which her very identity is in question. Sethe had originally defined herself as the mother who cared so much for her infant daughter that she would kill her in order to save her from slavery. But now she herself has become the infant daughter, the "teething child," the "chastened child."

Sethe has so succumbed to the archetypal presence of Beloved that she has become outright delusional in relation to the external world. While the women are preparing to rescue her, she spies Mr. Bodwin, the "good" white man who has come to pick up Denver for her new job at his house, and mistakes him for the slave master from whom, now as eighteen years before, she must protect her child: "he is coming into her yard and he is coming for her best thing" (Morrison 2004: 309). But this time, in a mad delusional frenzy, Sethe tries to kill the slave master, not her daughter. But, as she rushes at Mr. Bodwin with an ice pick in her hand, she is disarmed before anything irreparable can happen.

At this point Beloved suddenly vanishes from the scene—nobody is sure how. Her mysterious disappearance again signals the touch of the supernatural and the archetypal that plays around her as a figure, who is neither altogether human nor altogether divine. She is a phenomenon for which people, baffled as to the nature of her true identity, are prone to use the pronoun "it." In initiatory terms, Beloved is the transformational image that brings Sethe's crisis to a point of almost intolerable intensity. Beloved triggers in Sethe's mind the archetypal power of the Mother–Daughter dyad that years before had prompted Sethe's earlier arrogating to herself the inhumanly archetypal power to kill her own child. But now Sethe must confront this power not only in personal terms (hence her attempts to "explain things" to Beloved), but also in archetypal terms (hence her sinking into madness), as she is increasingly possessed by the power of the mythic configuration. This part of Sethe's ordeal is fraught with danger; in fact, her very life is at stake.

Unexpectedly, it is Paul D who reappears in the narrative at this juncture as the ultimate midlife mentor, who will guide her from madness over to the other side into safety. He has spent several months living in a church basement, and has just heard of the astonishing rescue scene and of the unexplained disappearance of Beloved. Drawn by his renewed love for Sethe, he comes to her home in her hour of deepest need, bringing with him, as before, his positive animus qualities ("the thing in him, the blessedness [Morrison 2004: 319]), but now also a midlife mentor's concern for the archetypal dangers Sethe has been facing:

> At the kitchen table he sits down. Something is missing from 124. Something larger than the people who lived there. Something more than Beloved or the red light. He can't put his finger on it, but it seems, for a moment, that just beyond his knowing is the glare of an outside thing that embraces while it accuses.
>
> (Morrison 2004: 319)

Paul D's final mentoring role is to deliver the words of wisdom that Sethe needs in order to escape death, and to be reborn at age forty, transformed by her ordeal into a woman who can exist on her own, no longer identified with the maternal role whose archetypal energy had prevented her from loving herself, totally inflated as she was with the archetypal pattern of the Mother protecting the Daughter, her "best thing," who had been once lost to her in death, but now has returned. (In her identification with this archetypal pattern, Sethe lives out something analogous to the Greek myth of Demeter yearning for her daughter Persephone, lost to Death, but then returning with the flowers of spring.) Paul D's message to Sethe, the teaching that will bring her back to herself as someone worthy of her own love, is this: "you your best thing, Sethe. You are." To which she replies wonderingly: "Me? Me?" (Morrison 2004: 322).

That is the end of the novel, except for a lyrical postlude that celebrates the mystery of Beloved, taken away, like Persephone, by Death, and carried down to the underworld:

> everyone knew what she was called, but nobody anywhere knew her Name. Disremembered and unaccounted for, she cannot be lost because no one is looking for her, and even if they were, how can they call her if they don't know her name? Although she has claim, she is

not claimed. In the place where long grass opens, the girl who waited to be loved and cry shame erupts into her separate parts, to make it easy for the chewing laughter to swallow her all away.

(Morrison 2004: 323)

No doubt, Morrison's Beloved has no individual name (she is simply—generically—the "beloved"), partly because she represents allegorically the loss of name caused by the anonymity of enslavement. But Morrison's allegory of the tragic history of slavery is given mythic power by its lyrical evocation at the end of the novel of the archetypal mystery of the Lost Daughter and the Mother who lost her, as in the myth of Demeter and Persephone. And the power of the myth itself is explicated and exorcised by Paul D's message that the archetypal weight of a myth, like the full weight of history, is more than any human individual—or any human mother like Sethe—is capable of bearing for long.

Notes

1 By contrast, Robert Graves's 1934 novel *I, Claudius*, a basis for the later successful BBC TV series (1976) starring Derek Jacobi, presents Livia as a brilliant and murderous psychopath.
2 This scene can be viewed as Fellini's homage to a notorious scene in Bunuel and Dali's film *An Andalusian Dog* (1929), in which a grand piano is shown being dragged into a room with a priest and a dead horse attached to it. It probably was intended, here as in Fellini's film, to symbolize psychological baggage (the young man's Catholic education, for instance) that has yet to be dealt with consciously.
3 Not all scholars accept the *Uttara Kanda* as the final book of Valmiki's text, believing it to be a later addition. The radical critical perspective it introduces is thus seen as highly controversial, in that it undermines the patriarchal justification for Rama's treatment of Sita.
4 The Spanish term *a lo divino* (literally, "in a divine or mystical manner") refers to a reworking of a secular love lyric into a devotional hymn, as for instance in some of the mystical poems of St. John of the Cross.
5 Alice Walker was later to portray Jung as a sympathetic mentor figure in her 1992 novel *Possessing the Secret of Joy*. There is no evidence, however, for Toni Morrison having been influenced by Jung in any significant way when she was writing *Beloved*.

Chapter 5

Homer's *Odyssey* and midlife transformation

Although the *Odyssey* deals primarily, as its title indicates, with the adventures of Odysseus, it also includes significant sections concerning his wife Penélopê, four books largely dedicated to his son Telémakhos, and a key episode centered around the figure of the young Phaiakian princess Nausikaa. Initiation paradigms, differing according to stage of life and gender, are important subtexts, since all four characters need to be prepared to assume new roles in life. Odysseus, erstwhile hero of the Trojan War, and then a roving pirate at the start of his long journey home, needs to be made ready to assume the generative role of a good king of his island of Ithaka, which he left twenty years before in order to join the Greek forces besieging the city of Troy. His wife Penélopê, surrounded by young suitors who vie for her hand and tyrannize her household, needs to prepare herself, once her husband returns, to assume full powers and dignity as his consort and queen of Ithaka. Their son Telémakhos, in order to be his father's ally in the final battle against the suitors, needs to metamorphose quickly from a brooding adolescent into the kind of young hero his father was earlier in his life, and the young princess Nausikaa must prepare herself for marriage and motherhood. The theme of initiation and transformation lies thus at the very heart of the *Odyssey*. However, for the purposes of this chapter, we will focus only on the midlife protagonists Odysseus and Penélopê. The *Odyssey* is, no doubt, chiefly concerned with the adventures and return home of Odysseus. But his wife Penélopê is given a major supporting role as a long-suffering and faithful woman undergoing a midlife transformation, and her new-found courage and strategic abilities prove crucial for the resolution of the problems of the epic's finale.

At the time when he set out for Troy, Odysseus had left behind an infant son, so he was presumably in his twenties at the time of his departure. Since the Trojan War lasted ten years, this would put him in his thirties at the beginning of his journey home, and in his forties when he finally arrived, since his return took about ten years—a plausible length of time for such an epic midlife transformation to take place. Homer's evocation of the ten years of Odysseus' return home constitutes an oneiric text rich in mythological fantasy and psychological insight. Told mainly in the first person in Books 9–12 by a shipwrecked Odysseus who has taken refuge at the court of Alkinoös, king of Phaiakia, it has the feel of a profound psychological self-confession wrapped up in a mythological narrative. As an inner history disguised as the story of wanderings across the Mediterranean in a fairyland of seductive nymphs and monsters of various sorts, the mythological phantasmagoria of Books 9–12 contrasts vividly with the epic realism of much of the rest of the *Odyssey*.

As John Finley pointed out in *Four Stages of Greek Thought*, Homer's age

> thought, not through analyzed ideas, but through ideas interfused with the full play of the senses. For the Greeks a chief impulse to such a way of thinking was the great skein of legend, myth and folktale . . . It was mythology that supplied a way of seeing reality in the full color of the senses.
>
> (Finley 1966: 34)

Homer's primary mode of thinking is "mythological thinking," an archaic mode of thought that was soon to be displaced in Greek cultural history by "conceptual thinking," which substituted for poetic mythological thinking "a world of concepts rather than figures, of prose rather than verse, of analysis rather than myths" (Finley 1966: 35). It is this latter mode of philosophical and analytical thinking with which we are thoroughly familiar today, as it operates through abstract ideas and theories, rather than through mythological stories and symbols. One might be tempted in modern times to scorn mythological thinking as childish and primitive, but such was not Jung's opinion, who wrote:

> The protean mythologem and the shimmering symbol express the processes of the psyche far more trenchantly and, in the end, far more clearly than the clearest concept; for the symbol not only contains a visualization of the process but—and this is perhaps just as important—it also brings a re-experiencing of it, of that twilight which we can learn to understand only through inoffensive empathy, but which too much clarity can disperse.
>
> (Jung 1968: 199)

Thus Odysseus' mythological self-reflective narrative may in some ways be better suited to communicating the mysterious nature of the midlife ordeal he went through than any theory that one could use today to reduce his transformation to abstract categories and make it comprehensible in terms of some overriding conceptual framework, even a Jungian and Eriksonian one! Modern readers need to relax their consciousness into the oneiric world of the "shining mythologem," and to reexperience its mysterious twilight charm.

Odysseus, temporarily stranded near the end of his wanderings at the Phaiakian court of King Alkinoös, boasts that his name has already become famous throughout the world. But, having said this, the self-proclaimed legend in his own time leads the court of Alkinoös quickly to the realization that their guest is no longer to be completely identified with his own myth; the hero he was in his youth has been transformed by experiences that no longer fit the pattern:

> I have been detained long by Kalypso,
> loveliest of goddesses, who held me
> in her smooth caves, to be her heart's delight,
> as Kirkê of Aiaia, the enchantress,
> desired me, and detained me in her hall.
> (Homer 1963: 146)

Thus, with his mention of Kalypso and Kirkê, strong images of female power have entered Odysseus' legend—the female power represented by the two *belles dames sans merci* to whom he has been in thrall during most of the ten years of his adventures in Neverland. But now, he goes on to tell the Phaiakians, he is a different man—a man who longs only for home and family and for the regaining of his kingdom: Odysseus will make use of all the resources of myth and folktale to convey to his listeners how he has changed in terms of a symbolic representation of a midlife transformation, whose key elements include the initiatory themes of mourning the demise of a blindly self-assertive youthful hero myth, dealing with troublesome dimensions of the shadow, confronting the sometimes overwhelming female power associated with the resurgence at midlife of the anima, getting the guidance of a midlife mentor, and finally acquiring a new generative identity.

As regards the resurgence of the anima, Homer is obviously fascinated with one particular dimension of the traditional tales concerning Odysseus (assuming he did not invent the episode to begin with—there is no evidence one way or another): that of Odysseus' long years of submission to the nymph Kalypso. In fact, once the short invocation to the Muse and the preamble are over, the *Odyssey* had gotten underway with a short description of how "her ladyship Kalypso clung to him in her sea-hollowed caves" (Homer 1963: 1). Thus the adumbration of the unusual theme of the submission of the hero to the power of a semidivine woman is the first stated theme of the epic. It is restated shortly afterwards during the Council of the Gods, at which Athena laments Odysseus' thralldom to Kalypso, and seeks Zeus' approval to intervene in his fate and to free him from the clutches of the lovely nymph.

Since the first four books of the *Odyssey* will be mainly devoted to the theme of the growth into manhood of Odysseus' son Telémakhos, this episode is a false start for the epic, and the beginning of the tale of Odysseus requires a retelling in Book 5 of the council of the gods on Olympus, which took place at the beginning of Book 1. Once again, Athena starts off her speech to her father Zeus by lamenting Odysseus' thralldom to a nymph. Zeus gives in to her request to do something for Odysseus, and sends the god Hermês to order Kalypso to release him. Since Homer's intention is to highlight the power of Kalypso and the powerlessness of Odysseus to escape her, the first description we have of Odysseus is of him sitting on the shore of her island, "as a thousand times before," who "racked his own heart groaning, with eyes wet / scanning the bare horizon of the sea" (Homer 1963: 83). This repeated stress laid on the theme of the power of Kalypso at the opening of the narrative concerning Odysseus should remind the reader that the *Odyssey*, as a story of Odysseus' ten-year return to Ithaka, allots most of those years to his captivity on Kalypso's island of Ogygia, a somewhat timeless twilight realm, where endless repetition of forced sex at night and bouts of anguished homesickness by day occupy most of this most unheroic hero's time. Kalypso is irresistible; she "holds him by Necessity." A short while later in Book 5 the narrative becomes more specific, lest the reader remain puzzled as to how this reversal of male and female power expressed itself and how it began in the first place:

> The sweet days of his life time
> were running out in anguish over his exile,
> for long ago the nymph had ceased to please.
> Though he fought shy of her and her desire,
> he lay with her each night, for she compelled him.
> (Homer 1963: 85)

Thus the presence in the text of Kalypso's female power totally deconstructs the myth of the hypermasculine hero. Odysseus is in a state of liminality: he is no longer the young hero he used to be, and is not yet the mature king he is destined to become.

But it must be remembered that the Kalypso episode, although it occurs at the beginning of the story of the return of Odysseus in the *Odyssey*, is placed near the end of the sequence of the events making up his ten years of wanderings. It is also important to note that the Kalypso episode had begun differently from the way it ended. Kalypso herself reminds Hermes that, at the outset, she saved Odysseus' life after all his shipmates perished in the storm that overwhelmed them after they had sacrilegiously eaten the Cattle of the Sun. Indeed, in return for his accepting to become her husband, she has promised him immortality and eternal youth. But Odysseus' submission to female power—to the power of fascination and control of the anima—is a mixed blessing for him. This is made clear in the text by the anguish and grief, which replace what one must assume to be his initial gratefulness to her for saving his life and for the sensual gratification of the first years of their relationship. The symbolic and intrapsychic dimension of their relationship is wonderfully symbolized by its mythological setting. Kalypso's island Ogygia, whose name may mean "antique" or "very ancient" (Homer 1964: I, 294), is described at the opening of the *Odyssey* as an island set in the navel (*omphalos*) of the sea.[1] Thus, both by its allure of timelessness—the relative timelessness of the archetypal dimension of the anima (cf. Kalypso's promises of immortality and eternal youth), and by its association with the archetypal mother, to whose body Odysseus remains symbolically attached at the navel, Ogygia is a place doubly associated with female power, that of the archetypal mother as well as that of the anima. For Odysseus, Kalypso's island was, physically and psychologically, a prison. It was the site of his sexual slavery and of his increasingly painful state of liminality. The outcome of his ordeal, however, was a midlife transformation desirable not only as a stage of life transition, but also as a psychological necessity, for Odysseus, the savage hypermasculine warrior of the Trojan War and ruthless pirate of the beginning of his journey home to Ithaka, must not only become capable of regaining his kingdom against overwhelming odds (sheer physical heroism will not be enough for this feat), but also of reuniting with his queen Penélopê and then of ruling as a fair and just king. His reintegration into civilized and peaceful society requires him to become a new man, and submission to the power of Kalypso is an important part of the process that will prepare him for this new stage of life.

But how did Odysseus get into this midlife crisis in the first place? The oneiric text of the adventures of Odysseus before he arrives on Kalypso's island are organized in a pattern of two short adventures followed by one long one. Even though the weight of symbolic significance may be said to correspond to the comparative length of the episodes, the shorter episodes add something to a growing richness of its oneiric presentation of midlife themes. The first short adventure (the battle with the Kikonês) still participates in the epic mode that might have governed the whole sequence, if a psychic journey into a phantasmagorical land of monsters and nymphs had not been on the epic's agenda. Odysseus' adventures began as soon as he has left Troy with his ships, and at first they are narrated in an epic realistic mode. Having sacked Troy (it was he who devised the winning stratagem of the Trojan Horse), Odysseus had led his men in the sack of another city, Ismaros—so far, nothing new, in that the sack of the Kikonian city was like a quick replay of the sack of Troy. It was business as usual for Odysseus and his men: they sack the city, kill the men and enslave the women and children.

But it soon turns out that Odysseus' luck as a sacker of cities has changed. His men refuse to obey his orders to take to sea immediately, and this gives time for those from Ismaros who fled his onslaught to return in full force with numerous allies, and many of his men lose their lives in the ensuing debacle. This defeat, coming as it does at the beginning of his journey home, has an ominous significance for the future: the once invincible hero now has trouble getting himself obeyed by his own men, and disaster begins to dog his footsteps.

The next episode takes Odysseus and his men to the coast of the land of the Lotos Eaters, who live in a drugged state of lethargy and forgetfulness, which is very tempting for some of Odysseus' men to live in also. The point of this oneiric episode is that, once again, there is mutiny afoot. Three of his men—men he has chosen for reliability—become curious and ingest a bit of the magic drug, and then no longer feel like going home to Ithaka, and wish only to live with the Lotos Eaters forever. Such is their resistance to continuing their journey home that Odysseus has to drive them back on board by force. With the Lotos Eaters episode an important theme—the desire to forget about homecoming—makes its appearance in the *Odyssey*, and it begins to undermine its dominant theme as an epic of homecoming. The journey of Odysseus, now launched into the world of the "shining mythologem," comes to resemble less and less the epic narrative of a journey home, and more and more the symbolic representation of an inner journey, whose various episodes become the mythological means for Odysseus of communicating to the Phaiakian court the psychological evolution of his inner states of mind. The Lotos Eaters episode shows that the psychic momentum of Odysseus' heroic drive is beginning to lose steam, and that the desire to move ever onwards towards home and family is weakening. In a word, *enantiodromia* is beginning to set in, with antiheroic lethargy and weakening of the will as its first symptoms.

The third episode (the Kyklops) is a long one, and one of the most memorable in the *Odyssey*; it was also a favorite scene for Greek vase painting. When viewed as something other than a purely sensational piece of storytelling, however, its psychological dimension becomes quite intriguing, for the savage one-eyed giant Polyphêmos whom Odysseus will blind with a sharpened olive stake presents a strange shadow analogy to Odysseus himself. Although Odysseus tells his tales in a rather self-justificatory manner, presenting himself typically as the innocent victim of his men's disobedience or of a god or goddess's irresistible power, he clearly has a large, uncivilized shadow side that he has been living out as a sacker of cities roving the sea in search of slaves and booty. In fact, not to put too fine a point on it, he has become a pirate and an enemy of civilized life and of the rule of law. As the captain of his ship and master of his men, he is himself a kind of seafaring Kyklops, living a lawless life of uncivilized barbarism. Thus the Kyklops Polyphêmos can be seen as representing symbolically Odysseus' own shadow, although Odysseus himself is mainly unaware of their psychic kinship, seeing him only as a horrible man-eating monster.

The link between Odysseus and his monstrous shadow is not completely unconscious, however, as the text, proceeding as usual through the process of mythological thinking, indicates on two occasions. Odysseus leads the men of his own ship on an explorative walk into the land of the Kyklops, and has brought along food and some good wine, as though he has sensed that he is about to meet someone already connected to him by secret bonds and hidden affinity. Although he presumably intends to use the food and wine he has brought along as a trick in order to gain the monster's good graces, his gift also constitutes a gesture of relatedness, since the sharing of food and drink is the most archetypal form of human communion. Thus Odysseus has already intuited his own brutal and uncivilized shadow projected onto the Kyklops, who is indeed someone he already knows in a dimly conscious way as his other self, as his dark shadow brother. However, the monstrous Polyphêmos, when he finally makes his appearance, will turn out to be almost as dangerous and threatening for Odysseus as Mr. Hyde was for Dr. Jekyll. This episode in the *Odyssey*, expressing symbolically as it does the latent affinity between the Kyklops and Odysseus, is a marvelous example of Homer's mythological thinking at work.

Although Odysseus initially fooled the brutish Kyklops by identifying himself as Outis or "No-Man" (a clever idea he should have stuck with), after he escapes him and sets sail, he taunts the monster from his ship, in spite of the protestations of his men, and reveals his true name. This is a tragic mistake. Giving his true name creates a new and totally unnecessary bond between himself and the Kyklops, who promptly takes advantage of this new information and prays to his father Poseidon to punish the man he now knows is Odysseus; and this is what the god of the sea does, delaying his return to Ithaka with storms, high waves and winds. Odysseus in this scene has acted out the immature, boasting, blindly self-assertive hero role and has shown a tragic inability to control his *thymos*, a difficult to translate Homeric term that designates his aggressive warrior energies or "blind self-assertion." Fitzgerald's translation gets the sense of the repetition of *thymos* in the Greek text, first translated as "glorying spirit," and then as "anger":

> I would not heed them [his men] in my glorying spirit,
> but let my anger flare and yelled:
> "Kyklops,
> if ever mortal man inquire
> how you were put to shame and blinded, tell him
> Odysseus, raider of cities, took your eye:
> Laertês' son, whose home's on Ithaka."
> (Homer 1963: 160)

By now the inner affinity and the unconscious psychic connection between the two of them—the heroic sea captain and his "monster"—have been firmly established in the reader's mind, but it is also clear that Odysseus tragically underestimates the power of this connection. Odysseus' failure to deal prudently with his Kyklops shadow marks a deciding moment in his homeward journey, in that, from now on, rather than being a direct voyage home to Ithaka, it will become, thanks to the enmity of the Kyklops' father, the sea god Poseidon, a long and circuitous route, that will take ten years and will result in the death of all of Odysseus' men as well as in Odysseus' solitary shipwreck on the island of Kalypso and a long period of midlife liminality. Through a failure to recognize and respect the full power of his shadow, he has given it a large measure of control over his destiny.

The next episode (Book 10) adds a significant touch to Homer's symbolic representation of an inner psychodrama portrayed via mythological thinking in the narrative mode of folktale and myth. The arrival at the island of Aiolos, king of the winds, demonstrates yet one more time Odysseus' new pattern of failure as commander and hero;[2] in psychological terms, his youthful heroic self is now something that he is no longer able to manifest as well as he did earlier in his life as one of the great young heroes of the Trojan War. Odysseus—typically, one must say—reveals his weaknesses somewhat grudgingly and inadvertently. He tells the Phaiakian court how Aiolos has given him all the unfavorable winds tied up in a bag, with only the favorable west wind left free to waft him homewards. Once again, if one looks closely at the narrative, the ensuing disaster appears to be primarily Odysseus' fault, although he is quick to shift blame onto his men. After nine days and nights of managing the sails by himself, he falls asleep just at the moment when—ironically—he is in sight of his own native shore. His men are suspicious (their suspicions say much about the lack of confidence that prevails between Odysseus and his men, as does his refusal to let anyone else tell him) as to what booty the captain might be hiding from them in the bag, and so they untie it; immediately all the unfavorable winds spill out and blow him and his men back to the island of Aiolos.

The key element in the Aiolos episode is the motif of sudden and involuntary sleep, and from now on this motif plays an ever more important role in Odysseus' symbolic psychobiography and confession—at first negatively, and eventually positively, as we will see. It is Homer's way of designating what Jung liked to call an *abaissement du niveau mental*—a sudden drop in the level of consciousness. In the previous episode, Odysseus and his men had put out the Kyklops's eye, after the monster had fallen into a drunken sleep. Now it is the turn of Odysseus. Demonstrating once more his inner affinity with the monster shadow figure, he falls asleep and then realizes that disaster has struck him while he slumbered. Exhausted as he is, Odysseus' suddenly falling asleep is all the same peculiar, since it happens just as he sees some men building fires on the shore of his own island of Ithaka (the men were probably building beacon fires for the benefit of the unknown ship they had just sighted [Homer 1964: I, 267]). Was his sudden sleep pure coincidence? Or was it more likely an *abaissement du niveau mental* accompanied by unconscious acting out of secret desires—here, perhaps the desire *not* to go home? Why would a man fall asleep just as his homecoming journey was about to be crowned with success? Perhaps, one suspects, because he did not really want to go home at all, whether he realized it consciously or not. The motif of sleep here is easily translatable in psychological terms as a sudden lapse into unconsciousness that allows for an unconscious wish to be fulfilled—in this case, the continuation of his wanderings, and not the homecoming he consciously wishes for. Or perhaps it is that something in Odysseus' psyche did not wish him to go home just yet—that the activation of an archetypal process of midlife transformation was pushing him into greater and greater liminality. The savage and uncivilized city-sacking Odysseus was not *ready* to reenter civilized society, until a midlife transformation had prepared him for that reentry. His falling into the unconscious at this crucial moment is followed, once he awakens, by a desire to kill himself by throwing himself overboard. The appearance of the motif of symbolic death marks the moment at which his long initiatory ordeal actually begins; from now on, he will not be making a quick home-coming, but rather be involved in a long process of midlife transformation.

The next short episode (the Laistrygonês) raises the specter of some more unfinished psychological business for Odysseus, and prepares the way thematically for Odysseus' arrival on Kirkê's island and his first confron-tation with what was one of the most terrifying things for the patriarchal hypermasculine hero to run up against: superior female power. Up to this point, as during the ten years of the Trojan War, Odysseus' relationship with women, like those of his fellow Greeks in the war camp, had been almost entirely that of master to slave, captive women being used either as useful workers or as concubines. In either case, the power balance was totally one-sided in favor of male dominance. But now that he and his men have landed on a new shore, the balance begins to shift. This new land's very topography suggests the archetypal feminine, when viewed from a negative patriarchal perspective in terms of confinement and entrapment:

> A curious bay with mountain walls of stone
> to left and right, and reaching far inland,—
> a narrow entrance opening from the sea
> where cliffs converged as though to touch and close.
> (Homer 1963: 168)

Their search party asks directions from a young woman fetching water, who, with a casual wave of her hand, points them in the direction of her father's palace. But there, rather than a king, they discover first an embodiment of terrifying female power: "a woman like a mountain crag—and loathed the sight of her" (Homer 1963: 168). The ogre queen calls out to her husband the ogre king, who then devours one of the men; the scene presents an obvious parallel with the cannibalistic Kyklops episode, but this time with the initial foregrounding of *female* power in a horrific form. In the ensuing battle with the Laistrygonês, more of Odysseus' men perish, trapped in the narrow bay. It is as though, symbolically, as more and more of his men meet their doom, more and more pieces of Odysseus' soul are being lost, swallowed up by unconscious forces he cannot effectively control. As he loses men, his power as a leader is diminished, that is, his area of conscious control becomes smaller and smaller. It is, in a mythic mode, the evocation of the beginning of a near psychotic breakdown, when archetypal contents of the collective unconscious start to overwhelm him.

The next long episode deals with the year-long sojourn on Kirkê's island, and it initially follows the folktale pattern of the dangerous encounter with a beautifully attractive female demon. The analogy with the two previous episodes (the Laistrygon ogre queen and the Kyklops) is made explicit with the mention of the same anticipatory anxiety on the part of Odysseus' men, who dread exploring this new place marked by the smoke of some habitation in the forest, because they remember how badly things turned out with the Kyklops and the Laistrygonês. But the witch Kirkê at first seems harmless— just "a young weaver singing a pretty song" (Homer 1963: 172). She proves to be a wonderful hostess as well, but welcomes the men with food and wine only in order to put a magic potion into the wine that makes them forget— like the lotos of the Lotos Eaters—the desire to return home. And then she magically turns them into swine. Swine, of course, are destined eventually to be eaten and so Odysseus' men are clearly on the way to becoming Kirkê's dinner, just as some of them had become food for the Kyklops and the Laistrygon ogre king—the switch from male to female cannibalism (of a sort) is significant. Once again, but this time through his absence, Odysseus shows himself unable to protect the lives of his men from danger; the once young hero is not as good at dealing with monsters as he used to be!

The Kirkê episode is a magnificent evocation of the ambiguous power and charm of the anima, which is quite unmatched in ancient Greek literature. Everything about Kirkê is ambiguous, from her initial description as a semidivine figure reminiscent of the ancient Mediterranean goddess the Mistress of Animals (tame wolves and mountain lions attend her) to the beguiling songs she sings at her loom, apparently those that a pretty, young weaver would sing, but in fact more like those of a Greek Lorelei luring passing sailors to their doom. Her female power turns out to be more than Odysseus can confront on his own, and the patriarchal hero requires the assistance of the god Hermês in order to avoid being what Fitzgerald translates as "unmanned," but which can be more directly translated as "castrated." And yet, after Odysseus has protected himself from her spells and the threat of castration thanks to Hermês' advice (the god tells him to draw his sword and make her swear an oath not to harm him) and the magic talisman he gives him, he is able to induce her to reverse the metamorphosis of the men turned into swine. Interestingly enough, after she does so, the men appear younger, more handsome and taller after their involuntary metamorphosis, and altogether better off for their short experience of living in porcine bodies—having regained, so to speak, some of their animal spirits after the trauma of the Kyklops' cave. As for Odysseus, Kirkê invites him to leave behind the hectic and heroic days of his youth and to savor a life of leisure and luxury spent in her company. But his year's stay with the nymph Kirkê and her maids represents for Odysseus not just a time of R&R for the weary warrior, but an important educational experience. The savage youthful hero, sacker of cities and enslaver of women, gets to know the feminine as an equal partner, and learns how to savor with her the peaceful pleasures of sensuality and "joy" (*euphrosyne*)—the relaxed *joie de vivre* that has been conspicuously lacking in Odysseus' life as a young warrior, who took himself and everything he did very seriously, even though, as we have seen, stagnation and *enantio-dromia* have recently been setting in, as his sun begins its descent at the approach of midlife.

His love affair with Kirkê will eventually lead Odysseus into the depths of the unconscious. Kirkê sends him on a journey to the Land of the Dead, a confrontation with the archetypal world that will change him forever. For Kirkê not only provides a sensual education for the hero; she also plays a positive psychic mentoring function in his life. Jung wrote of his own first experiences of the anima, that she had appeared to him first in a dream he had when he was thirty-seven. In this dream, Jung's anima took the form of a playful little young girl with golden blond hair (Jung 1963: 171–172); this playful girl reminds the reader of Kirkê as she first appeared as a young weaver singing a pretty song. For Jung, there was something momentous in the anima's appearance in his life:

> The soul, the anima, establishes the relationship to the unconscious. In a certain sense this is also a relationship to the collectivity of the dead, the land of the ancestors. . . . Like a medium, it gives the dead a chance to manifest themselves.
>
> (Jung: 1963: 191)

And this is in fact the symbolic role Kirkê will play for Odysseus, when at the end of his stay she sends him off on a journey where he will meet and converse with the spirits of the dead.

Initially, though, Kirkê proves to be such a charming lover and companion that a whole year flies by in her company, and Odysseus' men are eventually forced to remind their captain that it is high time that they were on their way home to Ithaka. But, once again, ambiguity is the prime characteristic of Kirkê. She insists that, in order to sail home safely, they must chart a course via the Land of the Dead at the far reaches of the world. Her directions make no practical geographic sense, and cause Odysseus and his men no end of anxiety, since, Hades being known as a land from which no traveler returns, they reasonably fear that she is sending them to their deaths. (The threat of death is a major initiatory motif, as we have seen.) But, apparent ambiguities aside, Kirkê claims to be motivated by her conviction that only the ghost of the dead prophet Teirêsias can give them final directions for their voyage home. So her instructions constitute the sort of ambiguous anima advice that is both reliable and unreliable, and that has both positive and negative dimensions. But, by sending Odysseus and his men on a journey to the Land of the Dead, Kirkê also establishes a link in the text between herself and another major mentoring figure in Odysseus' life, the sage Teirêsias, in much the same way that, in Jung's account of his waking visions of the winter of 1913–14, the beautiful blind girl Salome was linked with the white bearded prophet Elijah and the figure of Philemon who developed out of him (Jung 1963: 181–185), the anima thus leading to the emergence of the mentoring figure of the Wise Old Man.

After the pleasant and relaxing year spent with Kirkê, her injunction to sail back home via the Land of the Dead comes as a terrible shock; the men set sail "in tears, with bitter and sore dread" (Homer 1963: 185). In terms of its length, the *katabasis* of Odysseus and his men is the most important episode of his wanderings, as it takes up the entirety of Book 11. In terms of symbolic significance, it is also the most complicated and puzzling episode, and is reminiscent of the bizarre phantasmagoria of images in Jung's account of his fateful midlife confrontation with the unconscious. Every encounter with the spirits of the dead moves Odysseus further and deeper into the twilight world of the archetypes. Once in Hades, Odysseus first meets with the shade of Elpênor. This curiously clueless young man had had too much wine to drink on the evening of the departure from Kirkê's island, and the next morning had stumbled from his cool sleeping spot on the roof, had fallen off the ladder, broken his neck and died. His ridiculous, poignant and unheroic death went strangely unnoticed by everyone; even during the journey to Hades no one had missed his presence. And yet, as the first of the shades to appear to Odysseus, he is given unexpected prominence in the text, as though some great symbolic significance were attached to him, forgettable though he had otherwise been in his life as in his death. He is described at the end of Book 10 only as the youngest of Odysseus' men, and as "no mainstay in a fight nor very clever" (Homer 1963: 182). Yet Odysseus "wept for pity" (Homer 1963: 186) when he caught sight of Elpênor's shade in Hades.

So why is the seemingly unimportant Elpênor so important for Odysseus? First of all, it may be because the death of the young Elpênor marks symbolically the death of his own youth. Odysseus has entered fully into his period of midlife liminality with this journey to the Land of the Dead, and Elpênor's death reminds him that his own youth is past; this is partly what he mourned when he "wept for pity" for Elpênor. It is not that Elpênor represents his own youthful heroic side, however. It is rather the careless and carefree unconscious side of youth that he laments. In Elpênor's death there is a lesson for Odysseus, too: if he is to survive his midlife ordeal, he will need to be careful and alert, and leave youthful carelessness and unconsciousness behind.

Odysseus reports the long conversation he had with the shade of Elpênor, at the end of which he promised the young man to give his ashes the proper rites when they return to Kirkê's island. In fact, Elpênor has his own ideas about how he wishes his death to be commemorated, and gives precise and somewhat unusual (and, as we will see, symbolically significant) directions to his captain: to plant his own oar on top of his funeral mound, which will thus become a kind of memorial to an unknown sailor, which will be visible to all who sail by it in the future. As soon as he returns to Kirkê's island, Odysseus will do exactly as requested. And yet these are puzzlingly impressive funeral rites for such an unheroic young man. But reading the *Odyssey* as an oneiric text from the perspective of archetypal psychology provides, once again, an opportunity to focus on symbolic detail. Such a reading allows for Odysseus' fantastic storytelling to be treated as a true account of his psychic journey and inner transformation. The precise details concerning Elpênor's last rites are a case in point, since they suggest that this sad episode is not only an occasion for Odysseus to bid farewell to his own careless youth, but points towards something potentially significant in another way as well. That is because the striking image of Elpênor's oar planted in his funerary mound (a powerful transformative image in its own right) is repeated in slightly different form later in Book 11, when Teirêsias tells Odysseus that, after his victory over the suitors, he must journey inland on foot, carrying his own oar on his shoulders until he is so far away from the sea that landlocked landlubbers cannot distinguish it from a winnowing fan. Then he is to "implant [his] smooth oar in the turf" and "make fair sacrifice to Lord Poseidon" (Homer 1963: 189). This correspondence of imagery between one oar (Elpênor's) and the other is intriguing, and cries out for symbolic interpretation. It is the Homeric text itself that will provide the clues, and they suggest that the image of Odysseus' oar, implanted on the turf like Elpênor's oar was fixed on his barrow, adds something significant to the symbolic import of the initiatory theme of the death of Odysseus' youthful self at midlife; we will return to this point shortly.

One would expect the meeting of Odysseus with the wise prophet Teirêsias to have occurred right away in the narrative of the *katabasis*, but Homer, one suspects, has manipulated for his own purposes traditional epic narrative material dealing with Odysseus' journey to Hades—thus the unexpected priority he gives to the appearance of Elpênor's ghost. Only then does Homer have Odysseus proceed directly to his fated encounter with Teirêsias. As befits the message of a mentor for Odysseus' midlife initiation, Teirêsias' words of wisdom are short and to the point; Fitzgerald translates them as "denial of yourself, restraint of shipmates" (Homer 1963: 188). But this is not really a felicitous translation of "son thymon erykakeein kai hetairôn" (*Odyssey* 11.105). The problem is the almost untranslatable word *thymos*, which designates in Homeric Greek the seat of the vital and aggressive passions that can make a warrior great, but can also lead to unrestrained anger. What Teirêsias literally urges Odysseus to do is to "build a barrier [*erykakeein*] around his *thymos* and that of his shipmates." The advice points him in the direction of cultivating a midlife heroism of restraint and reflection, in contrast with the heroism of rashness and blind self-assertion characteristic of youthful heroism, as imaged for instance in Jung's figure of Siegfried. It points Odysseus in the direction of the kind of mature heroism of endurance, that he will need when he arrives back on Ithaka, when he will have to patiently suffer the blows and insults of the young usurpers of his kingdom without reacting angrily, careful not to give himself away while disguised as an old beggar. (The second part of the advice—to restrain his men's *thymos* as well—does not prove effective, and Odysseus will return home alone.)

Teirêsias accompanies his advice with a curious directive. After he has slaughtered the suitors who have occupied his palace, Teirêsias says, Odysseus is to undertake a final journey, whose symbolic richness is concentrated on the image of the oar first mistaken for a winnowing fan, and then implanted in the ground. Here is the full text of what for Odysseus constitutes the *rite de sortie* of his midlife transition, a ritual designed to signal his establishment in a new kind of wisdom and in a new kind of identity:

> But after you have dealt out death—in open combat
> or by stealth—to all the suitors,
> go overland on foot, and take an oar,
> until one day you come where men have lived
> with meat unsalted, never known the sea,
> nor seen seagoing ships . . .
> The spot will soon be plain to you, and I
> can tell you how: some passerby will say,
> "What winnowing fan is that upon your shoulder?"
> Halt, and implant your smooth oar in the turf
> and make fair sacrifice to Lord Poseidon.
> (Homer 1963: 188–189)

Let us examine the symbolic images one by one. "Going alone on foot" would be for Odysseus symbolic of a loss of heroic and kingly status, since ordinarily a princely personage such as he would have gone in a chariot accompanied by attendants (this is, for example, how his son Telémakhos travelled to Sparta in Book 3). As for his journey inland, it is a kind of pilgrimage away from the sea to a landlocked place where no one recognizes him as a legendary warrior and sea captain. There Odysseus, king of Ithaka, glorious son of Laertês, will sink to the status of a nobody like

Elpênor, a common man, unremembered and unmemorable. It is a loss of his identity as a young hero: he has now become anonymous. As for "planting his oar in the turf," if we decode the enigmatic language of Teirêsias, it is clear that Odysseus is being told to commemorate in the symbolic gestural language of ritual the Elpênor-like end of his own rash youth, the end of his pretensions to glory and of the self-assertive heroism that served him so well in youth but which has increasingly proved to be counterproductive. In Teirêsias' mythological and symbolic evocation of this last journey, once Odysseus has finished the pilgrimage and performed the accompanying rituals, he is ready to assume a new and generative identity, that of the Good King, and then, after a long and benevolent reign, to die, "wearied out with rich old age, your country folk in blessed peace around you" (Homer 1963: 189). Teirêsias' description of this final moment of his journey inland can be seen as the ritual commemoration of the end of Odysseus' youthful heroic pretensions, and the beginning of a stage of life in which generativity will be his dominant virtue, which is what he will need in order to fulfill the role as good king and father of his people.

Teirêsias has also asked Odysseus to "make fair sacrifice to Lord Poseidon" before he sacrifices to all the other gods. This, too, is an enigmatic injunction: why tell Odysseus to sacrifice to the sea god who delayed his voyage home for so many years, and why honor Poseidon in a land so far from the sea? It is the text of the *Odyssey* itself, and not the broader cultural context of the Greek myths associated with Poseidon, that provides the clue for a symbolic interpretation. It was in the course of Book 8, just before Odysseus had identified himself and had begun telling his own story to the court of Alkinoös in Book 9, that the bard Demodokos had assigned to the god Poseidon a most intriguing role in the mythological scene that was the substance of his song. Demodokos told the story of the adulterous love affair of Aphroditê and Arês, and how Aphroditê's husband, the lame blacksmith god Hephaistos, had caught the pair *in flagrante delicto* with a light and almost invisible net that fell and ensnared the couple on their bed of love. All the Olympian gods came to see the sight, and all were greatly amused, with the exception of Poseidon, who remained strangely serious, taking the side of Arês and vociferously offering to guarantee the fine that Ares would need to pay as penalty for his adulterous act. Thus the specific associations generated in this scene define Poseidon, in terms of mythological thinking, as *the god who befriends and champions adultery*. Now Odysseus by the time of his return to Ithaka has been spending most of his time in the semidivine arms first of Kirkê and then—for long years—of Kalypso; this may not have technically constituted adultery from a patriarchal standpoint (neither nymph being human, nor for that matter married), but it did constitute a case of long-term and, at least until near the end, remorseless unfaithfulness to his wife Penélopê. Odysseus, typically self-justifying, presents himself to the Phaiakians primarily as an ill-fated wanderer yearning for hearth, home and family, who has been the hapless victim of the desire of the two goddesses Kirkê and Kalypso. But this is only half true. We know that Odysseus clearly enjoyed being with Kirkê, so much so that his men finally had to remind him that a year was time enough, and that now they should be sailing on home. As for Kalypso, while it is true that their relationship had eventually turned into a kind of sexual servitude for Odysseus, this was only after the goddess's sexual allure had disappeared for him. So it is evident that, at least at the beginning of his relationship with Kalypso, Odysseus was a willing victim of her desires and of his own. But this evasiveness is typical of Odysseus' sidestepping of inconvenient facts, and typifies his avoiding revealing his shadow side—here his midlife sexual shadow side. Odysseus' midlife story, in the context of the mythological narrative that is its vehicle, involves a lot of sex away from his wife—years of it—to the point where he has finally become tired of it, and yearns for home. Perhaps this is not an unusual experience for men at midlife, although not every man is as able as Odysseus to ultimately escape from his Kalypso.

But where was Poseidon in all of this? It is obvious that, were it not for the anger of Poseidon, furious at Odysseus because he blinded his one-eyed son the Kyklops,[3] and were it not for his suspicious failure to stay awake within sight of Ithaka, Odysseus would have been long ago safe at home in the arms of Penélopê, and both Kirkê and Kalypso would never have known the delights of his company. By sacrificing to Poseidon according to Teirêsias' instructions, Odysseus has acknowledged, at least by implication, the crucial role that Poseidon, friend and ally of Arês' adulterous adventure, has also played in his own life as regards his adultery with Kirkê and Kalypso—love affairs that kept him away from home for almost ten years just as effectively as the storms sent by Poseidon. By ritually honoring the god who championed Arês' adultery with Aphroditê, he is symbolically saying farewell to such an adulterous life of sexual excess, and making himself ready for settling down permanently with Penélopê. Thus there is in the text of the *Odyssey* a complex network of symbolism associated with Poseidon, and simply defining him as Odysseus' divine enemy does not tell the whole story. Poseidon is also an archetypal force that keeps Odysseus at sea and away from home, and, as a kind of mentor in spite of himself, the god has his own role to play in the midlife education of Odysseus. In seeking his own godly revenge, he enables Odysseus (indirectly, no doubt) to satisfy his desire for a greater experience of life and of feminine sensuality and *joie de vivre*, and to become better acquainted with the anima power that has hitherto remained unconscious in his hypermasculine warrior soul. Poseidon also helps him (more directly, this time) to fulfill his inner need for a long period of liminality, before the sacker of cities can be ready to reenter civilized society.

The symbolic equation mythical underworld equals psychological unconscious existed already with Freud, who put as an epigraph to his book *The*

Interpretation of Dreams the lines of Virgil *flectere si nequeo superos Acheronta movebo* (if I cannot prevail against the Olympian gods, at least I shall stir up the underworld).[4] The slow unrolling of events in Book 11 of the *Odyssey* constitutes a sort of diorama, which for its richness of detail is unparalleled in accounts of journeys to the Land of the Dead, exceeded only by Dante's amplification in his *Inferno* of Virgil's imitation of the Odyssean account in Book 6 of the *Aeneid*. If Dante's midlife journey to hell clearly has deep spiritual significance, Odysseus' *katabasis* has at least deep psychological significance. It is, so to speak, an encounter with the contents of a Greek patriarchal hero's unconscious at midlife. It also constitutes an oneiric text of the greatest value for the understanding of one relatively stable archetypal component of the male psyche, that is, the initiatory impulse that can force itself on a man at midlife.

What Odysseus finds in Hades is thus a mixture of the archetypal and the personal, starting with the strong feelings and emotions as regards the mother–son bond, what Stephen Dedalus in Joyce's *Ulysses* famously called "*Amor matris*: subjective and objective genitive" (Joyce 1986: 23), that is, both the child's love for the mother as well as the mother's love for her child. Odysseus' poignant meeting with the shade of his mother Antikleia, who, he now realizes, died of grief over his long absence, is the one moment in the *Odyssey* where Odysseus sheds tears for a woman. He tries desperately to embrace her shade, but his hands find only thin air. But then he asks her (in a phrase that we will see significantly paraphrased at the end of his *katabasis*): "or is this all hallucination, sent against me by the iron queen, Perséphonê, to make me groan again?" (Homer 1963: 191).

Thus the mythological narrative suggests that behind the power of his personal love for his mother and his mother's love for him stands the august archetypal figure of Perséphonê, Queen of Hades, whose divine feminine power he fears, in typical patriarchal fashion, as malevolent and deceitful. It is Perséphonê who, in Odysseus' imagination, is the mistress of ceremonies of this phantasmagoric procession of the shades of the dead, of this resurgence of the archetypal feminine within the hypermasculine hero's psyche at midlife. As his mother disappears from his sight, it is Perséphonê who sends to him a long procession of the famous women of myth and history, including Epikastê (an alternative name for Jocasta), the mother and wife of Oedipus—a passage Freud should have marked, for it shows the fear of incest with the mother as one of the chief components of the male heroic psyche, which, in its struggle to achieve hypermasculine ideals, represses much of the feminine component of the psyche, including quasi-incestuous ties with the mother. This description of the procession of the spirits of famous women and mothers of heroes is unexpectedly long, and is placed near the middle of the *katabasis* narrative, so that its central importance is highlighted. Such is the emotional effect on Odysseus of this evocation of his memory of the pageantry of the Eternal Feminine that, for

the only time in his storytelling at the court of King Alkinoös, the loqua-
cious hero suddenly falls silent, stunned into silence, one might surmise, by
the overwhelming feminine power represented by the ghostly procession of
famous women.

When Odysseus resumes his narrative, it is to evoke the presence of his
onetime commander at Troy, Agamemnon. Their long conversation
together is permeated with the typically hypermasculine fear and distrust
of female power. Agamemnon in Hades is obsessively fixated on the last
moments of his life on earth: his murder by his wife Klytaimnéstra in
connivance with her lover Aigisthos. That memory is almost all he can bring
himself to talk about. He exemplifies a state of midlife stagnation now made
permanent through death; his attitude of rigidity and resentment poisons
what could have been a wonderful reunion of heroes and comrades in arms.
Agamemnon's hatred and distrust of women extends even to Odysseus'
proverbially faithful wife Penélopê, and he warns him cynically to return to
Ithaka in disguise, in order to be sure of her faithfulness before he reveals
himself to her: "the day of faithful wives is gone forever" (Homer 1963: 200).

If the resurgence of the feminine has been the thematic concern of the
first half of Odysseus' narrative of his experiences in Hades, the second half
is oriented around a midlife redefinition of heroism as generative and
patient rather than, as in Odysseus' youth, as self-assertive and impulsive.
Such midlife heroism is generative also in contrast with Agamemnon's
midlife rigidity, resentment and stagnation. The ghost of Akhilleus represents this to some degree. Akhilleus in the *Iliad* was the prototype of the
youthful hero, whose rashness and egomania were part and parcel of
his capacity to "fight like fire." But in Hades the shade of Akhilleus seems
to have become middle aged; Akhilleus has lost his desire to lord it over
others as once he did in his youth. When Odysseus seeks to console him
for his early death and for his now-insipid afterlife as a shade in Hades
by reminding of how his friends "ranked him among the immortals" for
his power and glory, Akhilleus is quick to reply that he would rather be the
hired hand of a poor landless man than to reign over all the spirits of
the dead.

But if Akhilleus is disenchanted with the self-assertive heroic ideals of his
youth as far as he himself is concerned, and distressed that he is no longer
able to provide protection for his aged father (he "cannot be that man [he]
was on Troy's wide seaboard" [Homer 1963: 201), he is nevertheless full of
admiration and generative feeling for his son Neoptolemos. Odysseus'
assurance that his son has proved to be the youthful hero he once was
himself allows him to leave Odysseus' company in a joyful mood. Akhilleus
has thus discovered in Hades his own limited form of generativity, nar-
cissistically directed towards his own son, no doubt, but still representing a
movement in the right direction, in terms of moving out of self-involved
bitterness, resentment and midlife stagnation.

But such is not the case with the great hero Aîas, whose ghost Odysseus meets next. Aîas lost the competition for the arms of the dead Akhilleus, which were awarded instead to Odysseus. Enraged by this failure to have his valor given what he felt was its proper reward, Aîas went committed suicide out of raging despair at the insult to his honor (a midlife ordeal gone terribly wrong, one might say). Even in Hades, Aîas refuses to speak to Odysseus, and leaves his presence before they can be reconciled. Aîas' youthful heroic egomania has become a permanent part of his postmortem identity. He is now stuck, like Agamemnon, in brooding resentment, rigidity and stagnation.

Agamemnon, Akhilleus and Aîas symbolize rather poignantly the fading value of youthful self-assertive heroic ideas for Odysseus at midlife. (It is interesting to note in this context that the subject of the maddeningly enchanting song of the Seirênes—melodious female monsters, that Odysseus encounters later on his return from Hades—is their "song of Troy," with its evocation of youthful heroism now gone forever; it is this fierce nostalgia, and not, as one might expect, their sexual allure, that almost drives Odysseus to distraction.) But it is the appearance of Heraklês that provides him with a positive example of a new type of heroism more suited to mature adulthood. Heraklês represents for Odysseus an augustly impressive transformative image of heroic energies yoked to tasks for the benefit of the world—to the full weight of the work of the world that falls squarely on the shoulders of men at midlife, as contrasted with the personal glory associated with the brilliant exploits of youthful heroism. Heraklês speaks to Odysseus as one midlife hero to another, emphasizing their common life-experience of suffering and ordeal, but he also speaks as a midlife mentor who can encourage Odysseus to persevere in his labors with patience and endurance.

After Heraklês has faded from sight, Odysseus would like, he says, to see other great heroes such as Theseus and Peirithoös, who also undertook journeys to Hades, but something suddenly throws him into a panic:

> But first came shades in thousands, rustling
> in a pandemonium of whispers, blown together,
> and the horror took me that Perséphonê
> had brought from darker hell some saurian death's head.
> I whirled then, made for the ship.
>
> (Homer 1963: 206)

Two things are to be noticed here that are of prime importance for interpreting the psychological significance of Odysseus' panicky departure from Hades. First of all, what panics him is not actually catching sight of another set of shades approaching, but rather the very *thought* that Perséphonê *might* be sending his way something even more frightening; in other words, it is his imagination that spooks him, not an actual experience. Secondly, as regards the nature of the imagined image, one needs to note that Robert Fitzgerald's translation is misleading.[5] What Homer says Odysseus imagines is that what Perséphonê is about to make him see is not, as Fitzgerald would have it, a "saurian death's head" (whatever that might be: a giant reptilian skull?) but, literally translated, "a Gorgon head of some terrible monster" (*gorgeiên kephalên deinoio pelôrou*). What Odysseus imagines is thus the snaky-haired head of a Gorgon, tongue hanging out, whose gaze can turn a man to stone—which can petrify the patriarchal hero with fear. This "Gorgon-head of a terrible monster" is an archetypal image of Female Power at its most horrific, the worst nightmare of the hyper-masculine imagination. It is something, the bare imagining of which, makes Odysseus panic and run. It is a frightening image of elemental female power, an archetypally "vulval" image that the phallic hero cannot bear to face, even in imagination. This frightening image of female power that Odysseus cannot bring himself to face even in his imagination is not only the proximate cause of his sudden flight from Hades; it is also a fore-shadowing of what he will have to face eventually for many long years: ineluctable female power in the form of Kalypso, Homer's vision of the Eternal Feminine in all her seductive as well as devouring and containing dimensions. The mere thought that so frightened him in Hades is exactly what Odysseus' hypermasculine warrior culture had repressed: its own fear of its female opposite. And so it will become one of Odysseus' midlife psychological tasks to come to terms with it, not to run away from it.

For the second part of his journey—the voyage to Ithaka after his return from Hades to Kirkê's island—Odysseus receives life-saving instructions from Kirkê, who seems once again to be stepping into a mentoring role. Earlier, when she had sent him on his way to Hades, it is clear that, from the standpoint of folklore, she was playing the role of the dispatching king who assigns heroic tasks for the hero to perform as part of his initiatory trials—in Odysseus' case, a *katabasis*, a journey to the underworld. When he and his men return, Kirkê hails both him and them as *disthanees*, "twice dead"—a word, as Stanford notes on *Odyssey* 12.21–22, that occurs here for the only time in Greek, and is perhaps a neologism coined by Homer for this almost unique situation. The initiatory resonance of the term is clear: the initiate, who like all mortals will eventually experience physical death, dies also a symbolic death—is "twice-dead"—and is reborn with a new identity. But what is this new identity? What exactly has Kirkê taught him as one of his midlife mentors?

Odysseus could have said of Kirkê, as Socrates said in Plato's *Symposium* of the woman Diotima (Plato 1999: 37) that she had been his teacher in matters of *eros*, of love and sensuality. Providing him with good food, sex and physical comfort is her way of helping to ease Odysseus into the world of the feminine and to grow beyond the one-sided hypermasculine heroic identity with its typical fear and disdain for the feminine and feminine sensuality. Staying with Kirkê prepared Odysseus for the journey to Hades, an initiatory *katabasis*, with the object of making conscious for him the limitations of the self-assertive young hero archetype as well as the counterbalancing power of the feminine in the form of his dead mother, the great ladies of myth and legend, his fear of Perséphonê's deluding power, and of the vulval image of the fearsome Gorgon head.

What is strange, however, is that, while Kirkê and Teirêsias both warned Odysseus about the dangers of eating the Cattle of the Sun, neither was able to foresee the immensity of the problem that Kalypso would represent for Odysseus, and this betrays a significant blind spot in their instructions to him. The wise old man Teirêsias was, no doubt, also unable to foresee the dangers represented by the female monsters (the Seirênês, Skylla and Kharybdis) that the nymph Kirkê is able to tell Odysseus how to confront successfully; these picturesquely monstrous creatures readily appear, to the modern reader schooled on Freudian psychology, to illustrate the hypermasculine patriarchal hero's fear of the female sexual organs they stand for as vulval symbols, and one senses that Odysseus, under the tutelage of Kirkê, has eventually left such residual adolescent fears behind. But the archetypal Eternal Feminine represented by Kalypso is another matter entirely; no one has prepared him—not Kirkê, not Hermês and not Teirêsias—for *Her*. It is on the island of Kalypso that Odysseus reaches the realm of archetypal female power that can no longer be vanquished or managed by the ruses of the trickster hero, and he is caught there in a long period of midlife liminality, which only ends when another archetypal female force, that of Athena, decides to set him free.

But why has Athena waited so long to help him? The absence of Athena from Odysseus' years of wandering and the long years of his captivity on Kalypso's island is more than a bit of an enigma.[6] One possible psychological explanation is that Odysseus was not ready for her final mentoring, until he had come to terms with the feminine and with the process of integrating it, at least to some degree. For Odysseus, after his long stay with Kalypso, is a changed man. He has been forced to live isolated (no male companions) in the feminine world, and to submit to Kalypso's domination—to live with her beyond the point of satisfaction of his own sexual desires and needs, and to experience her needs and her power over him fully. She has been a most important part of his midlife education. But even when she has been forced to release him on the instance of Hermês acting on the behest of Athena, Kalypso has her own agenda, which is to possess him forever, and so she never ceases to be tricky and devious, the ultimate image of the ambiguous anima for him. And, like the anima, she is a jealous mistress, who resents and resists his determination to rebuild a relationship with a real woman, his long-abandoned wife Penélopê. Since Kalypso cannot disobey the command of the gods to release him, she supplies him with tools to use in building a ship, and then presents him with a "scented cloak" (Homer 1963: 88) as a parting gift.

But, even then, their story is not quite over. As Homer implies somewhat obliquely, Kalypso's scented cloak turns out to be a dangerous gift that almost brings about his undoing during the storm Poseidon raises, just as he is in sight of the land of the Phaiakians. It is strange that Odysseus the experienced mariner would have forgotten to take off the now waterlogged cloak, which could only have weighed him down perilously in the raging seas, but he does, and the scented cloak nearly drowns him:

"Now the big wave a long time kept him under,
helpless to surface, held by tons of water,
tangled, too, by the seacloak of Kalypso"
(Homer 1963: 90)

If the cloak had drowned him, Kalypso, through her ambiguous parting gift, would have been successful in keeping him away from all other alluring females. Perhaps causing his death might also have been her way of punishing him for scorning her offer of immortality and eternal youth. But fortunately a savior appears in the form of the sea nymph Ino, who emerges from the waves and tells him to shed Kalypso's cloak, and replaces Kalypso's near fatal gift with a lifesaving one, her own veil. He is then able to save himself by swimming to shore. From this point in the narrative onwards, the forces of the feminine become consistently positive and helpful for Odysseus. Having once been a young girl, born as a daughter of King Kadmos of Thebes, but then having been metamorphosed into a minor goddess of the sea, Ino herself represents a kind of bridge from the supernatural to the human social world that Odysseus had left behind during his stay with the goddess Kalypso. The veil she gives him allows magically for this bridging of the two realms, acting as a kind of talisman, and once he has used it as such, he is told to return it to the sea as soon as he arrives safely on land.

This motif of the helpful young girl, an image of the positive anima (cf. the first image Jung had of his anima, who took the form in his dream of his young daughter), is developed at greater length in the following episodes where the Phaiakian princess Nausikaa rescues the shipwrecked Odysseus and helps him find asylum at her father's court. In his dealings with Nausikaa, Odysseus is a model of male respect for her and for the women servants who accompany her on the beach. His newly acquired respect for women is a direct result of his integrating his own feminine side, since, for a man, respecting women properly is a natural consequence of honoring the feminine inside himself. Thus Odysseus is very careful not to take advantage of Nausikaa's girlish fantasies of marriage with a handsome stranger, and his later farewell to her acknowledges his full debt of gratitude to the teenage girl who had saved his life, and he promises to invoke her for the rest of his life as a goddess (Homer 1963: 139). Nausikaa has also guided him towards a new attitude of respect for female authority in a nonsexual and more maternal context. She indicates that the true power in the Phaiakian royal family is her mother, Arêtê, and so she is the one, and not her father, King Alkinoös, whom he should beg first for protection.

The Phaiakian episode also contains the first of several appearances of Athena in Odysseus' life, after many long years of absence from it. From now on, Athena will be his last and most important midlife mentor, although she often disguises herself in ways that fool even the trickster Odysseus. Athena first appears, consonant with the motif of "the helpful young girl," after Nausikaa has left Odysseus to make his way to the Phaiakian palace, as a girl carrying a water jug. The banality of the image—what could be a more common sight in ages past than a young girl like Victor Hugo's Cosette fetching water from a well?—hides a wonderful symbolism, which is that of a goddess hidden in the most humble of female forms.[7]

The wanderings of Odysseus end with his brief stay with the Phaiakians. Homer's description of his return to Ithaka is accompanied by a symbolic image of death and rebirth that is developed with great ingenuity. The Phaiakians have agreed to take him to Ithaka on one of their ships, but once Odysseus is on board he falls fast asleep. When they arrive on the shores of Ithaka, they have to carry him still sleeping onto the beach, along with the various gifts they have given him. This deathlike sleep is transformative for Odysseus, containing as it does symbolic resonances of initiatory death and resurrection. The nature of his transformation begins to become apparent when Odysseus wakes up and shortly afterwards greets a young man, apparently a shepherd, who is walking along the shore. Odysseus, with none of the arrogance of an older man of aristocratic status that would once have made him demand deference and respect from a mere shepherd youth, now beseeches him most humbly for protection, "touching your knees," he tells him, "as I might ask grace of a god" (Homer 1963: 237). His supplication echoes his words of farewell to the princess Nausikaa, whom he promised always to remember as though she were a goddess.

In this case, of course, there is more than a little irony, for the young shepherd is actually the goddess Athena in disguise, who from now on until the end of the *Odyssey* will play the role of his last and most important midlife mentor. When she reveals her identity after a long conversation during which he has told her a pack of lies concerning his own identity and past history, she takes on the form of a tall and beautiful woman, and gives him the advice that he will need to follow if he is to regain his kingdom and kill the usurping suitors who have been plaguing his wife:

> Patience, iron patience, you must show;
> So give it out to neither man nor woman
> That you are back from wandering. Be silent
> Under all injuries, even blows from men.
>
> (Homer 1963: 240)

What Athena enjoins upon Odysseus is a new kind of midlife heroism of caution, discipline and restraint, and her injunction emphasizes what in Hades Teirêsias had told him and Heraklês had exemplified for him, namely, that youthful heroic energies need to be carefully controlled, and the ability to suffer and endure patiently needs to come to the fore. What Odysseus requires at midlife is not the Siegfried- or Akhilleus-like youthful heroic self-assertion and "fighting like fire," but rather the skill, patience and determination that allow Heraklean generative labors to be undertaken and brought to a successful conclusion.

Odysseus' midlife transformation has prepared him for the challenges of returning to Ithaka and regaining his throne. Thus he does not betray his disguise as an old beggar, and is careful to reveal his true identity even when the suitors mock and threaten him with violence, and even when he is overcome with emotion when he sees his wife after twenty years of absence from her side. His newly found respect for women, evident already in the way he had promised to pray to Nausikaa as though she were a goddess, is confirmed ritually by the prayer he makes to the local nymphs of Ithaka, who guard the cavern on the beach where he is storing the gifts the Phaiakians gave him. Athena has just dissipated the fog that hid the familiar landscape of Ithaka from him:

> Then indeed Odysseus'
> heart stirred with joy. He kissed the earth,
> and lifting up his hands prayed to the nymphs:
> "O slim shy Naiadês, young maids of Zeus,
> I had not thought to see you ever again!
> O listen smiling to my gentle prayers."
> (Homer 1963: 241)

Having learned through suffering and long experience to respect the power of the feminine in himself and in the world, Odysseus is now a new man, one who is ready to reunite with his queen in a balanced partnership.

By the time he arrives home, his wife, Penélopê, has also changed; she is in the process of becoming a new woman, having been involved in a midlife crisis and transformation of her own. Homer does not focus anywhere near as much attention on her transformation, no doubt, but its evocation, for all its relative brevity, is touching and profound. One can glimpse in the *Odyssey* a text based on traditional epic material concerning male heroic themes, the androgynous mind of the visionary poet at work, probing the archetypal dimensions of a woman's midlife initiation, representing it in mythological and symbolic terms—whether with complete accuracy or not being, of course, an always pertinent question in the case of a male author, even one as great as Homer.

As we have seen earlier, one possible archetypal paradigm for a woman's midlife initiation process—there may well be others—has the onset of the crisis experienced as a *crisis of abandonment*, during which time the woman feels cut off from her traditional familial supports, especially her husband and children. Such is the case with Penélopê at the opening of the *Odyssey*. She has been left at home by her seafaring husband for many long years, and seems to spend a lot of time weeping on her bed for Odysseus. At the opening of the *Odyssey*, her agony awakens once again when she hears her court bard Phêmios singing the tale of "The Homecoming of Akhaians," and she is so overcome by despair that she asks him to stop. But her young son Telémakhos objects, and this novel independent mindedness on his part makes her begin to realize that he is at last becoming a man, and is no longer under her control.

Her ordeal is intensified when she discovers a few days later that Telémakhos has secretly left home to go on a dangerous night sea journey to find information about his father's whereabouts. He has left her on her own without even telling her in advance, and now she fears for his life, for she has been told that the suitors are plotting to kill him on his return. This revelation brings on more of the weeping and wailing we have come to associate with her.

However, this image of a passively suffering and helpless Penélopê is not the only image of her that Homer gives us in these early scenes of the *Odyssey*. She is also shown to be someone with unexpected shadow traits, which, as Jung often said, are not only negative drawbacks, but also can be of positive benefit, since they sometimes include repressed attitudes that might in fact further an individual's psychological and social development. At midlife the shadow can come roaring out of its cage, sometimes with extraordinary results. In Penélopê's case, the suitors acknowledge that in the last three years she has become unexpectedly clever and cunning, and has held off from committing herself to marriage with any of them by claiming that it is necessary, before she takes a new husband and enters into a new set of family obligations, for her to finish weaving a shroud for her father-in-law, Laertês. The suitors are quite angry when they discover the trick she has been playing on them. But, also quite impressed with her cleverness, they declare that, for cunning among women, "history cannot show the like" (Homer 1963: 22). The reader will remember, although the text does not make the comparison between them explicit, that it is just for such clever trickery that her husband was famous—it was Odysseus, after all, who had devised the trick of the Trojan Horse that brought about the sack of the city of Troy. So Penélopê at the beginning of her midlife transition has begun the process of making herself into her husband's equal in cunning, and will soon become the originator of the trick that will enable Odysseus to kill the suitors and regain his kingdom.

The narrative initially focuses on the image of Penélopê bedeviled by a crowd of rowdy young men, suitors who wish to force her to abandon all hope of reuniting with Odysseus, and to give her hand in marriage to one of them. The internal intrapsychic correspondence of this social harassment by the suitors is the plight of a woman passively submitting to an animus attack, which threatens to take her over and to destroy her bond of relationship with her beloved husband. The effect of her son's sudden departure intensifies the pressure of the situation, since she now fears for the life not only of her long-lost husband, but also of the son who has been her hope and mainstay throughout her years of pain. It is at this point in the narrative that Athena begins to play a mentoring role in her life, as she also has been doing roughly at the same time for Odysseus. In order to soothe Penélopê's spirits, Athena sends her a dream. The dream figure she sends to console her is that of her sister Iphthimê, whom she has not seen for ages. She unburdens her soul to this consoling vision of her sister, explaining how much she has missed Odysseus and how now she fears for the life of her son. Her sister, however, reassures her that Pallas Athena will protect Telémakhos, and tells her that it is the goddess who has sent the dream in order to calm her fears; she refuses, however, to give any information about the missing Odysseus.

The last books of the *Odyssey* pick up the story of Penélopê from where it left off in Book 4. Homer supplies a number of intriguing details concerning the midlife transformation she is undergoing. Now that the ruse of her daily weaving and nightly unweaving has been uncovered, she has been forced to confront the suitors' insistent demands more directly, especially since she now knows that they are plotting to kill her son. Just as Telémakhos had put boyish shyness aside and been able to stand up to the suitors like a man in Books 1–2, so Penélopê in Book 17 assumes an unaccustomed voice of authority, and calls on them forcefully to stop their abusive activities. Back in her chamber where one has seen her mainly passively suffering from the suitors' harassment and weeping on her bed for Odysseus, she is now shown entertaining unexpectedly violent and murderous thoughts about them: "may death relieve us . . . of all the suitors!" (Homer 1963: 329). To her maidservant Melantho who has been cursing the old beggar (who is actually Odysseus in disguise), she also threatens death (Homer 1963: 356). Her shadow side has thus provided her, like Inaana, with the aggressive energy that enables her to stand up to abuse, and has given her access to murderous thoughts and intentions that stand in complete contrast with her former posture of passive suffering and anguish.

Throughout this crisis it is Athena who acts as her midlife mentor, just as she does constantly throughout the end narrative for Odysseus. For Penélopê she provides significant behind the scenes help, guiding her towards actions that will ultimately benefit herself and her husband— actions that require her to act differently than she has ever acted before, and to present herself differently, confident in her seductive power as a beautiful woman. Inspired unconsciously by Athena to make a blatant display of her beauty to the suitors, she allows this shadow seductiveness to allow her to act totally out of her character: "knowing no reason" and "laughing confusedly," she tells her maid that "I have a craving / I never had at all—I would be seen / Among those ruffians" (Homer 1963: 341). Athena makes her more beautiful than ever during the sleep she sends upon her. And now that the chaste and timid Penélopê has been transformed into a daringly seductive woman, she blatantly solicits the desire of the very men who have tried to reduce her to submitting passively to their will, and uses her beauty as a powerful arm in her struggle against them (Homer 1963: 342). This most untypical flirtatious activity on her part beguiles all the suitors into giving her precious gifts, and Penélopê then goes back upstairs to her room.

But the sleep that made her so beautiful and seductive also brings her renewed anguish, to the point where she wishes for death. This death wish introduces the initiatory motif of symbolic death that is such an important part of the initiatory pattern of death and resurrection, and will occur again at much greater length in another prayer Penélopê makes to the archer goddess Artemis, begging her to slay her with one of her arrows. This marks the moment of her utmost despair—ironically, since Odysseus is already present on Ithaka and in their palace, but disguised as an old beggar. Unbeknownst to his wife, this disguise is part of his plan to take the suitors by surprise and to slaughter them before they know what is happening.

However, the success of Odysseus' audacious plan is mainly due to Penélopê, for it is she who will devise the test of the bow, which for her is ostensibly designed to allow one of the suitors to prove his right to her hand in marriage, but in fact will allow Odysseus to put his hands on the formidable weapon that can kill the assembled suitors at a distance—the only means, in fact, he might hope to use successfully in order to achieve victory when so outnumbered by the suitors. Penélopê's last trick is thus her best one, whether she is fully conscious of it or not, and it turns out to be a most murderous one. This is hardly the type of plan one would have expected a woman to have thought up, consciously or unconsciously; later, in a scene where the ghosts of the slain suitors are shown conversing in Hades, they assume (understandably, but incorrectly) that Odysseus put her up to it— that "he assigned his wife her part" (Homer 1963: 450). But that is not how Homer describes it happening, as he has Penelope tell the old beggar—her husband in disguise (does she possibly already suspect who he really is?)— that she herself will "decree a contest" (Homer 1963: 371), which, in fact, will be an exact reenactment of the contest through which Odysseus first won her hand in marriage, but now put to an ironically new and original use. She describes it in precise detail as clearly her own idea: to challenge the suitors to string Odysseus' powerful bow, and then to shoot an arrow through the socket holes of twelve axeheads lined up together and embedded upright at short intervals in the dirt floor of the great hall. "The one who easily handles and strings the bow / and shoots through all twelve axes I shall marry," (Homer 1963: 371) she declares. But, in fact, consciously or unconsciously, she has devised not a marriage contest but the perfect strategy for Odysseus' imminent slaughter of the suitors. It should be emphasized that, up to this moment, Odysseus' own strategizing has only gone to the point of planning to have all the weapons and armor removed from the great hall, so that he and his son, each armed with a spear, a sword and a shield, might deal with the large crowd of unarmed but angry suitors. This is arguably not such a great plan, even if Odysseus remains blithely certain that Athena and Zeus will see them through, no matter what (Homer 1963: 299). Penelope's plan, on the other hand, offers a much greater chance of success, even if it does so through providing an occasion for the slaughter that she never makes explicit. Nevertheless, whether the result is consciously planned on her part or not, it is she who deserves the credit for devising the ultimately successful strategy that will enable Odysseus to triumph. Penélopê herself will carry the bow into the hall where the suitors are assembled, wear the quiver over her shoulder, and declare the contest open. As a once weepy woman most unexpectedly transformed into a master strategist, it is her finest hour.

Since, as we have seen, there is no indication in the text that anyone other than Penélopê had devised the fiendishly clever test of the bow (even Athena's inspiration is not hinted at), it is clear just how radically she has been transformed. She has integrated devious and murderous shadow energies, and it is surely significant that when the suitors are being slaughtered downstairs she is sleeping soundly upstairs, waking up the following morning to exclaim that "I had not dozed away so tranquilly since my lord went to war" (Homer 1963: 429)—a wonderful touch on Homer's part, as it indicates the deep if partly unconscious satisfaction she must have taken in the bloody murder of those young men who had been pestering her for marriage and making her life a misery. She has so well integrated contra-sexual masculine energies that she is able to plan like a man—to act as a superlative warrior strategist by originating and setting up the test of the bow. She has now become, in fact, the equal of her husband when it comes to trickster ingenuity. This will be shown, once again, after the suitors have been slaughtered. Wishing to be absolutely sure that the man who has slaughtered them is her long-lost husband, she orders her attendants, with a combination of apparent tact and hospitality, to place Odysseus' own bed for the 'stranger' to sleep in outside the actual bedchamber, where she would have shared it with her husband, had he actually returned. This trick is sufficient to clear her doubts, for Odysseus at this point bursts out angrily, protesting that no one should have dared to cut away his bed from the olive trunk rooted in the ground that had served as its original support—and only Odysseus could have known this fact. So her last trick is cleverly devised in order to make sure, beyond a doubt, that the hero who has shown up at her door to free her from the suitors' unwanted attentions and abuse is indeed Odysseus.

The *Odyssey* might well have ended with the slaughter of the suitors and the happy reunion of husband and wife, but it does not. However, it seems to me, especially as regards the ideal of midlife heroism, the heroism of self-restraint and patience, that Odysseus is now coming to represent, sometimes in spite of himself, that the ending of Book 24 is quite appropriate. From a realistic standpoint, the slaughter of the suitors could only have led to a formidable confrontation of Odysseus and his small band of supporters (his son Telémakhos, his old father Laertês, and a few servants that had remained faithful to him) with the combined force of the suitors' enraged relatives, a much larger group hell bent on avenging the deaths of their sons and brothers. In such a confrontation, one could foresee tragic consequences for Odysseus and his little band, and that is exactly what Book 24 shows about to happen. Even though Odysseus and his men are woefully outnumbered, this valiant handful of rash and impulsive self-asserting heroes—even his old father Laertês seems to have regained momentarily the spirit of his youth—is on the point of leaping joyfully into the fray against a swarm of enemies, fully expecting, against all odds, to exterminate them all. But realism would have suffered in such an insanely optimistic outcome, so Homer declined the option. A tragic denouement would have been a more plausible option to choose, but, if chosen, it would have made Odysseus pay with his life for his regressively youthful rashness and impetuosity, and so would have provided a thoroughly disappointing and depressing end for the story of the adventures and homecoming of Odysseus.

So Homer chose a third option, and the option he chose was, I think, not only an original one, but also the one most consonant with Odysseus' new status as a midlife hero. What Homer did was this: he had Athena bring the battle to a halt just as it was beginning; she did this with a loud shout "that stopped all the fighters in their tracks," seconded by a thunderbolt from Zeus. And there is a good moral tagged on to the end of the epic, since Athena's last words to Odysseus sum up the new kind of midlife heroism of restraint he should be content with now: "Son of Laertês and the gods of old, Odysseus, master of land ways and sea ways, command yourself. Call off this battle now, or Zeus who views the wide world may be angry."

It is a happy ending, and Odysseus chooses to act wisely and prudently: he "yielded to her," with the result that "his heart was glad" (Homer 1963: 462). Athena's peremptory command to him (in Greek, a brief and brutal *ischeo*, "hold!") reminds the reader of Teirêsias' terse and laconic advice to "build a barrier around his *thymos*," and could likewise be translated at greater length as "get a handle on yourself and your impulsive youthful heroism before it is too late." One way or another, her intent is clear: Odysseus must find a new way at midlife to be a hero.

Of course, this ending, satisfying as it is in some ways, also suffers from a certain lack of realism. It is all very well for Odysseus and his small band of men to choose peace over war, but why should the relatives of the suitors be expected to give up their vendetta to avenge the deaths of their best and bravest young heroes? So a deus ex machina is still needed in the end, and it is Zeus who will take on this role: he magically erases from the suitors' relatives' minds all memory of the loss they have suffered! Once this providential amnesia is in place, Athena can proceed to settle things in a civilized fashion, with terms of peace that she devises, appropriately enough, as she continues to intervene at the very end in the form of the wise midlife mentor . . . named Mentor.

Notes

1 Homer 1963: 3. Fitzgerald here translates *omphalos* not as "navel" but as "middle," thus missing some of the symbolic resonance of the word used in the Greek text (*Odyssey* 1.50).
2 Jonathan Shay, in his book *Odysseus in America* (2002) has highlighted the tragic and even criminal weaknesses of Odysseus as a commander; see especially the chapter "Odysseus as a Military Leader," 231–241.
3 Is it possible to interpret the blinded Polyphêmos as a symbol of the blind sexual desire of the one-eyed phallus? If so, this would implicitly set Odysseus up for his lengthy period of sexual infatuations both with Kirkê and with Kalypso, as the victim of his own blind sexual desires.
4 Virgil, *Aeneid* 7.312.
5 I suspect that Fitzgerald was misled by W.B. Stanford's note on the Greek text of *Odyssey* 11.634, where Stanford had translated the phrase as "the grim spectral head of some dread monster," opining that *gorgo* in Homeric Greek "is probably a general term for a fearful spectre . . . not especially one of the Gorgons." Stanford's remark is clearly speculative.
6 Jenny Strauss Clay has argued, in *The Wrath of Athena* (1983), that there is good reason for seeing the offended goddess Athena's anger as the key to the enigma.
7 The same idea of a powerful goddess appearing in such a juvenile form is present in one cult tradition of the Hindu goddess Kali, where the priests at her great temple at Dakshineshwar, on the outskirts of Calcutta, affirm that one of the primary forms of the goddess is a divine eight-year-old girl.

Chapter 6

Tragedy, inflation and midlife transformation

There is no reason to assume that a midlife transition will automatically proceed easily and effortlessly according to archetypal plan. An archetypal template is not equivalent in this respect to an animal instinct, however much Jung may have been inclined to draw the analogy on numerous occasions, returning frequently to the example of weaver birds weaving complicated nests as evidence of an inner behavior pattern. But human beings are clearly not as completely run by their instincts as weaver birds are. For humans, archetypes have "suggestive effects," not controlling effects. Writing late in his life to a student of biology, Jung qualified his theory of archetypes in the direction of probable, rather than of inevitable, outcomes:

> for me the archetype means: an image of a probable sequence of events, an habitual current of psychic energy. To this extent it may be equated with the biological pattern of behavior.
>
> (Jung 1975: II, 505)

The archetype of initiation would be triggered by any situation involving the need to move on to a new stage of life. But the outcome of this process may just as well be resisted—or even aborted—by the person involved. For better and for worse, human beings have something that deserves to be called free will.

For Erikson, too, the successful resolution of "phase-specific psychosocial crises" is by no means guaranteed. As regards midlife, the transitioning to it may be stalled, resulting not in generativity (the "syntonic quotient") but rather in self-absorption and stagnation (the "dystonic quotient"). As Erikson writes in *The Life Cycle Completed*:

> The syntonic supports growth and expansion, offers goals, celebrates self-respect and commitment of the very finest. Syntonic qualities sustain us as we are challenged by the more dystonic elements with

which life confronts us all. We should recognize the fact that circumstances may place the dystonic in a more dominant position.

(Erikson 1997: 106)

Other negative factors that may come to dominate include for Erikson
authoritism or "the ungenerous and ungenerative use of sheer power for the
regimentation of economic and familial life," which he calls "the opposite
of true authority" (Erikson 1997: 70). "Rejectivity" is another. If generativity is a form of caring that is "the expression of a vital *sympathetic* trend
with a high instinctual energy at its disposal," writes Erikson, "there is a
corresponding *antipathetic* trend," which he labels "rejectivity." He defines
rejectivity as "the unwillingness to include specified persons or groups in
one's generative concern—one *does not care to care* for them" (Erikson
1997: 68).

In the tragic vision of life, things do not have to turn out well; in fact,
they probably will not. In tragedy, if the worst can happen, it probably will.
And, even in the best of circumstances, disaster is just around the corner.
When it comes to the question of the literary genre of tragedy and the
theme of midlife transformation, it would not be appropriate, however, to
define what is tragic solely in terms of a negative outcome of a crisis.
Sophocles' tragedy *Philoctetes*, for instance, exemplifies the type of tragedy
with a happy ending that Aristotle was quite willing to accept in his
definition of the genre. Even *Oedipus the King* points at the end to some
later and happier dimension to Oedipus' fate as an exiled and lonely
wanderer, foreshadowing his apotheosis at the end of *Oedipus at Colonus*.
In the end, what makes for a tragic protagonist is the acceptance of the
burden of a fate and the resolution of a crisis, one way or another. And
transformation is the key factor for both. At the end of the play the tragic
protagonist is a new man or woman.

There was no lack of tragedies in ancient Athens where a positive
resolution of the crisis proved to be impossible and the transformation too
late in coming to do the protagonist any good. However, even when the
outcome is tragic in the narrower sense of the term, and coincides with
the death of the tragic protagonist, a symbolic interpretation sees in the
hero or heroine's death a marker indicating that the character *as he or she
used to be* exists no longer—in other words, that a radical transformation
has occurred which has resulted in the "death" of the character's former
self. In such instances this "death" of the tragic protagonist is the culmination of a tragic ordeal in which the spectators can participate emotionally,
no doubt at a distance, but also empathetically, identifying themselves with
the character, and fearing the possibility of a similar fate for themselves.
Aristotle felt that this emotional participation on the part of the spectator
led to a therapeutic reduction of tension in the spectator's mind, especially
as regards the build up of a powerful, if unconscious, emotional overload

involving terror and compassion. The result of feeling intense fear and concern for a dramatic protagonist, with whose sufferings the spectator can to some degree identify, is that the spectator's unconscious emotional state is brought to consciousness, focused, intensified and then released in what Aristotle called a *catharsis*, a "purging" of excess emotion. This, Aristotle concluded, was the primary function of tragedy—that is, to provide a kind of social safety valve for a backlog of emotional agitation that, if allowed to pile up, might overpower both the individual and the collectivity alike. For any community, but perhaps especially for an urban community like that of ancient Athens, with people living together cheek by jowl, and fraught with social and class conflict, this social function of tragedy—to promote personal psychological balance and social peace and cohesion—would have been of great value.

Tragic theater in Athens thus provided emotional *catharsis* as well as entertainment of the highest order in the context of a religious festival oriented around the cult of the god Dionysus. But there was another social function that tragedy may have sometimes played for the ancient Athenians, and that was, I would suggest, to serve as *an esthetically distanced ritual of midlife transformation*. Some of classical tragedy's major themes turn out, upon further inspection, to be stage of life specific, in that they present a rich, in-depth dramatization of midlife transformation of the tragic hero or heroine's conscious attitudes and identity. This is true not only of some of the great dramas of fifth-century Athens, two of which—Sophocles' *Philoctetes* and Euripides' *Alcestis*—we will consider in this chapter, but also of the tragic theater developed in later ages under the direct or indirect stimulus of the ancient Greek models, as exemplified especially well for our purposes by Shakespeare's *Antony and Cleopatra*. If three such plays from centuries ago can speak directly to modern readers and spectators, offering them symbolic representations and transformative images that touch their souls and stimulate their imaginations, it is because the basic gestalt—the archetypal configuration—of midlife transformation has probably varied little if at all over the centuries.

The tragic theme of "learning through suffering" certainly has a general relevance for all stage of life initiations, but it has a particular relevance to the initiatory process that leads to midlife metamorphosis. But what is it that the midlife tragic protagonist specifically learns? In many cases, it is that the old identity established in youth is no longer valid, that is, is no longer adapted to the new circumstances, whether internal (psychological) or external (social), of middle age. This recognition can be resisted, and usually is resisted, at least at first. "I am the man/woman I always was!" But this proud boasting is based on a potentially dangerous illusion. Not recognizing the futile nature of the attempt to cling to the past can be dangerous, in that it opens the door to a compensatory fantasy that is all the more powerful for being illusory and unadapted. A grandiose fantasy of being as strong, as beautiful and as invulnerable as one was in the golden days of one's youth may be greatly energized by an influx of unconscious contents, powerful and largely unintegrated by the conscious mind, which morphs into a willful denial of reality and can generate an *inflated* state of mind that can verge on the delusional. The more people at midlife deny reality—the reality of growing older, of leaving youth behind—the more the inflation can take possession of them, with the result that they take themselves, consciously or unconsciously, for a kind of god or goddess through their overidentification with the archetypal fantasy of still being as young and as vigorous as ever. (The promise of eternal youth is part of Kalypso's bag of tricks.) The subsequent process of disidentifying with the archetypal fantasy leads to what Jungians call "deflation." After the intoxicating pleasures or grandiose sufferings of inflation, this sudden coming down to earth, this taking on of a new and modestly human identity more suited to one's actual stage of life, can be painful in the extreme. Change, rebirth and transformation are born from the anguished experience of a symbolic death. By giving dramatic representation to this theme of initiatory transformation at midlife, Athenian tragedy remained true to its probable origins in the rites associated with Dionysus, the "twice-born" god who became the patron deity of theater, and who could be represented simply by an empty dramatic mask symbolizing his status as the god, not only of physical and psychological transformation, but also of theatrical metamorphosis.

Jung was no doubt correct in insisting that "more aesthetic forms of experience must be carefully distinguished from those which indubitably involve a change in one's nature" (Jung 1971: 52). But, while tragedy may lack the indirect transformative power of ritual, not to mention the direct transformative power of personal psychological experience, one should not underestimate tragedy's power to stimulate a sense of the urgency at midlife of the archetypal challenge to change one's life through a process of suffering leading to insight. In so doing, tragedy must have performed cultural work of great value for ancient Athens, since no culture can grow and flourish unless there are large numbers of culture-building individuals who are willing and able to put their shoulders to the wheel at midlife and to *create*, *renovate* and *preserve* culture in larger and smaller ways according to their capacity. Tragedy must have been, at the very least, a reminder of the desirability of individual midlife transformation, since it represented symbolically, at least to some degree, the underlying archetypal pattern that presided over its unfolding. Tragedy also provided a philosophical and psychological outlook, couched primarily in the language of myth, which could serve as midlife transformation's guiding principles. If one were to restate these latent principles as simple admonitions, they would be primarily, "don't be rigid and rejective; don't cling to superannuated and overly youthful ideals; recognize and honor the power of the gods" (in

Jungian terms, the power of the archetypes of the collective unconscious); and, finally, and most importantly, "be willing to accept a fate that involves suffering, change and transformation." Even in radically different social settings—Elizabethan England or mid-seventeenth-century France—tragic theater arguably acquired some of its cultural prestige from the way it was able to put itself at the service of a societal need to stimulate the growth and development at midlife of culture-building individuals, that is, of genuinely mature and generative people, who had successfully undergone midlife transformation, and who were hence in a position to make their own distinctive contributions to culture and society. Thus the importance of the "cultural work" of tragic theater cannot be reduced to its effect of emotional catharsis, its esthetic beauty or its entertainment value. It could also help stimulate, educate and foster a social desire for midlife transformation, without which civilized generative values could not maintain themselves, let alone flourish. Without large numbers of people becoming generative, especially at midlife, a civilization is ultimately doomed. Recent examples certainly are not lacking of untransformed and ungenerative middle-aged self-promoters wreaking havoc in the economy and in political life. In large numbers, such pseudo-adults can bring a society to the brink of disaster.

Consequently, one can understand the crucial nature of this social need for midlife transformation on a large scale by considering what happens when it is not met successfully. In such cases, the alternatives would be either a youth culture left to its own devices coexisting precariously with a culture of uninitiated and regressively immature pseudo-adults (which may explain some of the stranger aspects of recent American culture), or a culture run by a hidebound authoritism and mindless adherence to rules and regulations resulting from the rule of the authoritarian *senex*—the tyranny of old men and women, hostile to change and cultural innovation, as has been the case in many pre-modern societies. But stagnation and rejectivity, the qualities most associated with failed midlife initiation, are also perennial threats to the welfare of even advanced modern societies, not to speak of the less progressive ones.

The specific psychic process that Jung associated with midlife was, as we have seen, that of *enantiodromia* (reversal). Jung borrowed the term from the Greek philosopher Heraclitus, and used it to designate a midlife reversal of values, the emergence of the unconscious opposite. In other words, the content of the new stage of midlife is to some degree predetermined by the values that have been dominant during the time of youth and young adulthood, for which this content will, at midlife, constitute a compensatory set of new values. But the creative reversal of values at midlife that Jung describes is by no means automatic, and the process can be aborted for a number of reasons. Fearing new and unfamiliar values and perspectives, a person at midlife may become more rigidly attached to the ideals of youth, or sink into sentimental nostalgia for the life patterns established in youth. The psychic pain of transformation as well as the disorientation inspired by a sense of dissolution and loss of identity are a normal part of the initiatory process of symbolic death and rebirth, and these may be something from which people at midlife understandably shrink. Regression is thus as much a real possibility at midlife as progression. Jung labeled this regression a "diminution of personality" that "is known in primitive psychology as 'loss of soul.'" (Jung 1971: 53). Its symptoms are

> listlessness, moroseness and depression. One no longer has any wish or courage to face the tasks of the day. One feels like lead, because no part of one's body seems willing to move, and this is due to the fact that one no longer has any disposable energy.
>
> (Jung 1971: 53)

Jung's description of "loss of soul" provides a good psychological picture of what Sophocles evokes at the opening of his tragedy *Philoctetes*. The middle-aged Philoctetes had been in his youth the squire of Heracles and the one, according to some accounts, who lit the funeral pyre on which the great hero had immolated himself. (Heracles did this in order to escape the excruciating pain caused by wearing the garment soaked in the blood of the centaur Nessus, which his first wife had sent him inadvertently—she thought what was a fatal poison was actually a love potion—as a gift for his second marriage.) As a reward for this service to his master, Philoctetes became the possessor of Heracles' great bow. But, in spite of his uniquely close connection with the greatest of all Greek heroes, Philoctetes was later cruelly abandoned on a desert island by his fellow warriors sailing to participate in the siege of Troy. After having been bitten by a snake, he had developed a festering and incurable wound whose noxious odor, combined with his constant cries of agony, made him an intolerable presence for his Troy-bound fellow warriors. His tragic exile and enforced solitude were actually the result—he found out only later—of his trespassing accidentally onto the sacred precinct of the desert island's local goddess Chryse ("the Golden One"), and it was her sacred serpent that had bitten him and caused his festering wound. So he was left by his comrades to stay on Chryse's island for almost ten long years, miserable and isolated, in a state of midlife liminality that had no end in sight.

As Sophocles' tragedy opens, Philoctetes' long period of midlife liminality and isolation (comparable in many ways to Odysseus' stay on the island of Kalypso, as we will see), although it has apparently induced a permanent state of stagnation and stubborn resistance to midlife transformation, is about to come to an end. His old enemy Odysseus and Achilles' son Neoptolemus have arrived on his desert island to offer him the possibility of returning with them to Troy, since he, as the possessor of the bow of Heracles, has been prophesied to be the key to the taking of the

city. But Philoctetes refuses this golden opportunity out of bitter resentment for the way his fellow Greeks treated him, when they mercilessly
abandoned him years before. He continues to cling to his misery and to his
intense regressive longings to return home to his father. Fortunately, at the
very end of the play a vision of the spirit of Heracles provides him with the
transformative image whose inspiration he needs for his midlife metamorphosis into a generative hero, who will fight at Troy on behalf of his
fellow Greeks, and pull himself out of his morass of personal misery.

In the symbolic terms of Sophocles' oneiric drama, Philoctetes may be
said to have moved from an unconscious identification of himself as a
miserable, if sacred, victim of a goddess's anger to the conscious recognition that the gods will give him a better fate, if only he chooses to play a
generative role in the final conquest of Troy. In Jungian terms, one can say
that he succumbed to a negative *inflation* with an archetypal content of the
collective unconscious. In his seminar in English on Nietzsche's *Thus Spake
Zarathustra*, Jung made a point concerning midlife that has direct relevance
to the study of this particular tragedy and of tragedy in general. Midlife,
Jung says, "is the age when the ego purpose normally fades from life and
when life itself wants to accomplish itself, when another law begins." It is
the age, to speak in the archaic mythological language of the classical
world, when the gods intervene in a human life—the age, as we have seen in
the case of Odysseus, when Athena suddenly intervenes and starts the
process of leading him back to Ithaka from the island of Kalypso. Jung
continues:

> In the middle of life a time comes when the inner sphere asserts its
> rights, when we cannot decide our fate, when things are forced upon us,
> and when it seems as if our own will were estranged from ourselves . . .
> We don't choose—it is chosen for us.
>
> (Jung 1988: II, 1195)

In his final adventure in Hades, it was the shade of Heracles who presented
Odysseus with a transformative image of the kind of heroism more suited to
the stage of midlife—the Heraclean heroism of endurance and generativity.
In Sophocles' tragedy *Philoctetes*, it is also a vision of Heracles that defines
a new fate for the suffering and self-pitying warrior, one that he would not
have chosen by himself—one rather that the gods (the unconscious) have
chosen for him. With Heracles as his "ghostly guru" and midlife mentor, he
will be able to move from stagnation to generativity, although it will take
him time (the length of the tragic play, in fact) to overcome his feelings of
resentment against Odysseus, his obsession with his personal misery and his
unconscious attachment to his status as sacred victim.

For both Odysseus and Philoctetes it was the power of a goddess—
Kalypso or Chryse—that had trapped them on a desert island. The desert

island is a wonderful symbol of liminality and of apparent stagnation (nothing much happens, except for a constant round of repetition, misery and self-indulgence), and it was the appropriate site for a painful midlife ordeal, without, however, any apparent purpose or foreseeable resolution. But, just as Odysseus' fate changes thanks to the intervention of Athena, so Philoctetes' fate changes when, ten years later, as the siege of Troy seems to be impossible to bring to a successful conclusion, Odysseus himself appears on the island, charged by the Greek commanders to bring him—by force, if need be—to Troy. His presence at Troy is absolutely necessary, because a prophet has declared that only the bow of Heracles, which is now in the possession of Philoctetes, who uses it to hunt small animals and maintain his miserable life as an ancient Greek version of Robinson Crusoe, has the power to bring victory to the Greeks at Troy. In Sophocles' play, Odysseus is portrayed as an unscrupulous bully, who orders Neoptolemus, the young son of the late great hero Achilles, to collaborate with his devious schemes to trick Philoctetes into surrendering his bow. Sophocles' Odysseus is in fact much what he was shown to be in Books 9–11 of the *Odyssey* during the early stages of his wanderings and midlife initiation: a trickster of dubious morals, although not lacking in courage and determination. The young Neoptolemus is thus put in a terrible moral dilemma. His resentment of Odysseus' blatant authoritism and his increasingly filial feelings of compassion for the plight of Philoctetes make it hard for him to betray the suffering hero, although this is what the commanders at Troy clearly ordered him to do, when they placed him under the authority of Odysseus. He is torn between the obedience he owes his superiors and his compassion for a lonesome castaway's anguish.

Philoctetes is nevertheless a problematic figure for Neoptolemus. His constant complaining and self-pity are off-putting, as is his refusal to go to Troy, even though a prophet declared that participating in the final victory would cure him of his disease and suffering. Philoctetes seems indeed to have fallen in love with his own misery, in the grip of a dystonic rigidity and rejectivity. Later in the play, Neoptolemus will finally lose patience with him, telling him bluntly that he has become a brutal and unthinking savage in his unwillingness to listen to good counsel.

However, Philoctetes is not simply a tedious and increasingly rigid mid-life neurotic; he is also, although without knowing it, a sacred victim of an offended goddess's anger. He has fallen victim to what Jungians call an unconscious psychological *inflation,* that is, an unconscious identification with an archetypal content—in his case, the sacred victim role as the negative archetypal pole of the self-assertive hero myth. If the positive pole of the youthful hero myth involves heroic deeds and hypermasculine self-assertion, its opposite pole involves unconscious subservience to the power of the feminine, which is what the youthful hero myth ignored in its drive for success. To be stuck in such a psychic situation is also to remain stuck in the unconscious grip of the anima. For Odysseus this feminine power took the form of Kalypso, and for Philoctetes that of the local goddess Chryse. (This paradoxical fate of the hypermasculine hero was also exemplified by Heracles' period of servitude to Queen Omphale, who made him dress in woman's clothing and work at the spinning wheel.) If Philoctetes perseveres in his sufferings, it is because he has identified, albeit unconsciously, with his sacred status as the victim of a goddess's anger. He will eventually be enlightened as to the divine origin of his peculiar inflated state of glorying in his misery, when Neoptolemus reveals it to him near the end of the play. Self-knowledge and insight are important in an inflation's resolution, in that they enable one to distinguish one's limited individuality immersed in real life from the archetypal syndrome with which one has become identified, consciously or unconsciously.

The classic example of inflation in Jung's work is his detailed study of Friedrich Nietzsche's identification with the archetypal Wise Old Man Zarathustra, who became for him a kind of mythic double or alter ego. Nietzsche expressed this feeling of inflated identification in a short poem "Sils Maria," the name of the Swiss village in the Engadine where he stayed for several summers in the early 1880s, and near which, on the south shore of the Lake of Silvaplauna (a spot now marked by a monument to the event), he claimed to have experienced—at midlife, when he was in his late thirties—the vision of a numinous figure he named after the ancient Persian sage Zarathustra. This vision of a midlife mentor or "ghostly guru," however inspiring it may have been for Nietzsche on a philosophical plane (he later credited Zarathustra with teaching him the doctrine of the Eternal Return), had, in Jung's opinion, disastrous psychological consequences for him. Jung felt a special affinity with Nietzsche, no doubt partly because he himself had also encountered at midlife a significant mentor and "ghostly guru" in the form of Philemon. His diagnosis of the causes of the tragic end of Nietzsche's career as a philosopher (Nietzsche became incurably insane in 1889) was that Nietzsche had failed to distinguish himself from the archetypal figure, and that this perilous state of inflation had never been resolved. If it had been, inflation giving way to deflation, then it would have been possible for Nietzsche to assimilate the teachings of Zarathustra— to integrate some of the archetypal contents he represented—but also to become aware of his own all-too-human limitations. The process of "deflation" (in ordinary language, realizing that one has developed a "swelled head") is a humbling but therapeutically beneficial experience, since only by anchoring oneself in one's ordinary human reality can sanity be maintained in the face of a nearly overwhelming flood of archetypal energies.

For Philoctetes, however, this therapeutic deflation is not a possibility, as long as he is unaware of the archetypal origin of his painful situation in the anger of an offended goddess. This ignorance on his part constitutes potentially another Homeric parallel, in that Odysseus in the *Odyssey* is equally unaware of the possible origin of his sufferings and wanderings and especially of his years of captivity on Kalypso's island, which may have ultimately been the anger of the goddess Athena; Jenny Strauss Clay has argued that the wrath of Athena is actually "a key to the structure of the entire *Odyssey*" (Clay 1983: 51). The parallel becomes even closer, if the name Chryse was originally another name for Athena (Sophocles 2004: xi). The opposite archetypal pole of the self-assertive hypermasculine hero is, as we have seen, "the sacred victim of a goddess's anger," mythologically exemplified in the case of the pan-Hellenic hero Heracles, whose very name ("the glory of Hera") denotes the anger of the goddess Hera, who perse-cuted him as the bastard son of her husband Zeus. Radical male heroic assertiveness, with its tyrannous attitude towards women, is understandably counterbalanced archetypally by radical subservience to female power. The resurgence of the anima at midlife marks the coming to consciousness of some of this archetypal female power, which is why the anima can be such a problem for a man, even though it is fair to say that "the mistress of our soul" is a creative problem as well. Philoctetes seems in this respect to have been overwhelmed by such typical anima affects as moodiness, self-pity, resentfulness, suicidal thoughts and a regressive desire to go back to his childhood home. It is as though a return to his father's patriarchal protec-tion seems to offer the prospect of shielding him from unconscious possession by the anima in the form of Chryse. But escaping the problem is not the answer. What Philoctetes needs to do is to become consciously aware of the presence of his anima, that is, in mythological terms, he needs to realize that there is an invisible goddess in his life, and that she does not wish him well.

Philoctetes' state of stagnation and rejectivity is one he cannot easily escape, not the least because he does not understand what the archetypal roots of his situation are; until Neoptolemus tells him, he has not a clue as to the existence of the goddess Chryse or the reason for her wrath. Thus his unconscious inflation with the archetypal "victim of a goddess' anger," the negative pole of the hero archetype, manifests itself consciously for him as a narcissistic preoccupation with his own status as a victim of his fellow Greeks, and more specifically of Odysseus and the two commanders Agamemnon and Menelaus, who decided to abandon him on the shores of the island ten years before. It is this victim status that he cannot let go of, and this is also understandable, because it constitutes for him a fascinating unconscious inflation with the negative pole of the hero archetype. He may not yet realize consciously the role an angry goddess has played in creating his tragic plight, but he has become his own worst enemy by clinging to his divinely ordained misery and the exalted status of sacred victim that comes from it.

Thus Philoctetes can be seen as an embodiment of midlife stagnation and self-absorption, unwilling to challenge the validity of the survival values that had enabled him, during his lost youth, to stay alive as a solitary castaway suffering from a very painful disease, but that now are threatened by a midlife *enantiodromia*. His survival had been a heroic achievement in its own way, no doubt. But, over time, Philoctetes let himself become defined neurotically by his misery—misery that, from another standpoint, was the result of no mere neurosis, but of a divine fate that has given him the opportunity to practice the heroism of survival and self-concern (the other side of the coin of heroic action and self-assertion, so to speak) under extraordinarily difficult circumstances. The war years, which his coevals the young heroes of the Trojan War had spent on the glorious battlefield, Philoctetes had spent, in a reverse but still parallel situation, not fighting enemies, but struggling to stay alive under the most difficult circumstances. This youthful survivalist heroism has served him well over the years, and he finds it hard to even consider letting go of this youthful heroic attitude, even though it is no longer suited to the new opportunities the arrival of Odysseus and Neoptolemus extends to him to leave his isolated misery behind, and to practice generative heroism at Troy. His mind is obsessed with a death-oriented regressive desire to go back to his father, even if he is in Hades: "I would seek my sire . . . in the realm of the dead" (Sophocles 2004: 189). Indulging such a suicidal fantasy would destroy for him any future possibility of change and transformation, and he seems close to indulging it, when, at his moment of deepest despair, he calls upon the chorus of sailors to bring him a sword, in order that he might "mangle this body utterly—hew limb from limb with mine own hand. Death, death is my thought now" (Sophocles 2004: 187–188).

Philoctetes' suicidal fantasy, however, can also be seen as marking a growing willingness on his part to die to his former self and to accept change on a deep level as part of a process of psychic death and rebirth. It is the young man Neoptolemus who turns out to be the initial catalyst for his acceptance of change. Son of the great hero Achilles, now dead, Neoptolemus finds in Philoctetes a surrogate father and Philoctetes responds in kind, frequently calling him "son," and treating him with all the desperate affection and concern of a man who has been cut off from human contact for many years. This empathic movement on Philoctetes' part towards generative feeling for Neoptolemus establishes a relationship of mutual trust between him and his new-found "son," and generates a progressive movement towards fatherly feeling in him that counters the regressive movement that continues to hold sway in his psyche, which would otherwise lead him to return, uncured and untransformed, to his own father.

But this movement towards paternal and generative feeling is not enough. Neoptolemus finally feels it is time to reveal to him the divine origin of his suffering and the archetypal foundation of his misery, which is the anger of the goddess Chryse:

Thou suffereth this sore plague by heaven-sent doom, because thou didst draw near to Chryse's watcher, the serpent, secret warder of her home, that guards her roofless sanctuary. And know that relief from this grievous sickness can never be thy portion, so long as the sun still rises in the east and sets in the west, until thou come, of thine own free will, to the plains of Troy, where thou shalt meet with the sons of Asclepius [the primal physician], our comrades, and shall be eased of this malady; and with this bow's aid and mine, shall achieve the capture of the Ilian town [Troy].

(Sophocles 2004: 205–207)

But, even after Neoptolemus assures him that the "sons of Asclepius" will cure his disease if he comes to Troy, and even after the young man changes sides and defies the authority of Odysseus, thus leaving Philoctetes free to decide what to do with his life, it is the regressive option of a return to his father that Philoctetes finally chooses. Although the young man Neoptolemus has transformed himself by defying the unjust authority of Odysseus and has in so doing thus fashioned himself into a self-assertive young hero no longer submissive to the pseudopaternal manipulation and authoritism of Odysseus, Philoctetes remains untransformed. Is it perhaps because a young man cannot ultimately play the role of an effective midlife mentor for an older man? Should not the midlife mentor more properly come in the form of an elder, of a wise *old* man, even of a "ghostly guru"?

Thus what does turn out to be the effective catalyst for transformation for Philoctetes is his vision of Heracles in the last scene of the tragedy. Just as Heracles represented for Odysseus the ideal of the mature heroism of endurance and generativity at the end of Book 11 of the *Odyssey*, so he does here for Philoctetes at the end of Sophocles' tragedy. Since the *Odyssey* was extremely well known to Sophocles' audience, Heracles' inspiring words to Philoctetes would have easily reminded them of what Heracles had represented for Odysseus in Hades as the numinous exemplar of heroic endurance and generative activity. At the end of Sophocles' play, Heracles expresses his teachings as much through his sudden dramatic appearance on stage as a deus ex machina as through his verbal message, as much through his "face" as through his "voice":

know that the voice of Herakles soundeth in thine ears, and thou lookest upon his face . . . give thou heed unto my counsel. First I would tell thee of mine own fortunes,—how, after enduring many labours to the end, I won deathless glory, as thou beholdest. And for thee, for sure, the destiny is ordained that through these thy sufferings thou shouldst glorify thy life.

(Sophocles 2004: 219)

The actual "labors" (*ponoi*) that Heracles enjoins on Philoctetes are clearly defined in terms of the epic tradition the audience would have been familiar with:

> with my bow shalt thou slay Paris, the author of these ills; thou shalt sack Troy; the prize of valor shall be given to thee by our warriors; and thou shalt carry the spoils to thy home, for the joy of Poeas thy sire.
>
> (Sophocles 2004: 219)

These labors—including the slaying of the Trojan prince Paris, whose abduction of Helen was the cause of the Trojan War—will "glorify his life" in the manner of any great exploit of a young epic hero; for instance, the slaying of Hector by Achilles. But the killing of Hector, Achilles' most glorious deed, as recounted in the *Iliad*, was shown to be motivated above all by a desire for personal revenge, since Hector had slain his best friend Patroclus. By contrast, the labors of Heracles were glorious deeds performed in a generative mode. The audience would have been familiar with these famous labors, which were frequently represented in the sculpture and the vase paintings of the time, and constituted the defining set of heroic exploits of the greatest of all Greek heroes. Of the twelve labors, at least seven would qualify as heroic forms of generative "community service," such as the elimination of dangerous or man-eating monsters and dangerous animals such as the Nemean Lion, the Lenean Hydra, the Hind of Ceryneia, the Erymanthean Bull, the Stymphalian Birds, the Cretan Bull and the Horses of Diomedes. In a similar fashion, Philoctetes' defining heroic deed will not only bring him personal glory, but will enable the Greeks to finally capture the city of Troy. In helping those who once betrayed him, Philoctetes will be acting in a way that is doubly generative, putting thoughts of personal revenge behind him in order to further the greater common good.

The mature generative mode is emphasized again, when Heracles states that Philoctetes will accomplish his glorious deeds in concert with Neoptolemus. They will be co-fighters, he says to his erstwhile squire, "like two lions roaming together, each one protecting the other" (Sophocles 2004: 221). Since each one is necessary to the other for the attainment of victory, their cooperation breaks the narcissistic pattern of isolated activity in which the youthful self-assertive hero is frequently trapped. It also establishes a generative bond between generations—between "son" and "father"—of the sort that is celebrated in the final pages of the *Odyssey*, where Telémakhos, along with his grandfather Laertês, becomes his father Odysseus' ally in defeating the suitors who have usurped his kingdom. The victory strategy foreseen by Heracles for Philoctetes and Neoptolemus also includes himself, although indirectly, as the third participant, since it is with the help of his legendary bow that Philoctetes will slay Paris and sack Troy. In this way a generative bond between three generations is reaffirmed and celebrated, much as in the *Odyssey* Odysseus is shown rejoicing in the presence of both his son and his father as the final battle against the suitor's friends and relations seems about to begin. Establishing and nurturing these intergenerational bonds is part of the generative task of midlife, and Heracles sees to it that Philoctetes will play his part in fostering them.

It is of key significance that Heracles associates the accomplishment of such heroic generative labors with a willingness to suffer (*pathein*). The emphasis on suffering is a major point of difference between midlife heroism and the heroism of the young self-assertive hero; for the latter, the key elements are swift action and quick glory. But for midlife heroism, patience and suffering are the key. The "sufferings" Heracles refers to, when he tells Philoctetes that "the destiny is ordained that through these thy sufferings thou shouldst glorify thy life" (Sophocles 2004: 219), must mean, not Philoctetes' ten years of suffering on his deserted island, but some unspecified aspect of his future heroic activity at Troy, for which the context of Heracles' own legendary Twelve Labors may provide a clue. As the former squire of Heracles, Philoctetes would have known that Heracles had accomplished his famous labors at the command of Eurystheus, an unpleasant and demanding taskmaster or "dispatcher king," and Philoctetes (and the Athenian spectators of the play) would easily have been able to draw the comparison between Heracles' legendary situation of painful submission to authority with his own future situation at Troy. As we have seen, Philoctetes' reluctance to go to Troy is partially caused by his hatred of the Atreidae, Agamemnon and Menelaus, the twin commanders of the Greek forces he blames for his ten-year exile on the desert island. By returning to Troy, he would be putting himself under the direct command of the very men he hates most—no wonder that he prefers to fantasize returning to the arms of his father, even in Hades! His stubbornly regressive revolt against authority demonstrates the type of sullen, rebellious temperament more typical, for better or for worse, of the young heroes Achilles and Neoptolemus than of the mature hero Heracles. "Suffering" is thus for Philoctetes implicitly linked to submission to established authority as a means of participating in furthering the cause of the common good, and to the substitution of generative, cooperative feeling for personal resentment.

Heracles also urges Philoctetes to practice *eusebeia*, often translated as "piety", which was an ancient Greek virtue concerned especially with respecting and honoring the power of the gods. *Eusebeia* can be seen as denoting an attitude analogous to the one Jung often urged on modern people, who needed, he felt, to realize that they were "not masters in their own house," but rather under the strong influence of the archetypes of the collective unconscious, the modern near equivalent of "the ruling principles, the gods" (Jung 1956: 105) of the ancient Greeks. Such a respectful and reverent attitude towards the gods, towards the collective unconscious or any other transpersonal dimension of life, would constitute a recognizably religious attitude, sometimes crucial for the successful resolution of a midlife crisis. For Jung felt, at least in terms of his own experience as a therapist, that midlife problems originated in a failure to discover some transcendental meaning in life. Jung thus believed that midlife is often the moment when a spiritual orientation becomes of prime necessity in a person's life. When purely personal ambitions and concerns can no longer inspire one's best efforts, the flow of psychic energy diminishes until a more transcendent and transpersonal goal makes its appearance. Such a transcendent goal is what the vision of Heracles indicates for Philoctetes.

Sophocles' decision to manage the end of his tragedy with Heracles suddenly appearing as a deus ex machina might seem, dramatically speaking, as some kind of theatrical trick. But, from the standpoint of archetypal psychology, the vision of Heracles provides a most appropriate resolution for Philoctetes' midlife dilemma. This is partly because Philoctetes' vision of Heracles constitutes for him not only a powerful transformative image, but also a religious experience as significant in its own cultural context as a vision of Christ or the Virgin Mary would be in the Christian tradition. As Jung said by way of conclusion in his Terry Lectures at Yale in 1937:

> religious experience is absolute . . . No matter what the world thinks about religious experience, the one who has it possesses the great treasure of a thing that has provided him with a source of life, meaning and beauty that has given a new splendor to the world and to mankind.
>
> (Jung 1960: 113)

Jung's lectures at Yale dealt extensively with the case of a man who believed he had cancer, even though no sign of it could be discovered even after many medical examinations. He suffered greatly from his fear of the disease, and this fear gradually came to dominate his everyday life; nothing could convince him that his terrible anxiety was not justified. However, the neurotic misery of this modern Philoctetes suddenly vanished after he experienced, at the end of a long series of dreams, a numinous vision of a mandala-shaped form. Without going into the details of the vision, it is crucial to appreciate the fact that the vision not only left him with "a feeling of most sublime harmony," but that it was also "a turning point in the patient's psychological development" (Jung 1960: 80). In its wake, his neurosis was cured. Jung commented at the conclusion of his lectures that

> the thing that cures a neurosis must be as convincing as the neurosis; and since the latter is all too real, the helpful experience must be of equal reality. It must be a very real illusion, if you want to put it pessimistically. But what is the difference between a real illusion and a healing religious experience? It is merely a difference in words.
>
> (Jung 1960: 114)

Such a healing religious experience was Philoctetes' vision of Heracles, and its effect on him was immediate: he decided then and there to go to Troy. At the very last minute, the direction of his future life veers away from continued stagnation and resentment.

The vision of Heracles is thus an effective catalyst for Philoctetes' transformation at midlife into someone capable of living a life of generative heroism. This transformation involved first of all, as we have seen, insight into the origins of his misery—in mythological terms, an understanding of the power of the *anger* of the goddess Chryse, which in Jungian terms would involve some degree of insight into the way the anima power of the feminine can disturb a man's life, until it is properly appreciated and partially integrated. As regards the factor of the partial and selective integration of anima contents, it is interesting to note that *anger* is the emotion that Philoctetes must reclaim for himself. In Jungian terms, he takes anger out of the control of unconscious anima resentment, making some of Chryses' anger his own in the context of his own life. In other words, he turns irrational resentment into lucid anger. "Resentment" is one of the irrational moods that Jung associated with anima possession in a man, and Philoctetes is defined dramatically by this mood, along with the corresponding anima mood of neurotic self-pity, at the opening of the play. Unfocused resentment can perpetuate the depressive feeling of always being the victim of practically everything and everybody. But resentment, when focused, can turn into anger, a clarifying feeling that can pull a man out of an anima mood and show him what his situation really is, and how it can be dealt with effectively. Jung himself once related in a seminar how he had spontaneously countered an intense anima mood in himself with a sudden burst of anger:

> I had been working very hard on my association tests and my walls were covered with charts, when my mother came unexpectedly to visit me. She looked all around my walls and said: "Do these things really mean anything?" What she said was thin as air but it fell on me heavier than tons of lead. I did not touch a pen for three days. If I had been a weak boy I would have been crushed and said, "Of course, it is no good," and given up. My mother would have said that she loved me and meant nothing by it . . . Well, I had a terrific fit of anger and then I could work again.
>
> (Jung 1984a: 97)

In the course of the drama, Philoctetes also manages to reclaim his anger from the depths of his depression and anima-induced resentment, and to focus it mainly on Odysseus for plotting to trick him and to steal his bow. This anger is a justified anger, and, as with Jung, it clarifies his sense of his situation, and pulls him out of his depressive anima mood.

But the vision of Heracles demands more of him than insight and anger; it demands of him *action*. However, taking action requires that he separate himself from an unconscious inflated identity as "the victim of a goddess's anger," since this inflation has reduced him to a miserably passive state that is incompatible with a new life of heroic action. From unconsciously acting out the negative pole of the hero myth, passive suffering, he is now called upon to consciously act out its positive pole, active heroic endeavor, in a mature (i.e., without immature resentment of authority figures) and generative mode. Thus the vision of Heracles inspires Philoctetes to consciously integrate into his life, through actions that will require acceptance of suffering and the ability to endure and persevere, the mature heroic archetypal energies that the myth and the ghostly presence of Heracles embody.

As the mythical embodiment of generative heroism, the figure of Heracles also appears—once again, in the nick of time—as midlife mentor in Euripides' play *Alcestis*, a play that is both tragic and comic in a way that makes it unique in what survives of ancient Greek drama, in which the generic boundaries of comedy and tragedy did not normally overlap. This unusual drama provides, as does the *Odyssey*, two parallel symbolic representations of a man and a woman both undergoing a midlife crisis. In Euripides' play, Heracles serves as the midlife mentoring figure for both of them, but the individual transformations of Admetus and his wife Alcestis could not otherwise be more different. As in the *Odyssey*, their parallel but dissimilar initiation processes offer an opportunity for analyzing the archetypal dimension of male and female midlife metamorphoses in terms of gendered divergences. Whereas the narcissistic husband Admetus undergoes an ordeal that forces him to acknowledge a mature self whose primary virtues turn out to be not heroism but generous hospitality, his wife Alcestis, cruelly abandoned to her fate by her husband, who allows her to die voluntarily in his place, returns from the borderlands of death as an impressive hero figure of great numinosity. When Alcestis reappears at the end of the play as a mysteriously veiled woman, it is as a transformed woman, whose heroic attributes now appear to link her—quite paradoxically, given the ancient Greek strongly patriarchal cultural context—with the pan-Hellenic hero Heracles himself. Indeed, her *katabasis* has transformed her into a figure who is, in her own way, on an equal footing with Heracles. The play's conclusion thus creates a gender bending reversal of traditional expectations, and it must have had some real shock value for the original Athenian audience. In fact, even a modern audience might be somewhat surprised by the way both partners in this unusual marriage have succeeded in integrating contrasexual attributes to a marked degree: the husband Admetus as the perfect hostess, and the wife Alcestis as the impressive hero.

The atmosphere of the opening of the play is somber. Alcestis has agreed to die in the place of her husband in a bargain brokered with the Fates by the god Apollo, and she is now preparing for her death. Comedy breaks through soon with the arrival of Heracles, a friend of Admetus who has not yet heard of Alcestis' death, and who therefore cannot appreciate the painful sacrifice Admetus is making by entertaining him as a guest when his household is in mourning. But, since Admetus keeps him ignorant of his wife's tragic death, Heracles is happy to drink wine by himself, soon breaking into song and behaving very much like a typical drunken figure in a satyr play.

However, in the midst of his drunken ravings, Heracles manages to give some good words of advice (*in vino veritas?*) to the servant who attends him and brings him all the wine he wants. In this seriocomic scene, the servant is the only one present on stage with him. But, at this private symposium, the wisdom Heracles proffers is more logically intended as a midlife message for Admetus, who is not present on stage but who is arguably its intended recipient, the servant listening for him by proxy, as it were. Heracles first pontificates drunkenly on the ineluctable nature of death:

> But listen to me. Take death.
> All men have to pay that debt,
> Yet not one man jack of them can tell
> If he'll be around tomorrow.
> (Euripides 1998: 31)

Platitudinous as his words may be, they constitute just the sort of stiffening medicine Admetus would need, since he, alone among men, had thought himself entitled to escape dying his own death by accepting the offer of his wife to die in his stead, discovering only when it is too late that confronting the fact of her death and self-sacrifice is almost more than he can bear. Admetus now needs to realize that he will still have to die his own death one day anyhow, perhaps even the next day, as Heracles warns him. As a growing awareness of the inevitability of death usually accompanies the midlife crisis, Admetus has forestalled this recognition only for a short time.

Fortune, Heracles goes on to say—again, drunkenly and sententiously— is mysterious: "it can't be foreseen or taught or caught by any trick" (Euripides 1998: 31). Consequently, a man should drink his wine and live his life one day at a time, leaving the rest to Fortune. This too is good advice for Admetus, who has tried to take complete control of his life and death and has now seen the disaster he has created in the process: both loss of reputation (he will now be infamous as the man who let his wife die for him) and loss of love (he realizes too late how attached he is to Alcestis). A rigid attitude of hypercontrol must be replaced, insinuates the drunken Heracles, with the wisdom of flexibility and with openness to the vagaries of chance, an attitude naturally fostered by the carefree spirit induced by drinking wine. As a successful king, father and husband, Admetus thought he had worked out everything in his life perfectly. He now realizes that such is not the case. His wife has died, his reputation is ruined, and he even bears the shame and sorrow of having asked his old parents to die for him, and then being publicly refused. (The scene between him and his irate father, who finds his son's proposal preposterous, is one of scurrilous comedy.)

Then Heracles lurches into giving another piece of sententious advice: honor the goddess Aphrodite:

> And one thing more: pay homage to the sweetest power of all.
> Aphrodite, mankind's most gracious goddess.
>
> (Euripides 1998: 31)

But this time it is not immediately clear how it might help Admetus put his life back together again. If Hera was the patron goddess of the marital bond, Aphrodite by contrast was considered to preside over sexuality in all its forms, both licit and illicit. But why should Heracles urge a friend, whose wife has just died for him, to get happily involved with sex again? One possible answer to this question becomes clear only in the last scene of the play, and will eventually require some psychological interpretation.

Euripides had introduced Admetus at the opening of the drama in the context of a powerful myth of death and resurrection, when he had the god Apollo's prolog reveal the mythological origin of the god's divine intervention to save Admetus' life. Apollo's son Asclepius, the inventor of Greek medicine, had been so gifted as a physician that he had been able in one instance to bring a man back to life. Zeus, furious that one of the basic laws of the universe—that all men must die—had been violated, struck Asclepius dead with a thunderbolt. Apollo then retaliated by killing the Cyclopes, sons of Zeus and forgers of his thunderbolt. The divine dispute resolved itself, as all such quarrels between the gods eventually did, with Zeus condemning Apollo to spend a short time on earth in the humiliating position of being the slave of a mortal man. Fortunately for Apollo, this mortal man turned out to be Admetus, who treated him with great kindness. In return for this good treatment, Apollo took it upon himself to convince the three Fates to allow Admetus to escape his fast-approaching fated death, if he could find someone who would be willing to die in his place. After everyone else, including his aged mother and father, had refused, his wife Alcestis finally volunteered to give her life for him.

Thus Euripides defines Admetus in mythic terms as the man who, thanks to his hospitality to the god Apollo, had successfully escaped his appointed rendezvous with death. In Jungian terms, Admetus is a man who has succumbed to the archetypal inflation of "escaping death." But "escaping death" can mean symbolically, in terms of the initiatory archetypal process of death leading to transformation, also missing out on the possibility of resurrection and rebirth—of psychological change and transformation. Admetus is stuck in a myth that one would associate most readily with one of the common illusions of youth, that is, with the myth that one will never have to die. So Admetus remains stuck in a narcissistic and regressive state of mind, which leads him to assume that it is up to his parents and wife to save him from death, no matter what the cost to them. His inflated state of mind leads him to believe that, as a personal friend and benefactor of the god Apollo, he is entitled to be spared the common fate of mortals, which is to die when their appointed time has come. Admetus' inflation could be labeled an "Apollonian" inflation, given the way Apollo is presented in the play. Apollo's special nature is defined, for the dramatic purposes of the play, by the second scene, a comic interlude in which Apollo and the god Death squabble and argue vociferously with each other. This scene defines Apollo, in the specific context of this play, as the divine (archetypal) principle antithetical to death—a definition that, of course, also suits his traditional mythological role as the father of Asclepius, the primeval physician who could resurrect a man from death. In his unconscious identity with Apollo—in his unusual role of having been the master of a god, who was his servant—Admetus was arguably led to fantasize himself as "Apollonian," that is, as someone who existed, as Apollo did, at the opposite pole from Death. This resulted in a delusional and inflated state of mind, which led Admetus to believe that he could share his patron deity's immortality, and to behave as if he, a mortal man, were entitled to be spared the agony of dying his own death.

Later in the play there is a refinement of this definition of Apollo as the polar opposite of Death through a latent but significant contrast between Apollo and Heracles. Heracles brings Alcestis back from the dead, but he brings her back radically *transformed*. Apollo, by contrast, could only forestall Admetus' death, leaving Admetus the same man he always was. This turns out to be an important distinction, and Nietzsche's key concept in *The Birth of Tragedy* of the opposition of the Apollonian and Dionysian principles has some relevance here as well. If one takes the drunken Heracles partly as a representative of the Dionysian spirit of death, dismemberment and resurrection, then by contrast Apollo would represent Nietzsche's Apollonian principle of individuation, which makes for the individual always staying the same, remaining true to a certain definition of self. But staying true to oneself also implies avoiding the initiatory process of transformation through symbolic death and rebirth. In terms of Jung's solar image, to remain the same at midlife would be like being the sun reaching its zenith and staying there forever, its values never subject to revaluation and never running into their opposites in the midlife process of *enantiodromia*. By contrast, Nietzsche's Dionysian delight felt at the annihilation of the individual would represent the opposite process of painful change and transformation through the ordeal of a symbolic death leading to metamorphosis, the "second birth" that is presided over by Dionysus, the twice-born god. It is this initiation process that Admetus, by choosing to accept Apollo's bargain with the Fates, has implicitly chosen to resist.

But his resistance turns out to have tragic consequences for him. Once the action of the play gets underway, it is clear that Admetus is overcome by grief at the prospect of his wife's imminent death. What seemed to him initially as an extraordinary stroke of good luck—the fact that he found someone to die in his place—turns out to be the opposite. Admetus is on the verge of a serious midlife depression, having lost both his wife and his good name at the same time. It had originally seemed natural to him that his mother or father should willingly die in his place, and he had become furious when they refused. But now that Alcestis *has* willingly died for him, his inflated and narcissistic image of himself has been deflated. He must now recognize himself in a diminished and deflated shadow form as someone without courage, morals or scruples—an unheroic man, if ever there was one. Admetus casts a long shadow indeed.

However, Admetus does have one redeeming virtue that will unexpectedly save him: his acute sense of hospitality. X*enophilia* (guest love) was a virtue that was highly esteemed in ancient Greece, and one that Admetus had demonstrated both in his earlier kind treatment of Apollo and now in entertaining Heracles as an honored guest, even while his house was in deep mourning. His unanticipated reward for this generous gesture of hospitality will be twofold: Heracles will his wife back from the dead, and will also initiate him into the new life that should be his at midlife. But what kind of life would that new life be? And what kind of new man would Admetus become?

Jung once told of the belated midlife transformation of another man whose good opinion of himself was in conflict with his true nature, and whose story had much in common with the story of Admetus, in spite of major cultural and situational differences, in that it was a midlife drama in a somewhat *comic* mode:

I know of a pious man who was a churchwarden and who, from the age of forty onward, showed a growing and finally unbearable intolerance in matters of morality and religion. At the same time his moods grew visibly worse. At last he was nothing more than a darkly lowering pillar of the Church. In this way he got along until the age of fifty-five, when suddenly, sitting up in bed in the middle of the night, he said to his wife: "Now at last I've got it! I'm just a plain rascal." Nor did this realization remain without results. He spent his declining years in riotous living and squandered a goodly part of his fortune. Obviously quite a likeable fellow, capable of both extremes.

(Campbell 1976: 13)

But does Admetus, in spite of his many faults, turn out to be "quite a likeable fellow"? Oddly enough, that is the conclusion Euripides seems to be moving towards by the end of the play.

Admetus had tried to be many things—good king, protective father, dutiful son, loving husband—and his decision to find someone to die for him tears the mask off all these respectable roles. He has alienated his two old parents; he has given his children the spectacle of a father who deliberately lets their mother die; and he has surely lost the respect of his subjects. He does try to salvage some semblance of lifelong marital faithfulness by giving in to Alcestis' deathbed request that he never marry again and force a stepmother upon her children. He even imagines having an image made of her that he will keep in his bed as a constant reminder of his promises of fidelity. He also announces after her death that from now on in his palace there will be no more festivity with music and dance. But he seems well on the way to forgetting his promise, when Heracles, having left the palace after discovering Alcestis' death, returns shortly thereafter with a veiled slave girl he claims he won as a prize in a wrestling match. What the spectators know, but Admetus does not, is that the "slave girl" is actually Alcestis, whom Heracles has heroically saved from the clutches of the god of death. As the last step in destroying Admetus' narcissistic illusions about himself, Heracles asks him to take the girl into his household for safekeeping. Admetus initially refuses, alleging that he would not be able to protect her from the advances of all the young men at his court. Heracles then asks him to take care of her himself in his own quarters; Admetus, true to his promise of postmortem fidelity to Alcestis, refuses indignantly. But Heracles again is quite insistent, asking him to take the veiled woman into his apartments, holding her in his own right hand—a gesture that would have reminded the Athenian audience of the marriage ceremony, in which the groom holds the bride with his right hand before lifting her veil. The scene is clearly fraught with comic irony, which reaches its apogee when Admetus reaches out to her, but turns his head to one side in order to avoid looking directly at her, stressing the extreme difficulty of what he is doing, by comparing himself with the hero Perseus beheading Medusa (Euripides 1998: 42). One imagines that this bathetic comparison would have brought down the house in the theater of Dionysos in Athens. Admetus, an amiable coward who was incapable of keeping his promise to the woman who died for him, is about to do exactly what he promised Alcestis not to do—take another woman into his chamber—and in the process outrageously compares himself with the great hero Perseus, who cut off the Gorgon Medusa's head! (Advised by Athena, Perseus had, in the well-known myth, turned his head to one side in order to see Medusa reflected in the polished surface of his shield, thus protecting himself from her petrifying gaze, while he sliced off her head with his sword.) The comic irony is crystal clear: Admetus, regardless of how he sees himself, is no heroic Perseus at all, but rather the opposite: a weak-willed and self-indulgent man who cannot stay faithful even for a day to the memory of the wife who died for him.

But the ultimate irony, of course, is that it is actually his wife Alcestis' hand he has taken. The poignant dramatic symbolism of this mock-heroic scene is obvious. Symbolically, Admetus—without yet knowing it—is marrying Alcestis for the second time; in modern terms, it is a kind of renewal of vows. Furthermore, there is a subtle sexual dimension to the scene. Alcestis is presented to him at first, not as the possibly intimidating and guilt-making figure of the heroic wife who died for him and came back from the dead (to haunt him?), but rather as a concubine, that is, in terms of the easy sexual availability of a young slave girl. Although his fear of the feminine is of mythological proportions (the allusion to the Gorgon's head possibly reminding the audience of Odysseus' panic at the end of Book 11 of the *Odyssey*, when he imagines the "gorgonesque head of a terrible monster" and bolts from Hades), the scene not only shows Admetus symbolically overcoming this fear ("cutting off the Gorgon's head"), but also as practicing the one virtue he seems capable of practicing, which is generous and unconditional hospitality.

Thus Admetus' attempt to refashion himself as the virtuous widower, which represents his last chance to salvage some shred of respectability from the shipwreck of his deflationary degradation, is doomed to failure, and, to follow the analogy of Jung's churchwarden, he is forced to see just what "a plain rascal" he really is. This honest insightfulness about himself at midlife involves coming to terms with his shadow, that is, with the fact that he is a liar and a cheat, who is incapable even for a moment of keeping his promises, as well as a coward, who is unwilling to face his own death. Why else would the drunken Heracles have proffered the advice of facing the inevitability of dying one's own death, living life to the full, and accepting the hazards of fortune? This is proper advice for a fun-loving rascal, not for a hero. And, since a hero is what Admetus most emphatically is *not*, it is time for him to stop deceiving himself and to accept his limitations with good humor.

But Admetus' midlife transformation, for all its comic dimension (realizing what a "plain rascal" he is), also has a more serious aspect, and that involves a coming to terms with his fear of the feminine. Admetus is the mythic paradigm of someone who has an extraordinary fear of death, and this implies that he is also, on some level, extraordinarily afraid of life. Fear of death and fear of life go together, because life and death are inextricably linked. And more particularly, one can say that what Admetus seems to fear in life is the simple fact of joyful sexuality, such as having a good time with a pretty young slave girl, even after his wife has just died for him. That is perhaps why the drunken Heracles's admonition "to honor Aphrodite" might be a totally unnecessary piece of advice for most men, but it makes perfect sense for someone like Admetus. But there is more. Since the young slave girl is actually his wife, Alcestis, in disguise, he is actually accepting her into his chambers as a woman who is guaranteed, by her status of slave, to be submissive to his desires, and as a woman who inspires neither fear nor guilt. Heracles has cleverly initiated a process whereby Admetus and Alcestis will put the past behind them (and what a dark past it is!) and once again enjoy a happy marriage together, including a renewal of the sexual pleasure they take in each other's company—something that might not happen if, for his part, Admetus were to be not only paralyzed by the guilt of having let her die in his place, but also overawed by what we will see is a transformed Alcestis, an Alcestis of numinously heroic stature, and not the wife he used to know.

For if Alcestis is initially presented to Admetus under the guise of a potential sexual playmate, that is not the only symbolic import of the last scene; if it had been, the play would have ended in a purely comic mode, with a husband discovering that the concubine a friend has brought to him was actually his wife in disguise. No doubt, there is such a comic dimension in the denouement, but the final image of Alcestis as the play comes to an end is much more serious and provocative. Her silence in the last scene is at first puzzling; one would expect her to have something to say to her husband at this dramatic moment of reunion, but in fact she says not a word. It has been argued that, since only two speaking actors were allocated to this particular play, there was no way to have Admetus, Heracles and Alcestis speaking on stage at the same time. Since it was the actor who played Heracles who probably had also been given the role of Alcestis, this actor would not have been able to play both roles simultaneously, and another actor in a nonspeaking capacity would have been delegated to play Alcestis as a silent role in the final scene. But Alcestis' silence was bound to be seen as puzzling by at least some of the spectators, and so Euripides provided a partial explanation by having Heracles say that Alcestis was still consecrated to the gods below, and would be allowed to speak only after the third day. A fair explanation—but is that all there is to it?

I believe that there is much more to it than that, and that Euripides has transformed a technical problem (the unavailability of a third speaking actor) into the occasion for a very impressive piece of stagecraft and visual drama. The unexplained silence of a veiled Alcestis on stage would have had an increasing dramatic effect. As Alcestis stands silent next to Heracles, it is the visual aspect of the drama that works the magic. Her standing silently on stage next to the august figure of the hero Heracles suggests analogies between the two figures that would have intrigued and challenged the Athenian patriarchal imagination. Their similarity was clear: both had just saved the life of someone else by confronting death and putting their own life in jeopardy; both, in other words, were heroes. Thus what Admetus sees, or would see if he knew what the audience was seeing, is his wife transformed into a hero, that is, into someone worthy of honor, rituals and prayers—a figure of mythological grandeur fully deserving to stand next to Heracles.

Honoring a woman as a hero was not entirely foreign to Athenian culture, however. The American School of Athens identified in the 1970s the remains of a shrine, in all likelihood the Leokorion, which was known to have been dedicated to the daughters of the Athenian king Leos, who were honored as heroines for having given their lives in order to stop a plague from decimating the population. Offerings to them consisted of gifts women would appreciate, such as mirrors and perfume boxes. But shrines to female heroes were, all the same, most uncommon, and that is why the words of the chorus, just before Heracles brought the veiled Alcestis on stage, would have had such an impact on the Athenian audience:

> Never think of her tomb as the same as the mounds
> Of the dead gone by, but more like a shrine of the gods
> And a pilgrim's place to pray. Climbing the path
> That winds along, a passerby will say:
> "Here lies she that saved her consort. Now
> She is a blessed spirit . . . Lady, I
> Salute you. Bless us." Thus will pilgrims cry.
>
> (Euripides 1998: 38)

The word *daimon*, that Paul Roche translates by "blessed spirit," was ordinarily used in ancient Greek to refer to the spirits of the great heroes of the Golden Age, whose help (as would be the case later with Christian saints) could be solicited through prayers and sacrifice. Thus, when the silent figure of the veiled Alcestis comes on stage at the side of Heracles, the audience was already prepared, following the lead of the chorus, to see her as just such a *daimon*.

The play is thus not only about how good luck came in the end to Admetus through his exemplary hospitality to Heracles, but also how Alcestis came to attain the status of a hero. Although the play remains focused on Admetus (Alcestis' speaking role ends with her farewell to husband and children a bit more than one third of the way through the play), Euripides has provided, as Homer did for Penélopê in the *Odyssey*, a parallel if more sketchy account of a woman's midlife transformation. Her spoken lines defined her early on in the play in recognizably conventional terms as a wife and mother. No doubt, she is already extraordinary in that she resolved, before the play began, to give her life voluntarily for her husband. However, while Heracles' moment of heroic resolve to rescue Alcestis is given full dramatic focus, the play does not show the equivalent moment when Alcestis decided to willingly give her life for Admetus; instead, her spoken lines portray her on stage as a fairly ordinary woman facing the poignant sadness of her approaching death, and realizing with some bitterness that if Admetus had died instead, she could easily have found a fine new husband for herself after his death. Her ordeal and anguish are evoked in recognizably human terms as part of the common tragedy of mortality. When she makes Admetus promise never to marry again, one suspects that it is perhaps not only for her stated reason (that a stepmother would treat her daughter badly and blight her chances for marriage), but also for shadow reasons involving understandable female jealousy—swearing to not remarry would be the least Admetus could be expected to do for her under the circumstances!

All this makes Alcestis' reappearance as an augustly silent figure all the more impressive. She has been put into juxtaposition with Heracles through the exact parallelism of their heroic acts: she has braved death in order to save Admetus; Heracles has braved death (by wrestling with the god Thanatos for her life) in order to save her. But her actual midlife transformation has happened off stage and in silence. The playwright, for whatever reason, has chosen to operate more via visual suggestion than via explicit verbal explanation, in order to present Alcestis as transformed into a heroic figure of mythic dimensions. We may thus view Alcestis by the end of the play as having undergone a remarkable symbolic process of midlife initiation, with its crisis of abandonment, and its latent archetypal pattern of ordeal, death, rebirth and transformation.

As for Admetus, although he may have attained by the end of the play a kind of honesty about himself and a respect for the feminine in the form of his wife that was sorely lacking when he allowed her to die for him, he seems to be much the same man he already was, minus the inflation and the self-deception, and so his was perhaps more of a partial than a radical transformation. It was his friend Heracles, a drunken but wise midlife mentor figure, who had reawakened the life-enhancing vitality of this "likeable fellow" full of weaknesses, but with one saving virtue (his capacity for unconditional and generous hospitality), and had thus enabled him to renew himself in the midst of his grief, anguish, guilt and depression. If nothing else, one can imagine him as no longer afraid of life and death. That would in itself be a significant change.

But for Alcestis the transformation was far more radical. Her initiatory drama could not have been more intense; her freely chosen self-sacrificial death eventually changes her completely. As in the case of Penélopê and Inanna, her integration of fearlessness and male heroic force is clearly suggested, and in the end a changed woman, having been through an extraordinary ordeal, she emerges fully in possession of herself. That perhaps explains her dignified silence in the last scene: she has no need to criticize Admetus or to resent the ordeal through which she has been put. Of course, the audience can only speculate after the play ends as to how Admetus and Alcestis might pick up their relationship. But one thing is sure: Admetus will never look on Alcestis in the same way again and, for him, as for the audience, the image of Heracles will always remain partially superimposed upon that of Alcestis, reinforcing her newly acquired heroic stature and showing how a particular form of male heroism—the life-saving generative heroism of Heracles—can be integrated into a woman's psychic life as well.

Surely one of the most memorable midlife romances in history involved the Roman general Mark Antony and Cleopatra, Queen of Egypt. The ancient historian Plutarch preserved their story for the ages, and his Greek text, translated into English (from the French of Jacques Amyot) by Sir Thomas North and published as part of *The Lives of the Noble Grecians and Romans* in 1579, was eventually to inspire Shakespeare, who in his early forties followed Plutarch's account quite closely in his tragedy *Antony and Cleopatra* (c.1607). Although the play might be thought of as a magnificent story of tragic love along the lines of *Romeo and Juliet* (a tragedy of young love written when Shakespeare was turning thirty), it is even more a story of death and transfiguration, with midlife transformation as the primary theme developed in the last two acts. By the end of the tragedy, Cleopatra and Antony are no longer what they were at the beginning, since each has gone through an ordeal that has changed them radically.

Antony at the opening of the play is presented as a great Roman general in the throes of a serious midlife crisis. After a long history of political and military successes in his earlier years, he has put his great name and reputation in jeopardy by falling passionately in love with the Egyptian queen Cleopatra. This is something that his fellow commanders, officers and men consider degrading and humiliating, especially for a Roman. His friend Philo represents the Roman consensus, when he criticizes the "dotage" that has made Antony "the bellows and the fan / to cool a gypsy's lust" (Shakespeare 1984: 41). But Antony, although he admits that some "gray / do mingle with our younger brown" hair, considers himself, for all his "grizzled head," to be the equal of any younger man:

> Yet ha' we
> A brain that nourishes our nerves, and can
> Get goal for goal of youth.
> (Shakespeare 1984: 41)

This illusion about himself—that he is as young as ever—is put increasingly to the test in the course of the play by his rivalry and then outright conflict with the younger general Octavius (the future emperor Augustus), whom he disparages as "the boy Caesar," and considers to be a mere "novice" who "wears the rose / of youth upon him" (Shakespeare 1984: 33). Although Octavius in turn considers him to be an "old ruffian" (Shakespeare 1984: 136), he has great respect for the hero Antony once was, and says so publicly in a long speech, in which he praises Antony's past fortitude and valor (Shakespeare 1984: 59–60). But, by the end of the play, Octavius will have put Antony in his place, first defeating him at the naval battle of Actium, and then at the siege of the Egyptian capital of Alexandria. Antony's painful realization will be that it is Octavius, and not he himself, who is now the young, successfully self-assertive hero. This realization does not come easily to him, for, if he is not the hero he once was, who is he?

Antony has also begun to have doubts about his relationship with Cleopatra. So far he has been able to balance successfully the Roman and the Egyptian sides of his life, even though his men grumble that he is betraying his Roman heritage of effective military action by leading a soft life in Egypt with Cleopatra, whom they stigmatize as a gypsy, a witch, a serpent and a whore. When Antony receives news of his wife Fulvia's death, his first reaction is to resolve to end his affair with Cleopatra: "These strong Egyptian fetters I must break / Or lose myself in dotage," he says, declaring, "I must from this enchanting queen break off." "She is cunning past men's thought," he muses; "would I had never seen her" (Shakespeare 1984: 49–50).

Antony has come at midlife to a fork in the road, and is unable to decide which path to follow: the Roman path of military glory, or the Egyptian path of sensual passion—all for love, and the world well lost. He first tries to shore up his Roman side and by strengthening his alliance with Octavius and accepting the hand of his sister Octavia in marriage. But this political marriage yields to the force of his passion for Cleopatra, whose seductive ploys he finds impossible to resist, and his alliance with Octavius is soon over. Antony's military star begins to set, when he makes the bad strategic error of taking Cleopatra's advice to fight Octavius by sea rather than by land, and then compounds the error by losing the naval battle of Actium, because he allowed himself to leave the battle to rush after her "like a doting mallard" (Shakespeare 1984: 121) when she panics and flees from the battle in her ship. Antony blames her for his defeat, but is also honest enough to admit that his own fault was in being powerless to resist rushing after her:

> Egypt, thou knew'st too well
> My heart was to thy rudder tied by th' strings,
> And thou shouldst tow me after. O'er my spirits
> Thy full supremacy thou knew'st, and that
> Thy beck might from the bidding of the gods
> Command me.
> > (Shakespeare 1984: 124)

In the end, it is the Egyptian path of sensuality and passion, and not the Roman path of military glory and heroism, that Antony chooses to take, and this choice involves him in a period of subjugation to the feminine,

which makes him less and less of a general, and more and more of a lover—
Cleopatra's doting lover. Since Antony has always taken pride in being the
descendant of the great hero Hercules, it is all the more disquieting for his
soldiers, when they hear strange music playing at their camp at Alexandria,
to realize that

> 'Tis the god Hercules, whom Antony loved,
> Now leaves him.
>> (Shakespeare 1984: 140)

However, as the action of the play reaches its culmination, Antony, left
by Hercules, is actually in the process of *becoming* Hercules—but not the
heroic Hercules, vanquisher of monsters, but rather the suffering Hercules,
brought low by a woman. In the well-known myth, Hercules had decided to
remarry, and was perhaps surprised when his first wife Deianeira sent him a
beautiful garment as a wedding present. But Deianeira had a reason for this
apparent generosity. Years before, at her own wedding, the centaur Nessus
had tried to rape her, and, dying from the arrow that Hercules shot into his
side, had told her to take a vial of his blood; if ever her husband should lose
interest in her, she was to smear a bit of his blood on an article of his
clothing; his blood would then prove to be a powerful love potion, that
would enable her to regain his love. In reality, however, this was a vicious
lie: the dying centaur's blood proved to be a fatal poison that burned
Hercules' skin atrociously when he put on the poisoned shirt. Unable to
take off "the shirt of Nessus," and realizing that his time had come,
Hercules built a funeral pyre and immolated himself upon it.

This is the mythic pattern to which Antony now conforms in his own
way, and it testifies to a fateful inflation on his part with the mythic figure
of his heroic ancestor. Believing that Cleopatra has betrayed him and gone
over to the side of Octavius, he falls into a rage and threatens her with
violence. As he rants and rages, Antony is in a near psychotic state, in
which he identifies himself with his mythical ancestor Hercules (Alcides):

> The shirt of Nessus is upon me; teach me,
> Alcides, thou mine ancestor, thy rage.
>> (Shakespeare 1984: 157)

But Cleopatra has not in fact betrayed him, and she now wishes only to find
a way to cure him of his insane rage. So she takes refuge in a tall monument
nearby, and has her servant tell Antony that she has committed suicide,
hoping that his grief for her supposed death will return him to reason.
Antony, however, is so shocked by the news of her suicide that he orders his
servant Eros to kill him with his sword, realizing in the end that he is no
longer the herculean Roman hero he once was, and that this youthful

heroic self needs to die. The scene in which he slowly has his armor removed represents symbolically his realization that he is "no more a soldier"—that he is no longer the hero he was in his youth, and that, from now on, the identity that corresponds to his actual situation and to his deepest feelings will be that of the lover of Cleopatra for all eternity:

> I will o'ertake thee, Cleopatra, and
> Weep for my pardon.
> . . .
> I come, my queen!—Eros!—Stay for me.
> Where souls do couch on flowers, we'll hand in hand,
> And with our sprightly port make the ghosts gaze.
> (Shakespeare 1984: 157)

But Eros (so named in Plutarch, and the name is wonderfully appropriate for the servant of the great lover Antony) cannot bring himself to kill his master, and takes his own life instead, leaving Antony to do the job himself:

> My queen and Eros
> Have by their brave instruction got upon me
> A nobleness in record. But I will be
> A bridegroom in my death, and run into't
> As to a lover's bed.
> (Shakespeare 1984: 159)

In spite of his desire to end his own life gloriously as he imagines Cleopatra has done, Antony botches his own suicide, confirming that, even as regards heroic suicide (a death much respected in Roman culture), he is not the hero he used to be. His last scene, in fact, is grotesquely unheroic, but at the same time completely appropriate to the grand passion that unites him to his lover. Cleopatra's maids have to heave Antony aloft into the upper story of the monument, where the once great hero finally takes his leave of the world lying in Cleopatra's arms. It is, in its way, a worthy end for Antony: he has been 'raised up' and consecrated in his new identity as Cleopatra's magnificent lover.

As for Cleopatra, once she has lost Antony to death she will undergo a midlife transformation of her own. She refers to her years of youthful folly (during which she had an affair with Julius Caesar and bore him a child) as her "salad days," when she was "green in judgment" and "cold in blood." But her passionate love for Antony has changed her. Coming into her own sexually and emotionally at midlife, she toys with an appealing inflation, which links her to the goddess of love, Venus, the divine model of seductiveness and sexual power. Antony's friend Enobarbus, who is suspicious of

Cleopatra, and admires her only reluctantly, nevertheless sings her praises enthusiastically as he describes her at a festival on the Nile:

> For her own person,
> It beggared all description: she did lie
> In her pavilion, cloth-of-gold of tissue,
> O'er picturing that Venus where we see
> The fancy outwork nature;

Even in her middle years, he says, she is as sexually irresistible as a love goddess, having access to archetypal powers of seduction that cause even the priests to bless her when she is feeling sexy ("riggish"):

> Age cannot wither her, nor custom stale
> Her infinite variety: other women cloy
> The appetites they feed, but she makes hungry
> Where most she satisfies; for vilest things
> Become themselves in her, that the holy priests
> Bless her when she is riggish.
>   (Shakespeare 1984: 77)

In a later scene, Caesar refers indignantly to a report that Cleopatra had dressed herself as the goddess Isis, and showed herself to the people, even going so far as to give audience in this mythological costume. Thus it is clear Cleopatra plays with the idea of being a goddess—a dangerous game, in that it is based on an inflation on her part with an archetypal content of the unconscious.

But it is not to be Cleopatra's fate to maintain this inflated goddess identity forever. Antony's death shocks her out of it, and in her deflated state she realizes that it is her fate, now that Antony is dead, to suffer the ordeal of utter abandonment, and to feel what any woman—even a milkmaid—would feel in such tragic circumstances:

> No more than e'en a woman, and commanded
> By such poor passion as the maid that milks
> And does the meanest chares [chores].
>   (Shakespeare 1984: 164)

Although she is urged to make an alliance with Octavius, now that Antony is dead, she is unmoved by such practical considerations, for she has had a dream, which, like Philoctetes' vision of Heracles, is for her both a religious experience and a transformative image. She tells her maids how Antony in the dream appeared to her as a numinous image of the Cosmic Man, or what Jungians would call the Self:

I dreamt there was an Emperor Antony.
Oh, such another sleep, that I might see
But such another man. . . .
His face was as the heav'ns, and therein stuck
A sun and a moon, which kept their course and lighted
The little O, the earth. . . .
His legs bestrid the ocean: his reared arm
Crested the world . . .
                              (Shakespeare 1984: 173)

Having dreamt this dream, she can no longer identify herself with her role as Queen of Egypt, or take steps to preserve her imperial power, even after Octavius promises to let her set her own terms of surrender, and to be, not her master, but her friend. But she does not believe his promises, and resolves to take heroic steps to end her own life—a resolve that she identifies with a kind of male heroism, and which clearly marks her capacity to integrate the kind of heroic masculine energies that were exemplified by her lover Antony:

My resolution's placed, and I have nothing
Of woman in me: now from head to foot
I am marble constant: now the fleeting moon
No planet is of mine.
                              (Shakespeare 1984: 179–180)

Thus she plans to trick Octavius, to evade cleverly the surveillance of his men, and to commit heroic suicide through the bite of an asp she has had brought to her hidden in a basket of figs.

Cleopatra's new identity becomes clear as she faces her heroic suicide. She rejects the inflated identity of the love goddess that she enjoyed as Antony's ever seductive and beguiling mistress, and rather seeks to be called simply his wife, something she has never mentioned before in the play, which represents the result of her deflated coming down to earth as a woman no different in her "poor passion" than the "maid that milks / And does the meanest chares":

Methinks I hear
Antony call: I see him rouse himself
To praise my noble act. I hear him mock
The luck of Caesar, which the gods give men
To excuse their after wrath. Husband, I come:
Now to that name my courage prove my title!
                              (Shakespeare 1984: 181)

Laying claim to this new identity as Antony's wife will cap Cleopatra's midlife transformation. Her life comes to a moving conclusion, as she confirms her new identity as his wife by a heroic suicide that is decidedly more effectively managed than Antony's had been. Her self-chosen death represents not only literally the strength of her heroic resolve, but also symbolically the radical nature of her transition into a new identity as wife. At the end of the play Cleopatra has attained heroic status through her brave and clever suicide, and a certain nobility as the consort of Antony, acknowledged even by the Romans. Antony and Cleopatra's joint funeral becomes, for Octavius and his soldiers, an occasion of "great solemnity," and Octavius now finds them "famous" rather than infamous, declaring that

> No grave upon the earth shall clip in it
> A pair so famous . . .
> (Shakespeare 1984: 183)

Throughout *Antony and Cleopatra* one looks almost in vain for a figure who could be said to play the role of midlife mentor. Cleopatra is no doubt advised by her women companions, but no one of them is of the stature to be seen as a mentor. But, for Antony at least, there is one character whose mentor status is indicated by the fact that he is a soothsayer, and so someone who is in touch with the gods and with the secret workings of fate. Early on in the play he alone understands the nature of the hidden dynamics of the relationship between the older Antony and the younger Octavius, which he explains in mythological and symbolic language as a conflict between their two guardian angels (spirits or daemons)—a conflict that cannot work to Antony's advantage, when the two Roman generals are at close quarters:

> Thy daemon, that thy spirit which keeps thee, is
> Noble, courageous, high, unmatcheable,
> Where Caesar's is not. But near him thy angel
> Becomes afeard, as being o'erpow'red; therefore
> Make space enough between you . . . .
> If thou dost play with him at any game,
> Thou art sure to lose; and of that natural luck
> He beats thee 'gainst the odds. Thy luster thickens
> When he shines by; I say again, thy spirit
> Is all afraid to govern thee near him;
> But he away, 'tis noble.
> (Shakespeare 1984: 78–79)

This was excellent advice. Unfortunately, Antony is unwilling to listen to it, and dismisses the soothsayer rudely. Had he listened to him, he would not have entered into a disastrous marriage with his rival's sister Octavia, and then provoked Octavius by quickly abandoning his new wife for Cleopatra. And—above all—he would have avoided direct confrontation with Octavius. Thus Antony had found in the soothsayer a midlife mentor of a sort, but failed to listen to him. Consequently, whatever transformation and realization he attained in the end came too late to do him any good.

As for Cleopatra, she seems to be very much her own guide, with no mentoring figure to assist her. But, upon further reflection, perhaps it is not fair to see Cleopatra as being totally on her own at her moment of midlife transformation. Cleopatra throughout most of the play is presented as charmingly seductive, but also as given to impulsive acts (cf. her sudden escape from the naval battle of Actium) and extravagant gestures, having Antony brought false news of her suicide being the most histrionic. She has in essence a youthful persona, which has served her well up to the point of Antony's suicide—a suicide provoked precisely by her most ill considered and impulsive action. But after his death her life takes a more serious turn, and increasingly she seems to assume the role of a dignified mature woman making carefully thought out decisions. Her new capacity for strategic thinking is manifested in her negotiations with Caesar, and especially in her plan to commit suicide in spite of Roman surveillance. From the last scene of Act IV to the end of Act V her language is serious and on a high tragic plane, with none of the banter and clever repartee that characterized it before. But who, if not Antony, had inspired this radical change of character? In her dream of Antony as "Emperor" and Cosmic Man she has clearly projected onto him the kind of calm, impressive authority that in reality was conspicuously lacking in his frantic life and grotesquely botched suicide, or for that matter in his near psychotic rages against her.

So it makes sense to see in Cleopatra's vision of Antony after his death both a transformative image for her as well an inner mentoring figure, with which the real Antony deserved to coincide to some degree, most notably through his love suicide. Thus it is this "ghostly guru" Antony, given new authority through Cleopatra's projection onto him of archetypal mentoring contents, who proves capable of convincing her through the example of his heroic suicide that it is indeed possible to die for love, with the world well lost. This is a lesson Cleopatra learned well and put into practice almost immediately, becoming in the process a figure now worthy of even Caesar's admiration. Just before her death, she has, like Antony, come into her own—too late to do her any long-term good, but still soon enough for her to finish her life as a woman radically transformed.

Chapter 7

Modernist midlife initiations: Marcel in Proust's *Time Regained* and Clarissa in Woolf's *Mrs Dalloway*

Two great writers of the period immediately after World War I, Marcel Proust and Virginia Woolf, intuited that the ordeal of the war had a latent affinity with the ordeal involved in individual transformation, particularly at midlife. Their novels *Time Regained* (1927) and *Mrs Dalloway* (1925) will provide us a rich illustration of the ways in which the modernist imagination could evoke the full process of midlife transformation. For both novelists, the collective suffering of World War I and its aftermath provided the historical backdrop for their narratives of symbolic death and rebirth at midlife.[1]

The length and brutality of the war brought mutilation and death to millions and extensive damage and destruction to many of northern France's most beautiful cathedrals, churches, cities and villages. Marcel Proust, whose love for Gothic art and architecture had been stimulated by his reading of John Ruskin and of the pioneering medieval scholar Emile Mâle, published an anguished article on the "assassinated cathedrals of France," at a time when the shock of the unparalleled destruction was making its impact, and the urgent need for postwar reconstruction and restoration was being confronted. In the case of his fictional narrator Marcel (a stand in for the author, but only up to a point), death and rebirth were internalized as symbolic themes in the midlife transformation of a failed writer, who suddenly experiences a rebirth into joy and creativity that is the dramatic culmination both of the long novel *In Search of Lost Time* and of its final section *Time Regained*. To what degree this initiatory transformation corresponded to the actual lived midlife experience of the author, who had been working on *In Search of Lost Time* from about the age of thirty-six to his death at age fifty-one, we have no way of knowing for certain. But this hardly matters, since what is important is not the possible autobiographical subtext in the life of Marcel Proust, but rather the fact that Proust succeeded so brilliantly in making Marcel's bizarre and almost miraculous midlife transformation not only plausible but fully comprehensible.

Time Regained from beginning to end is structured by the presence of a midlife initiation process that leads from stagnation to a new and generative identity for the narrator Marcel. The volume breaks into three parts of roughly equal length. The first part describes the effect of World War I not only in terms of general death and destruction, but also and especially in terms of its particular effect on Marcel's own life. Marcel had spent much of the war away from Paris in two different sanatoriums, in the second of which the "cure" (which did not cure him of anything, he says) was mainly through "isolation." Ineffectual as the cure may have been, in initiatory terms this long retreat into solitude may be said to have constituted for him a period of liminality—of separation from the social world and from familiar surroundings—in which the seeds for his future transformation were allowed to germinate. In fact, Marcel has nothing much to say about this period, except that "many years passed" (Proust 2003: 238) As time passed, even the memory of his romance with Albertine began to fade, to the point where he could no longer remember clearly the feelings he once had for the last great love of his youth. What was equally disconcerting for him was that his faith in the supreme value of literature and in his own potential as a writer had disappeared as well. Marcel is thus not only at a physical distance from his familiar social world in Paris, but also at an inner distance from his own life as constituted by memory and emotion. This leads him to a depressive state of stagnation, in which his hopes for the future disappear along with the vividness of his memories of the past.

The narrator makes two brief visits to wartime Paris in order to renew contact with the world he has left behind—the first time in 1914, the second in 1916. There the effects of the war have become more and more apparent, as the German front is only a short distance from the city. The sound of distant bombing, the presence of warplanes in the sky and nightly curfews make it clear that Paris is a city under attack. Not only has Paris changed, but Combray, the beloved village of some of the most significant and vivid memories of Marcel's childhood, has become the scene of one of the war's most destructive engagements; even its beloved church has been destroyed.

Along with this destruction in the physical world comes the death of friends and associates. In particular, Marcel is deeply troubled by the death of his aristocratic friend Robert de Saint-Loup, who died heroically in battle, covering his men's retreat. "For several days I remained shut up in my room, thinking of him" (Proust 2003: 146), writes the narrator.

> He must have been truly magnificent in those last hours. The man who throughout his life, even when sitting down, even when walking across a drawing-room, had seemed to be restraining an impulse to charge, while with a smile he dissembled the indomitable will which dwelt within his triangular head, at last he had charged.
>
> (Proust 2003: 232)

Marcel attends Saint-Loup's funeral in the soon-to-be-destroyed church of Saint-Hilaire in the village of Combray, and sees in him now not so much the individual who had been his friend, but a medieval knight who had died leading a charge, a noble scion of the ancient Guermantes family:

> This Guermantes had died more himself than ever before, or rather more a member of his race, into which slowly he dissolved until he became nothing more than a Guermantes, as was symbolically visible at his burial in the church of Saint-Hilaire at Combray, completely hung for the occasion with black draperies upon which stood out in red, beneath the closed circle of the coronet, the G of the Guermantes that he had again in death become.
>
> (Proust 2003: 232)

Behind this narrative of Saint-Loup's aristocratic funeral it is possible to see the mythological motif of the death of the young hero, and to appreciate the symbolic role it plays in Marcel's midlife crisis, where Saint-Loup's heroic and premature death helps bring the whole idealistic world of Marcel's youth crashing to the ground. Marcel himself is no longer the up and coming young hero of the literary world; his ambitions and talents have faded, and his middle age begins to emerge as a disappointing sequel to a youth full of promise.

Finally, to such scenes of death and destruction, with their initiatory resonance of symbolic death, are added scenes of decadence and regression. Marcel discovers that his older friend the Baron de Charlus has been sinking into a senile turpitude after a heart attack, and is rapidly becoming a shadow of his former self. "How unfortunate it is that M. de Charlus is not a novelist or a poet!" (Proust 2003: 204) he says to himself. But M. de Charlus had never been anything other than a dilettante when it came to art, and had unfairly accused the younger Marcel of being the same. But now Marcel fears that, in spite of his earlier ideals and aspirations, he may never become a great writer, and indeed that literature may not be the high calling he once thought it was. M. de Charlus, once a rather admirable figure for Marcel with his aristocratic devil-may-care dash and elegance, now in his dotage plays a kind of shadow role for Marcel, reminding him of the shipwreck of his own idealism concerning the value of literature, the failure of his high aspirations to realize themselves in the career of a writer, and the end of his youthful creative energy and originality. The decadence and turpitude of M. de Charlus's present life is an unpleasant reminder for Marcel that his own life is on the edge of a downward slope. He, too, is in the process of becoming the shadow of his former self, at least in the sense of identifying himself with a shadow that appears as dilettantish, frivolous, weak willed and incapable of the sustained efforts of genuine artistic creation. This shadow identification—fortunately Marcel will soon feel quite differently about himself as an artist—produces in him a midlife depressive state that was arguably the ultimate cause of his having committed himself to a sanatorium for several years, although without finding there any cure for his malady.

The homosexual brothel that M. de Charlus owns and sponsors, and that Marcel discovers accidentally when he suddenly seeks refuge in a building during a bombing alert, inspires him with even more somber shadow thoughts about the ultimate failure of will power as the origin of all vice. He judges the brothel's high-class clients severely: "the appearance of each one had in it something repugnant, a reflexion . . . of their failure to resist degrading pleasures" (Proust 2003: 210–211). In Marcel's opinion, what had brought them together in this degrading place was "that greatest of all vices, the lack of will-power which prevents a man from resisting any vice in particular" (Proust 2003: 212). Charlus himself now appears to Marcel as "this consenting Prometheus [who] had had himself nailed by Force to the rock of Pure Matter," although he allows that "in this Pure Matter it is possible that a small quantum of Mind still survived" (Proust 2003: 215). Charlus, for all his unruly white hair and beard, has become in his dotage, according to his faithful servant Jupien, nothing more than a big child. His childish regression comes as a great shock for the usually imperturbable narrator Marcel. One wonders why he reacts so strongly . . .

This moral censoriousness on the part of Marcel is indeed rather untypical of him, and has all the marks of a shadow projection. One begins to suspect that Charlus and the patrons of the brothel must remind him of some side of himself he would rather not look at too closely. This becomes evident when later he reveals to the reader what he considers to be the crucial event of his childhood. "The night that was perhaps the sweetest and the saddest of my life," he reveals, was when his mother, with his father's permission, for once agreed to stay with him in his bedroom and indulge his insistent desire for her presence as he fell asleep. That moment of indulgence marked, he believes, the beginning of "the decline of my health and my will, and my renunciation, each day disastrously confirmed, of a task that daily became more difficult" (Proust 2003: 287). It was this failure of will power that had led him eventually to become what he feels he is now, that is, a would-be writer, who has despaired of his capacity and will to realize his creative ambitions. This tragic failure of will that brought him to such a degraded state of mind was also what had brought Charlus and the high-class patrons to the brothel—depressing thoughts indeed!

Having finally left for good his sanatorium, the site of his long midlife liminal period, Marcel returns to Paris, and makes his way across the city to a reception and concert at the Guermantes townhouse. In initiatory terms, he is about to make his reentry into society. But, unfortunately, he is untransformed and in what appears to be a state of permanent stagnation. His fate seems to be to become once again the dilettantish man of the world he was before his reclusion. Only now it is worse, since he is acutely aware of what he takes to be his "lack of talent for literature" as well as of "the non-existence of the ideal in which [he] once believed" (Proust 2003: 238). Consequently, he feels that there is no point in depriving himself any more of the pleasures of social life, because

> the famous "work" which for so long I have been hoping every day to start the next day, is something I am not, or am no longer, made for and perhaps does not even correspond to any reality.
>
> (Proust 2003: 240)

He has accepted this particular invitation from the Guermantes, just as he anticipates he will accept many others of the sort as he resumes his career as a social butterfly, because he is now convinced that he is a failed artist, who has nothing better to do with his life.

But just as Marcel seems resigned to his melancholy fate, a miraculous process of transformation for him suddenly gets underway. It comes as a complete surprise to him:

> But it is sometimes just at the moment when we think that everything is lost that the intimation arrives which may save us; one has knocked at all the doors which lead nowhere, and then one stumbles without knowing it on the only door through which one can enter—which one might have sought in vain for a hundred years—and it opens of its own accord.
>
> (Proust 2003: 254–255)

For Marcel, it will be a totally unexpected sequence of events that will lead him to his rebirth as a human being and as an artist. Although Marcel's midlife initiatory process itself is genuinely bizarre in some of its concrete details, these concrete details can be taken as a good reminder of the unique personal nature of individual experience, even in the context of the archetypal. The sequence is ultimately comprehensible, however, in more general terms, as an experience of timelessness, joy and fearlessness in the face of death, even though the actual events that stimulate the process of transformation seem anchored in ordinary and even banal reality.[2]

The first of these "resurrections," as he calls them, takes place just as he enters the courtyard of the Guermantes townhouse. Moving quickly to one side to avoid an oncoming vehicle, he almost stumbles because of an unevenly placed paving stone and, for no apparent reason, all his discouragement disappears in an instant and he enters into a state of felicity, in which

> all anxiety about the future, all intellectual doubts had disappeared, so those that a few seconds ago had assailed me on the subject of the reality of my literary gifts, the reality even of literature, were removed as if by magic.
>
> (Proust 2003: 255)

Marcel then begins to have a sort of waking vision, in which his eyes are flooded with azure light, and he senses cool freshness in the air. He then tries to discover the origin of these visionary perceptions. The chauffeurs waiting in the courtyard are highly amused by the spectacle of Marcel rocking back and forth on his feet between the higher and the lower paving stone, but he persists, determined to discover just what lay behind his extraordinary emotional reaction to an ordinary event. He persists in forcing his mind to discover the origin of the "vision" of light and freshness that has flooded his mind, which has all but made the banal present-moment experience of the paving stones in the Guermantes courtyard vanish from his consciousness. And then suddenly he realizes that it is the vivid memory of being inside the fourteenth-century Baptistery of St. Mark's Cathedral in Venice, where stumbling on an unevenly placed paving stone had given him a similar jolt. It is this memory that has been "resurrected." But, if the initial present-moment experience seems quite banal, by contrast the resurrected memory joined with it awakens an esthetic joy and religious ecstasy associated with light, freshness and a sacred place.

This novel experience of the memory of a past moment flooding and almost overwhelming a present moment is repeated a few minutes later, as Marcel waits in the drawing room library for a pause in the concert going on in the next room, at which point he will be able to join the other guests. What triggers this particular ecstatic experience is, once again, a moment of the utmost banality: a waiter, trying unsuccessfully to avoid making any noise, inadvertently knocks a spoon against a plate. The resulting sound gives Marcel the same feeling of joy, but this time it is associated with a sensation of heat mixed with the smell of smoke and the freshness of a forest setting. He is able this time to quickly locate the memory that is the origin of this sensation. As he was traveling from his sanatorium to Paris, his train had stopped for a moment in a little wood, and a trainman had been knocking his hammer against a train wheel for some reason or another. Once again, the memory of that moment and of that sound, both to all appearances quite banal, turned out to be of great significance: it was at that moment that Marcel realized that the beauty of the light falling on a row of trees in the forest had failed to move him;[3] he had found the row of trees boring, both as a spectacle and as a subject for poetic description, and this proved to him once again that his artistic capacities had so atrophied that even his capacity to respond to Nature had simply disappeared.

But this briefly described "resurrection" is quickly followed by a third. A waiter brings him a selection of pastries and a glass of orangeade—again, there is nothing especially interesting in this banal experience. But it triggers a new ecstatic vision:

> I wiped my mouth with the napkin which he had given me; and instantly, as though I had been the character in *The Arabian Nights*

who unwittingly accomplishes the very rite which can cause to appear, visible to him alone, a docile genie ready to convey him to a great distance, a new vision of azure passed before my eyes, but an azure that this time was pure and saline . . . so strong was this impression that the moment to which I was transported seemed to me to be the present moment.

(Proust 2003: 258)

This memory concerns the hotel of a Channel resort he frequented in his childhood, and the precise trigger for it is the feeling of the rough texture of the napkin the waiter has given him. This tactile sensation brings to mind the feeling of the overly rough texture of the towel he used to dry himself with years before as well as the view from his hotel window onto the sea.[4] This merging of a past moment with the present moment fills him with feelings of an inexplicable delight. Once again, an ordinary experience has triggered the experience of something not only personally significant as a memory (the seashore resort of his childhood), but also archetypally numinous as a poetic evocation (the azure splendor of the sea), which fills him with joy.

At this juncture, Marcel realizes that he may be asked to enter the reception room at any moment, and that he must quickly, before the pause in the concert, seek to uncover the *meaning* behind these disparate experiences. Proust devotes the next thirteen pages of his text to the narrator's ruminations and reflections—something that in real narrative time could only have lasted a few moments. Marcel eventually comes to the conclusion that the cause of his blessed feeling of felicity and of deep sensation of renewal is his discovery that a part of his own being must be located outside of time, and that it is this extratemporal side of himself that is able to experience both past and present moments simultaneously. It is the rebirth or resurrection of this being in him that not only gives him an intense feeling of happiness, but also frees him from the fear of death:

A minute freed from the order of time has re-created in us, to feel it, the man freed from the order of time . . . one can understand that the word "death" should have no meaning for him; situated outside of time, why should he fear the future?

(Proust 2003: 264–265)

Thus Marcel's midlife initiation, with its ordeal, presence of death all around him, and the revelation of a new set of ideals to replace those he has abandoned, finally culminates in a spiritual rebirth thanks to several brief ecstatic moments, during which he attains to a kind of contemplation of eternity. His experience has all the elements of a religious conversion— without being clearly associated with any specific religion, however. Or rather, his experience is what William James would have recognized as a "variety of religious experience," an experience of a very personal sort of the timeless nature of the soul. Marcel's midlife transformation is thus first and foremost a spiritual transformation, and there are good reasons for Marcel to refer to the experiences that bring it on as "resurrections."

The specific message that accompanies Marcel's midlife transformation can be characterized as an individually crafted form of Neoplatonic mysticism. Underneath the banal sensory experience (the "sensation") of the present moment (the uneven paving stones, the sound of the spoon knocking against a plate, the stiff napkin) is hidden a corresponding experience in the past that can only reveal itself spontaneously through involuntary memory. But the point is not so much the specific nature of the experience or even the specific meaning attached to it, but rather the realization that in himself there is a timeless being who experiences both past and present simultaneously, and who is thus capable of seeing the world *sub specie aeternitatis*, that is, who can glimpse the timeless essence of things in the midst of the flux of ordinary sensate experience. The realization of this new being is the equivalent of a powerful transformative image of a highly spiritualized dimension.

For Marcel, underneath the "sign" there lies a "hieroglyph" (a "sacred sign"), the contemplation of which is analogous to the contemplation of the world of Ideas in Plato's philosophy, which is not too distant from Jung's theory of the archetypes as the basis of human experience. Marcel gives a particular example of this, highlighting the Platonic dimension of the teaching through the word "Idea" capitalized in the text:

> Every individual who makes us suffer can be attached by us to a divinity of which he or she is a mere fragmentary reflexion, the lowest step in the ascent that leads to it, a divinity or an Idea which, if we turn to contemplate it, immediately gives us joy instead of the pain we were feeling before—indeed the whole art of living is to make use of the individual people through whom we suffer as a step enabling us to draw nearer to the divine form which they reflect and joyously to people our life with divinities.
>
> (Proust 2001: 303–304)

Marcel's sense of rebirth into a timeless realm in which death has no existence involves an *askesis*, a difficult turning away from the world in order to plunge into one's own inner psychic depths. But the process is nevertheless made possible by ordinary sense experiences linked with the memory of past sense experiences.

Marcel's rebirth as a spiritual being—as someone whose innermost being is experienced as existing outside of time—coincides with his rebirth as an artist. He now feels himself to be willing (because he has regained his belief in the value of literature) and able (because he now feels full of creative energy and strength of purpose) to be a writer, and it is in relation to this new identity that the generative side of his midlife transformation makes itself evident.

For it is not only that Marcel feels able at last to write a great novel, and that such a task seems well worth doing to him. It is also that he feels connected to his future readers in an unusual way—that he feels able to help them significantly in their own lives. Marcel proposes to help his future readers change their lives in a radical way. His object is to help his readers attain through literature to a sense of their own "real life":

> Real life, life at last laid bare and illumined—the only life in consequence which can be said to be really lived—is literature, and life thus defined is in a sense all the time immanent in ordinary men no less than in the artist. But most men do not see it because they do not seek to shed light upon it.
>
> (Proust 2003: 298–299)

The generative function of the novel that Marcel now intends to write will be to provide an inspiration and a model for readers who wish to turn away from the surface of life and to dive into its depths:

> In reality, every reader is, while he is reading, his own reader, the reader of his own self. The writer's work is merely a kind of optical instrument which he offers to the reader to enable him to discern what, without this book, he would perhaps never have perceived in himself.
>
> (Proust 2003: 322)

Proust returns to this theme and to this optical simile in the final pages of *Time Regained*, when he again calls his future readers "readers of themselves," and states that reading his book would be a bit like a visit to an optician, who would say, "Look for yourself, and try whether you see best with this lens or that one or this other one" (Proust 2003: 322). Although some of what his readers will find in themselves, and what Marcel has found in himself, will remain subjective and incommunicable, the fictionalized account of his own discoveries—the translation into a public language of his own private, and to some degree incommunicable, inner text—will provide an inspiration for others to undertake similar journeys of in-depth self-exploration, during which they too will catch a glimpse of their inner self outside of time and of their own "real life."

Although he has lost the fear of death, Marcel admits that he is now worried that his death might prevent him from finishing his novel. This worries him, because his book would be a treasure that he could pass on to posterity—something that would enrich his readers with the same joy and expansiveness of spirit that he has now gained for himself. His subjective delight in contemplating the new identity as a writer to which he has acceded, is not primarily selfish and egotistical—or rather, its egotism is now useful to others. So now he fears death, not for himself, but for his book. The generative concern for others and for the work that will connect him with his future readers and will help make them into readers of themselves—of the book they all have inside them—is now of paramount importance, and has displaced the self-centered and morbid concern for his health that characterized his liminal phase of stagnation at the sanatorium.

Marcel's entry into a new stage of life characterized by creativity and generativity involves also letting go of his fixation on what he considers to be the primal scene of his childhood—the origin of his childish mother dependency, and of his corresponding ill health and lack of will power. This confrontation with his regressive infantile self occurs as another "resurrection of memory," although it is one that brings more psychological insight than joy. After the three ecstatic moments that changed his life, and after having reflected at length on their meaning, still waiting in the library of the Guermantes's townhouse, Marcel accidentally—synchronistically, Jungians would say—takes down from one of the shelves a copy of George Sand's classic novel for children *François le Champi* (1848) and desultorily opens it:

> I felt myself unpleasantly struck by an impression which seemed at first to be utterly out of harmony with the thoughts that were passing through my mind, until a moment later, with an emotion so strong that tears came to my eyes, I recognized how very much in harmony with them it was.
>
> (Proust 2003: 281)

This sorrowful impression plunges him into his own unconscious depths, and he reacts angrily, as though to the sudden appearance of a stranger who has come to do him harm. He then realizes with a start that this "stranger" is actually himself, that is, the child he once was, suddenly resurrected by his picking up a book randomly from the library shelf. But the book is of tremendous personal significance, for it is the book his mother once read out loud to him all night almost until dawn—a night that he considers to have been "perhaps the sweetest and the saddest of my life" (Proust 2003: 287). For it was on this night that his mother gave in for the first time to his pleas to stay with him (the goodnight-kiss scenario), and it is to her unfortunate collusion with his regressive and neurotic wishes that he dates "the decline of my health and my will, and my renunciation, each day disastrously confirmed, of a task that daily became more difficult" (Proust 2003: 287). So on this, the most beautiful day of his life, he says, there also appears the memory of the sweetest and saddest night of his life, which confirmed him in his unhealthy and neurotic dependency on his mother's affection, when he had succeeded for once in winning the Oedipal battle with his father, by taking his mother away from him and having her all to himself all night long. This Pyrrhic victory set him up, he believes, for a lifetime of morbid ill health and lack of energy and determination.

Proust does not say anything about the content of the children's classic itself, probably because it would have been familiar to most of his readers in France at that time. But for today's reader it needs to be noted that *François le Champi* has a plot that is quintessentially Oedipal. It is the story of a young peasant woman Madeleine who discovers a child abandoned in the fields (a *champi*, "field child") and raises the foundling as her own child. At the end of his teenage years the young man leaves her in order to strike out on his own. But when he returns several years later, he and Madeleine fall in love with each other and get married. In other words, François winds up marrying the only mother he has ever known. Proust did not need to underline the irony of his choice of the book that would have revealed to his narrator Marcel the depth and intensity of his Oedipus complex. Marcel's painful insight into the depths of his mother attachment enables him to recognize the continuing presence of the neurotic child within him, but then enables him to bid him farewell. His midlife coming to terms with the regressive pull of childhood memories is especially appropriate now that he has decided to undertake the great creative and generative work of his adult years.

As Marcel revisits the memory of his childhood's most significant moments, he remembers also that what had announced to him the imminent arrival of his mother in his bedroom for their Oedipally fateful goodnight kiss was the sound of the jingling bell of the garden gate. This was the little bell that let him know that at last M. Swann had left his family's dinner table in order to return home, and that his mother would be coming up the stairs to kiss him goodnight. The sound of the little bell becomes, in the last two pages of the novel, the reference point for the narrator's internalization of his childhood memories, which he now intends to use as material for his literary project:

> I was terrified to think that it was indeed this same bell which rang within me and that nothing I could do would alter its jangling notes. . . . In order to get nearer to the sound of the bell it was into my own depths that I had to redescend. And that was because the peal had always been there, inside me, and not this sound only but also, between that distant moment and the present one, unrolled in all its vast length, the whole of that past which I was not aware that I carried about within me.
>
> (Proust 2003: 529)

Time Regained thus ends with a farewell to childhood, but at the same time it heralds the composition of the novel to be written with these memories as some of its raw materials.

Two typical elements of the midlife transformation have not been discussed so far in relation to Proust's *Time Regained*: the resurgence of the anima and the appearance of the midlife mentor. As regards the first, it should be stressed how much Marcel at midlife is shown to be subject to moods of discouragement that must have had a strong anima component. If Jung's negative anima had once tried to convince him that his visions were "art," Marcel's anima did the opposite, and tried to convince him that he was washed up as an artist. Marcel's acute sense of failure as an artist has the hallmarks of an effect of a negative anima's subtly discouraging insinuations. His isolation for several years in a sanatorium seems to have brought this irrational discouragement to a head. But, after his trans-formative experiences in the library of the Guermantes townhouse, it is interesting to note how one particular figure suddenly stands out in the aging crowd at the reception in the concert room next to it. It is Mlle. de Saint-Loup, the daughter of his late friend Robert, and she seems to embody in this crowd of increasingly decrepit seniors the magical beauty of the ever youthful anima: "I thought her very beautiful," he says; "still rich in hopes, full of laughter; formed from those very years which I myself had lost, she was like my own youth" (Proust 2003: 507). This type of senti-mental effusion is not typical of Marcel, who tends towards more subtly introverted and complex expressions of feeling. No doubt, having experienced her unexpected and magical charm, Marcel quickly passes on to thoughts about the artistic masterpiece work he now feels able to undertake. But his fleeting vision of Mlle. de Saint-Loup has the effect of an invigorating encounter with the Muse, with the creative anima, full of life and hope for the future.

As regards the presence of a midlife mentor—or "ghostly guru"—this is a role best allocated to Charles Swann. "As Marcel grows up," writes Wallace Fowlie, "he acknowledges Swann's mystical paternity" (Fowlie 1975: 285). It is to the memory of Swann's habitual after-dinner departure through the garden gate at Combray that Marcel's memories turn at the very end of the novel, as we have seen. If the memory of his mother coming upstairs to give him the dangerously Oedipal goodnight kiss reveals the roots of what Marcel considers to be the tragic weakening of his will and of his eventual failure as an artist, the memory of Swann seems to represent that which in his childhood provided a temporary obstacle to this fatefully repeated event. In other words, Swann, in coming between him and his mother, had acted unknowingly as a kind of godfather figure. His was an adult male presence, which provided a salutary barrier between the child Marcel and his excessive and overwhelming desire for his mother's love and affection. Swann thus embodied a principle of psychological balance, whose full effect would not be felt until years later in the "resurrection" scenes of *Time Regained*. Also, in keeping with the somewhat reverential attitude the narrator maintains towards him later in his life, Swann, unlike so many other characters in the novel, is not shown as undergoing any significant negative alteration before his death; he remains in Marcel's memory as an admirable if somewhat limited man whose basic goodness, like that of Leopold Bloom in Joyce's *Ulysses*, is not questioned.

Swann's special place in the mind and memory of the narrator is shown by the way Proust commemorates him in *Swann in Love*, a short novella-length section near the opening of *In Search of Lost Time* that is often read separately from the novel itself, partly because it is somewhat disconnected from the rest of the long novel, being set back in time before the narrator's birth, and reads well as a short narrative text in its own right. It is as though the narrator, in attempting to understand and to represent his own life and his eventual transformation at midlife, needed first to go back to a time before his own birth in order to understand the young adult years of Charles Swann. Swann, after a period of intense erotic confusion and anguish, finally married his long-term mistress Odette, and thus bade farewell to the passionate anima obsession of his youth by marrying a woman, who, he recognized too late, was not really his type of woman at all. Recreating the life of the younger Swann was for the narrator an unusual move, to say the least, but one that seems in the end justified, if one considers how much Swann represented for the young Marcel a godfather figure, a "male mother," to use Robert Bly's term for the mentor (Bly 1992: 182). Swann continues beyond the grave (he dies less than half way through the novel) to influence the course of the life of his godson. Swann's tortured and obsessive love for the high-class courtesan Odette de Crécy, who both deceives and enchants him, as described memorably in *Swann in Love*, established the template for the narrator's own passionate obsession with Albertine. In short, it was Swann who provided Marcel with a model for part of his own youth, whether he realized it fully then or not.

But, unlike Swann, who married the great love of his youth Odette, Marcel never marries Albertine. He thus avoids making what he comes to feel was Swann's greatest mistake in life, which was to fail to realize that love can find its fulfillment only in art, not in life. Thus the "little musical phrase" of the composer Vinteuil's sonata, which had so ravished Swann's ear, had not led him in the end to recognize the superiority of art over life; this insight was beyond his capacity to realize and to apply to his own life. So Swann's ultimate midlife mentoring message, accepted by Marcel and realized fully after Swann's death, was a teaching given via negative example. Admirable as he was in so many respects, Swann was not an artist, and so, on this day of all days of midlife transformation, Marcel realizes that he must leave his mentor behind. Such is the nature of Marcel's new vision of himself that he can finally see Swann's personal limitations

and the mixed nature of his message: "art is important, but not as important as life and love." For Marcel, after his midlife transformation, the truth
is just the opposite: art is more important than life or love. Wallace Fowlie,
referring to Swann's death earlier in the novel, sees its ultimate significance
for Marcel as "the death of the old king [meaning] the birth of the new
king" (Fowlie 1975: 285). Swann, by compensating with his male presence
for Marcel's tragic Oedipal bond with his mother, but also by providing a
clear negative example of the failure to recognize in art a higher ideal than
life and love, became, through the power of the memory he left in Marcel's
mind, the "ghostly guru" of his midlife transformation and of his rebirth as
"a new king."

In Virginia Woolf's novel *Mrs Dalloway*, the fifty-two-year-old Clarissa,
on a sunny day in June in London not long after the war, suddenly feels
herself to be abandoned by those she loves most, and then emerges from
her quiet ordeal transformed into a woman confident in herself, fearless in
the face of death, and with a new understanding of the generative significance of her ability as a hostess to bring people together. *Mrs Dalloway*
was published in 1925 (two years before the posthumous publication of
Proust's *Time Regained*), when the author was in her early forties. As with
Proust, the novel is a chronologically compressed narrative, dealing with
the events of a single "day of all days." Clarissa's midlife transformation
may not seem quite as dramatic as Marcel's; it proceeds in small steps and
is evoked through subtle touches. But the same general archetypal paradigm of midlife initiation may be seen at work here as well as in *Time
Regained*, although in the differing mode of female midlife initiation we
have examined earlier.

By the end of that warm day in June, Clarissa's old friend Peter Walsh,
who has always been highly critical of her and of her frivolity and social
snobbism as a "perfect hostess", suddenly sees her at the party in the
last scenes of the novel in a totally different light. But what has happened
to Clarissa between morning and evening that has made Peter change
his opinion?

Clarissa's party is scheduled to be held in the evening, near the time of
the summer solstice. The sun, as it moves towards setting in the course of
this warm day in June, provides an obvious solar symbol in *Mrs. Dalloway*
for the decline in the second half of life. Woolf shares with Jung, but need
not have gotten from him, the image of the course of life as the rising and
the setting of the sun, with the moment of its greatest height at noon (and
particularly around the time of the summer solstice) marking the beginning
of the descent at midlife. And so it is with Clarissa, for "age had brushed
her; even as a mermaid might behold in her glass the setting sun on some
very clear evening over the waves" (Woolf 2005: 190). Clarissa finds herself
wondering on "this having done with the triumphs of youth, lost herself in
the process of living, to find it, with a shock of delight, as the sun rose, as

the sun sank" (Woolf 2005: 181). What she sees in herself now as a delight in the process of living is associated in her mind with the Shakespearean tag "fear no more the heat of the sun" (Woolf 2005: 182), part of a song in *Cymbeline* (IV.2), whose theme of death and of the end of youth Clarissa seems to have half forgotten, since she does not quote in her mind the rest of the stanza ending with

> Thou thy worldly task has done,
> Home art gone, and ta'en thy wages;
> Golden lads and girls all must,
> As chimney-sweepers, come to dust.

But Clarissa is not about to finish with her "worldly task." In the opening scene of the novel, she has sallied forth to buy flowers for the party she will host later in the day. As she walks, she relishes the ever-changing spectacle of London's street life. Poised between youth and old age, she is on the edge of realizing that her own sun has begun its inexorable descent: "she felt very young; at the same time unspeakably aged." At the same time, she begins to fear abandonment: "she had a perpetual sense, as she watched the taxi cabs, of being out, out, far out to sea and alone" (Woolf 2005: 8). In particular, she has begun to fear that she is about to be abandoned by her husband, Richard—a feeling that is reinforced by the arrival of a luncheon invitation to Richard from the sixtyish Lady Bruton that failed to include her. A serious cardiac episode ("since her illness she had turned almost white" [Woolf 2005: 36]) a short while before had resulted in her sleeping in an attic room separate from Richard, in a single bed, and the sight of this isolated bedroom arouses more depressive thoughts of loneliness. She feels that her time is running out: "narrower and narrower would her bed be. The candle was half burnt down . . ." (Woolf 2005: 30). Her fears of abandonment culminate in a sudden ordeal of anguish and despair:

> It was all over for her . . . Richard, Richard! she cried, as a sleeper in the night starts and stretches a hand in the dark for help. Lunching with Lady Bruton, it came back to her. He has left me; I am alone for ever, she thought, folding her hands upon her knee.
>
> (Woolf 2005: 46)

In fact, there is really no reason to suspect that Richard will abandon her. The reader knows that he has just purchased a bouquet to give to her on his return home, with the intention of assuring her that he loves her, although he will actually not be able to bring himself to tell her this. However, Clarissa's ordeal, although grounded on baseless fear, is real for her as an inner psychological experience of anguished abandonment.

Clarissa's morning peregrination through the streets of London is accompanied by thoughts of her own death. Then the song from *Cymbeline* reminds her of the tragic deaths that resulted from World War I, just recently ended. This motif of death, crucial for the initiatory theme of death and rebirth, finds poignant expression in the novel in the figure of Septimus Smith, a shell-shocked veteran of the war, whose delusional state of mind has brought his young Italian wife, Rezia, to utter despair. Their tragic fate is described at great length in the novel in a series of separate episodes culminating in the scene where Septimus commits suicide by throwing himself out of a window. Later in the day, at Clarissa's party, the wife of Sir William Bradshaw, one of the two doctors who had unsuccessfully tried to treat Septimus, describes to Mr. Dalloway how her husband had received a phone call announcing the suicide: "a young man . . . had killed himself. He had been in the army." Clarissa thinks immediately, "in the middle of my party, here's death" (Woolf 2005: 179).

The plot of *Mrs Dalloway* is not only oriented around the banal events leading to the party Clarissa will host later in the day. The unexpected arrival of Peter Walsh, her old friend and the man she almost married before she chose Richard instead, complicates matters greatly for her, and brings her midlife crisis to a head. For Peter had been not only her closest male friend in her youth, but also her severest critic; his censorious remarks still plague her memory. If the animus represents to some degree the internalized image of male chauvinist misogyny and its carping criticism of women and their ways, Peter, a man she has not seen in years, and who exists for her primarily as a memory of her youth, has, in her mind, taken on the aspect of a somewhat negative animus figure, the carping critic in her inner psychological life. "If he were with me now, what would he say?" she asks herself during her walk on the streets of London that morning.

> How he scolded her! How they argued! She would marry a Prime Minister and stand at the top of a staircase; the perfect hostess he called her (she had cried over it in her bedroom), she had the makings of the perfect hostess, he said.
>
> (Woolf 2005: 7)

When they finally meet again, Peter still plays in real life the role of carping critic. Having surprised her at home while she mends a beautiful party dress:

> "And what's all this?" he said, tilting his pen-knife towards her green dress.
> He's very well dressed, thought Clarissa; yet he always criticizes *me*. . . .

What an extraordinary habit that was, Clarissa thought, always playing with a knife. Always making one feel, too, frivolous; empty-minded; a mere silly chatterbox.

(Woolf 2005: 40, 43)

If Peter, with his knifelike cutting remarks, embodies the resurgence at midlife of the animus for Clarissa, his effect on her is not by any means wholly negative.

In fact, at this midlife junction, when Clarissa is taking stock of the life she has lived so far, Peter's criticism, once simply irritating and distressing to her, now challenges her to justify her life to herself and what she has made of it— not just having chosen to marry the dull but successful Richard Dalloway, but also having made herself into the "perfect hostess." Peter's reappearance forces her to rethink her life, and to validate for herself the personal values that lie behind the apparently conventional social role she has chosen for herself. As we will see, Clarissa's coming into her own at midlife involves not an external change in life style, but rather an internal change of attitude—an increased level of consciousness that involves gaining more insight into herself and coming to the realization that what Peter takes for female superficiality is actually her greatest strength: the love of life accompanied by the power to "watch" and "understand" it (Woolf 2005: 189).

The character of Peter Walsh provides Woolf with the occasion for representing a male figure undergoing a parallel midlife crisis, which the author evokes in some detail. Peter, who is fifty-three, just a year older than Clarissa, has just returned from India after many years of service to the British colonial government—years that have gone largely unrewarded, as he is now in limbo, without a job, casting around for whatever opportunities his friends such as Richard may be able to steer him towards. Before he left India, he had begun an affair with a twenty-four-year-old Englishwoman named Daisy, the wife of a major and mother of two small children. The purpose of his return to England is ostensibly to make legal arrangements for her divorce, so that he can get married to a young woman who is less than half his age. But, upon telling Clarissa all this, "he burst into tears; wept; wept without the least shame, sitting on the sofa, the tears running down his cheeks" (Woolf 2005: 45). Peter is in the midst of a midlife mess, emotionally as well as professionally. His love for Daisy has all the hallmarks of a midlife return to youthful romanticism inspired by the resurgence of his anima: "only one person in the world could be as he was, in love," thought Peter to himself, like a moonstruck teenager, and he firmly believed that he "was now really for the first time in his life, in love" (Woolf 2005: 47–48). This resurgence of the anima at midlife has gotten him into a serious midlife crisis, especially as he realizes now that it is not so much that he is in love with Daisy as that the young woman is in love with him, and that she is about to sacrifice her marriage for him. A certain cool lucidity takes over his mind, as he considers the difficult situation. Still, things could be worse: "he had not felt so young for years" (Woolf 2005: 51). His anima fascination, problematic as it is in terms of its social consequences, feels vivifying to him. Suddenly his gaze was arrested by the sight of a young woman who

> seemed, Peter Walsh thought (susceptible as he was) to shed veil after veil, until she became the very woman he had always had in mind; young, but stately; merry, but discreet; black, but enchanting.
>
> (Woolf 2005: 51)

He follows in the steps of this enchanting image of his ever-youthful anima, until she disappears behind a door. But shortly afterwards something happens to Peter—something genuinely visionary. Sitting on a bench in Regent's Park next to a "grey nurse" who is knitting, he falls asleep and has a long dream, in which he

> looking up, suddenly sees the giant figure at the end of the ride . . . advancing down the path with his eyes upon sky and branches he rapidly endows them with womanhood; sees with amazement how grave they become; how majestically, as the breeze stirs them, they dispense with a dark flutter of the leaves charity, comprehension, absolution, and then, flinging themselves suddenly aloft, confound the piety of their aspect with a wild carouse. . . . myriads of things merged in one thing; and this figure, made of sky and branches as it is, had risen from the troubled sea (he is elderly, past fifty now) as a shape might be sucked up out of the waves to shower down from her magnificent hands compassion, comprehension, absolution.
>
> (Woolf 2005: 55–56)

This maternally colored anima dream of trees turned into female figures,[5] and then into one single figure who offers him "comprehension" and "absolution," is an ecstatic moment for him—a glimpse through a dream into the archetypal world of the feminine, where "compassion, comprehension, absolution" are offered to him freely. From his fascination with the anima image he had projected onto a young woman in the street, Peter has followed the royal road of dreams into the depths of his unconscious, where he discovers the anima herself in a moment of visionary insight.

But to return to Clarissa: her midlife passage involves not only confronting the animus criticism she associates with Peter Walsh, but also the reemergence of her own shadow side. Clarissa has discovered that she is capable of feeling intense hatred: she hates Miss Kilman, her daughter Elizabeth's tutor. Or rather, she realizes, in what can be taken as a real insight into the nature of shadow projection, that

It was not her one hated, but the idea of her, which undoubtedly had gathered in to itself a great deal which was not Miss Kilman; had become one of those specters with which one battles in the night; one of those specters who stand astride us and suck up half our life-blood, dominators and tyrants; for no doubt with another throw of the dice, had the black been uppermost and not the white, she would have loved Miss Kilman! But not in this world. No.

(Woolf 2005: 12)

This "brutal monster," as she calls "this hatred," the resurgence of her shadow at midlife, has been plaguing her, especially since her illness:

the brute . . . made all pleasure in beauty, in friendship, in being well, in being loved and making her home delightful rock, quiver, and bend as if indeed there were a monster grubbing at the roots, as if the whole panoply of content were nothing but self love! this hatred!

(Woolf 2005: 12)

Miss Kilman does to some degree deserve this hatred, in that she has—or at least to Clarissa appears to have—an inappropriately close relationship with her young tutee, which the novel later analyzes as something close to a lesbian passion, or at least the passion of a frustrated woman at forty who feels that no man will ever care for her. But in this respect as in others, Miss Kilman presents a mirroring shadow image of Clarissa at her worst and most despairing. Clarissa is afraid she is losing both her husband and her daughter at the same time; Miss Kilman mirrors her fear of being past her prime and becoming unloved and abandoned. Miss Kilman is a religious fanatic who uses her religion to disguise her hatred of the world that she feels has treated her so badly; Clarissa's defining fault is also hatred: her hatred of Miss Kilman. Clarissa wants desperately to hold on to Elizabeth; so does Miss Kilman. Miss Kilman also presents the negative image of someone who is not dealing well with her midlife passage; at age forty she is besotted with Clarissa's seventeen-year-old daughter, Elizabeth, and this attempt to satisfy the unfulfilled needs for intimacy of her youth is regressive and—as the narrative makes clear—probably doomed to failure. Woolf also presents Miss Kilman's religious conversion as a regressive move that consolidates an attitude of rejectivity, the dystonic opposite of syntonic generativity, that in Kilman's case expresses itself in her resentment of the happy and the prosperous, and in the kind of Christian moralism that delights in the anticipated punishment of sinners.

But Clarissa, at least at some moments, has the moral strength and the self-deprecating humor that allow her to withdraw her shadow projection from Miss Kilman—the shadow projection that had turned her daughter's lonely and frustrated tutor into a veritable monster:

> Odd it was, as Miss Kilman stood there (and stand she did, with the power and taciturnity of some prehistoric monster armoured for primeval warfare), how, second by second, the idea of her diminished, how hatred (which was for ideas, not people) crumbled, how she lost her malignity, her size, became second by second merely Miss Kilman, in a mackintosh, whom Heaven knows Clarissa would have liked to help. At this dwindling of the monster, Clarissa laughed.
>
> (Woolf 2005: 123)

It might even be said that Clarissa, who is altogether a little too submissive and conventionally nice (to her husband, to her social world, to Peter), integrates in the latter part of the novel some of the shadow nastiness represented by Miss Kilman, although she expresses it in her own more refined way; and that this partially integrated side of her shadow allows her to be more active and aggressive in resisting Peter's carping criticism and in standing up for herself and the choices in life she has made.

The shadow contains repressed contents of all sorts, including memories repressed for reasons of social convention and a concern for respectability. The need to return to one's memories of youth and childhood at midlife, and the need to revisit and finally understand them, is part of the process of coming to terms with the shadow at midlife, and this process finds expression with Clarissa, as it did with Proust's narrator Marcel. In fact, the parallelism between Clarissa and Marcel in this respect is quite striking, as each protagonist's single most obsessive memory of youth involves the scene of a kiss. With Marcel, it was the desperate waiting for his mother's presence and bedtime kiss (a wish finally granted) that became the locus of a long-term neurotic conflict only resolved at midlife. With Clarissa, it is the moment before her marriage to Richard Dalloway, when she and her best friend Sally Seton, a girl whose flaunting of convention was notorious in their circle, were walking up and down on the terrace of her family's country house:

> Then came the most exquisite moment of her whole life passing a stone urn with flowers in it. Sally stopped; picked a flower; kissed her on the lips. The whole world might have turned upside down! The others disappeared; there she was alone with Sally.
>
> (Woolf 2005: 35)

Revisiting this memory enables her to conclude, philosophically, with the distanced appreciation of a midlife perspective, that "this falling in love with women" was also a form of love. "Take Sally Seton; her relation in the old days with Sally Seton. Had that not, after all, been love?" (Woolf 2005: 32). So there is, it would seem, a repressed lesbian side to Clarissa's shadow that she is now able to acknowledge, understand and integrate as "another form of love."

If Marcel's move into midlife generativity involved writing a novel, Clarissa's involves giving a party. This is something she has done many times before as the "perfect hostess" of Peter's critical strictures, and Peter believes that Clarissa is just repeating herself—that she is bound to a conventional pattern of social activity that has not varied for years. From such a critical perspective, her party-giving would represent more stagnation than generativity. But, as the events of the day unroll, Clarissa comes to new realizations about herself that change completely the perspective she has on her party-giving.

First of all, she realizes that both her husband and Peter are wrong about her:

> Her parties! Both of them criticised her very unfairly, laughed at her very unjustly, for her parties. That was it! That was it! Well, how was she going to defend herself? Now that she knew what it was, she felt perfectly happy. They thought, or Peter at any rate thought, that she enjoyed imposing herself; liked to have famous people about her; great names; was simply a snob in short. Well, Peter might think so. Richard merely thought it foolish of her to like excitement when she knew it was bad for her heart. It was childish, he thought. And both were quite wrong. What she liked was simply life. "That's what I do it for," she said, speaking aloud, to life.
>
> (Woolf 2005: 118)

As she continues in this line of thought, she imagines Peter once again playing the role of her relentless critic (the negative animus side of his relationship with her):

> But suppose Peter said to her, "Yes, yes, but your parties—what's the sense of your parties?" all she could say was (and nobody could be expected to understand): They're an offering; which sounded horribly vague.
>
> (Woolf 2005: 118)

Clarissa, as she rests "cloistered" on her sofa, is experiencing at this moment of introspective solitude a major shift in consciousness about herself. Rather than seeking to avoid or deflect the criticism of Peter, she is now countering his criticism directly with a clear analysis of how she really feels about life (she simply loves it!) and the offering she makes to life (her parties). And what are parties for her? she asks herself. She continues to refine her analysis of giving parties as a generative activity, the one such activity of which she is eminently capable, and this analysis leads her to a transformative image of great emotional intensity:

Here was So-and-So in South Kensington; some one up in Bayswater; and somebody else, say, in Mayfair. And she felt continuously a sense of their existence; and she felt what a waste; and she felt what a pity; and she felt if only they could be brought together; so she did it. And it was an offering; to combine; to create; but to whom?

An offering for the sake of offering, perhaps. Anyhow, it was her gift. Nothing else had she of the slightest importance; could not think, write, even play the piano.

(Woolf 2005: 119)

The irony of the novel's last scene is that while Clarissa assumes Peter has come to her party only to flaunt his usual critical attitude towards her, in fact he is now struck with admiration for her:

What is this terror? what is this ecstasy? he thought to himself. What is it that fills me with extraordinary excitement? It is Clarissa, he said. For there she was.

(Woolf 2005: 190)

In this way the reader senses indirectly, through Peter's reaction to Clarissa, how momentous and impressive is her quiet transformation into a newly confident woman. She has come into her own at midlife, and can understand and validate the generative nature of the values that express themselves in a number of ways in her life, especially in giving a party. For giving parties is clearly the way Clarissa can manifest what Erikson called the midlife virtue of "care," defined as "a widening commitment to *take care of* the persons, the products, and the ideas one has learned *to care for*" (Erikson 1997: 67). It is her one fully realized form of creativity, and, although the act of giving a party is the same as always, the spirit now is clearly different, in that she is now fully conscious of the deep and almost sacred meaning for her of giving parties—bringing people together as an offering to life—and realizes that it can no longer be associated, as Peter once felt, with "imposing herself" and showing off the famous people who are her guests. Giving a party is her personal form of creativity, not an excuse for indulging self-absorption or stagnation.

Is there any glimpse of a midlife mentor in the story of Clarissa's midlife transformation? There is, in a rather unexpected form. There is an old lady who lives across the road from Clarissa, of whom Clarissa can catch sight from her window, but with whom she has never spoken. Woolf's representation of Clarissa's mentor for this midlife transformation is thus most unusual, in that there is no actual conversation between her and Clarissa; it is a relationship solely based on the realization of an unexpected inner affinity; the sight of the old lady has constellated in Clarissa's psyche the archetypal figure of the Wise Old Woman:

Big Ben struck the half-hour. How extraordinary it was, strange, yes, touching, to see the old lady (they had been neighbours ever so many years) move away from the window. . .

(Woolf 2005: 124)

Clarissa sees in the simple image of the old lady in one room, and herself in another, a powerfully transformative image, which becomes a kind of revelation of the very mystery of life:

that's the miracle, that's the mystery; that old lady, she meant, whom she could see going from chest of drawers to dressing-table. She could still see her. And the supreme mystery . . . was simply this: here was one room; there another.

(Woolf 2005: 124–125)

Although they have lived across from each other for years, her relationship with the old lady across the way is almost pure fantasy on Clarissa's part. The old lady is a screen on which she has projected her need for an older midlife mentoring figure, a Wise Old Woman, who could provide her, through Clarissa simply seeing her,[6] and then by being seen by her in turn, with a mentor's message, the key to what she considers to be the "supreme mystery."

The final appearance of the old lady is clearly synchronistic—it constitutes a meaningful coincidence for Clarissa and confirms the mentoring nature of the old lady's presence across the way. At the crucial moment when Clarissa realizes that she has "done with the triumphs of youth" and has "lost herself in the process of living," she leaves her guests and walks over to the window, parting the curtain in order to look at the night sky:

Oh, but how surprising!—in the room opposite the old lady stared straight at her! She was going to bed. . . . It was fascinating to watch her, moving about, that old lady, crossing the room, coming to the window. Could she see her? It was fascinating, with people still laughing and shouting in the drawing-room, to watch that old woman, quite quietly, going to bed.

(Woolf 2005: 181)

At this moment Clarissa's thoughts return to the young war veteran Septimus Smith (although she does not know his name), the news of whose suicide had so disturbed her as her party was getting under way. But now her feelings about his suicide have changed:

The young man had killed himself; but she did not pity him, with all this going on. There! The old lady had put out her light! the whole house was dark now with this going on, she repeated, and the words came to her, Fear no more the heat of the sun. She must go back to them. But what an extraordinary night! She felt somehow very like him—the young man who had killed himself. She felt glad that he had done it; thrown it away.

(Woolf 2005: 181–182)

Thus by the end of the novel Clarissa has accepted and even welcomed death as a necessary part of her life and of her party—as something just as necessary and normal as the old lady putting out her light. She feels a curious identity with the young man and his freely chosen death, perhaps because he represents for her the symbolic initiatory death that has led to her transformation on this "extraordinary night."

Notes

1 Mathew V. Spano's unpublished thesis "Hermann Hesse's Use of German Romanticism and Indian Spirituality in the Resolution of His Mid-Life Crisis" (2002), shows in rich and persuasive detail how the author of *Siddhartha* (1922) and *Der Steppenwolf* (1927) used his own midlife crisis experience as a springboard for an anatomy of midlife transformation via the medium of fiction. A longer list of modernist midlife heroes would certainly include Leopold Bloom in *Ulysses* (1922), an avatar of the fortyish fellow Odysseus in the *Odyssey*.
2 I have argued elsewhere that these "resurrections," although their immediate content may seem to be so highly individualized and private as to escape any attempt at symbolic interpretation, actually refer to the symbology of the Roman Catholic Mass, itself a ritual of death and resurrection. See S.F. Walker 2003: 390–411.
3 Cf. Monet's famous series of paintings of light falling on a line of poplar trees.
4 In French *serviette* can mean both "napkin" and "towel."
5 Woolf's evocation of this anima dream may well owe something to Paul Verlaine's poem "My Familiar Dream" ("Mon rêve familier," in *Poèmes saturniens*, 1866), where the anima-like figure also combines maternal love, understanding and forgiveness.
6 Cf. the Hindu concept of *darshan*: getting inspiration and guidance by simply looking intently at a spiritual figure.

Chapter 8

Some classical Hindu perspectives on midlife

The discovery of classical Indian civilization, thanks to the editing and translation of ancient Indian texts by Western scholars in the eighteenth and nineteenth centuries, was as momentous in its way as the rediscovery of ancient Greece through the recovery, editing and translation of Greek texts in the Renaissance. This discovery coincided with the realization that Sanskrit, the primary vehicle for classical Indian culture, was a not too distant cousin of the European classical languages Latin and Greek. A whole new field of comparison was thus opened up as the West found that it had a sister Indo-European civilization in South Asia, whose epics, dramas, poetry and philosophical texts were strange and different, and yet distantly familiar. Three classic texts were translated almost immediately: the sacred text *Bhagavad Gita* by Charles Wilkins in 1785; Kalidasa's drama *Shakuntala* by Sir William Jones in 1789; and, again by William Jones, *The Laws of Manu* in 1794. The translation of these three canonical Hindu texts—first into English, and then into some of the major languages of Europe—guaranteed that their cultural influence would spread over the next two centuries in the West. In this final chapter, they will provide us with paradigmatic examples of midlife transformation in a non-Western cultural context.[1]

The Laws of Manu is a compendium of classical Hindu laws and customs, and it includes a presentation of the various stages of life as theorized by the Hindu mind of centuries past and, more particularly for our interests, a brief description of the midlife stage of *vanaprastha*, "forest dwelling" or—to use the subtitle that Henry David Thoreau gave his *Walden*, after he had perused Sir William Jones's translation—"life in the woods." *The Laws of Manu* states that the decision to enter this stage of life is recommended for those of the Brahmin caste, once they have seen wrinkles on their skin, white hairs on their head, and the birth of their grandchildren. No doubt, Henry David Thoreau went to Walden Pond unmarried and, at age twenty-eight his own "life in the woods" was atypical and premature by classical Indian standards, although in America it has been applauded as a highly idiosyncratic and significant gesture of great cultural value. Classical Indian *vanaprastha* involved typically a shift in residence for both the husband and the wife, with the wife either going to live with her sons, or joining her husband in a hermitage in the forest. Since in this stage of life *The Laws of Manu* urged on the couple the voluntary loosening of marriage and familial ties, the couple may be said to have cooperated with the archetypal programming that seeks to establish new values during the second half of life, and to have modified their lives accordingly. In modern America, by contrast, many couples become involved at the onset of midlife in bitter divorce proceedings, then remarry, and start the process of being young and starting a family all over again. America has, no doubt, been a shining example for over a century of a vibrant youth culture that has widely influenced the rest of the world. But, even for Americans, there is much that could recommend itself in the classical Indian *vanaprastha* paradigm, as it traces out a clear path for that revaluation of values that characterizes midlife *enantiodromia*, and thus works with, rather than against, the archetypal pattern of midlife transformation.

"Forest dwellers" were expected to devote themselves to high thinking and plain living, and to struggle to deepen their spiritual life through contemplative and ritual practices, not only for their own benefit, but also for the sake of the physical and spiritual well-being of others. They were thus enjoined to be "compassionate towards all creatures" and to "honour those who visit [the] hermitage with water, roots, fruits and almsfood" (Olivelle 2004: 98). They were urged to be generous to all who sought their aid: to "always be a giver and never a receiver of gifts" (Olivelle 2004: 98). Their lives were held up as a model of spiritual struggle and generativity in the second half of life. The description in *The Laws of Manu* prescribes for them increasingly severe ascetic practices, some of them fairly fanciful, as essential components of a self-imposed ordeal that has their spiritual transformation as its goal:

> He should roll on the ground or stand on tiptoes all day; spend the day standing and the night seated, bathing at dawn, midday, and dusk; surround himself with the five fires [four fires plus the hot summer sun overhead] in the summer; live in the open air during the rainy season; and wear wet clothes in the winter—gradually intensifying his ascetic toil. Bathing at dawn, noon and dusk, he should offer quenching libations to ancestors and gods, and engaging in ever harsher ascetic toil, he should inflict punishment on his body.
>
> (Olivelle 2004: 99)

The violence of some of these ascetic practices can be taken as indicating the spirit of accepting pain and anguish as part of the process of midlife rebirth and transformation.

In 1979 Erik Erikson wrote a preface and an essay for the volume *Identity and Adulthood*, edited by the Indian psychologist Sudhir Kakar. Kakar's opening essay establishes a clear but not exact correspondence between Erikson's stage of "adulthood" and the traditional Hindu *ashrama* (stage of life) of *vanaprastha*. This stage of life, coming after the stage of *garhasthya* (establishing a household) in young adulthood, marks a radical departure from the family centered life of the preceding *ashrama*. As Kakar explains:

> in the Hindu view the later part of the *garhasthya* stage and the *vanaprastha* both deal with generativity and care, one in the narrow sense and the other in a widened sense. . . . Care in the first case was limited to one's own immediate family . . . *Vanaprastha* was followed by an inner withdrawal from family affairs and family ties. The individuals, now being consulted by the community, practiced a widened concept of generativity. The care thus extended from one's own family to the community at large; a man's interest turned from the sphere of the family to the sphere of public affairs.
>
> (Kakar 1992: 9)

Favorably impressed by his discovery of the strength of Hindu religious aspirations, Erikson wrote in his own essay:

> Important among all the forms of generativity . . . is . . . a continuing self-generation, both in the mature personification of the roles of householdership and (as cultivated in all the world religions and specially also in the Hindu tradition) in the promise of an eventual self-transcendence.
>
> (Kakar 1992: 28)

We will find some of these midlife themes beautifully illustrated in Kalidasa's play *Shakuntala*, one of the first texts translated from Sanskrit into English, and long a favorite of Western readers. Like many other classical Indian dramas, it is a long play, with a large cast and many changes of scene. The production of such lavishly organized plays bears witness to the immense wealth of the Indian courts and cities that sponsored them, in contrast to the relative economy of available means of classical Greek drama, with its limited number of actors and simple stage scenery. Kalidasa's play has been compared with Shakespeare's *As You Like It* as a kind of pastoral with a serious point and an idyllic atmosphere. But this comparison hardly does justice to the dramatic complexity and thematic richness of Kalidasa's masterpiece. As Goethe famously put it, entranced as he was by his first reading of the play, "If you want heaven and earth contained in just one name, I say 'Shakuntala,' and all is said."[2]

As Goethe implies, *Shakuntala* does indeed begin on earth and end in heaven, or at least in a sacred space high in the Himalayas. This sacred space—the Himalayan hermitage of the semidivine sage Marica and his wife Aditi—becomes a place of midlife transformation for the wife Shakuntala as well as for her husband King Dushyanta, who had lost her years before, and now recovers her in the last act of the play. This development of the theme of a mutual midlife transformation for a couple can remind the reader of Euripides' *Alcestis*, or for that matter, but more distantly, of Shakespeare's *Antony and Cleopatra*. In all three plays, the identity of both the man and the woman are changed through suffering and ordeal, but with the woman's midlife transformation most clearly and dramatically articulated.

The earlier youthful identities of Shakuntala and Dushyanta are constructed around their romantic roles of a beautiful young orphan raised by the hermit Kanva as her foster-father in his forest ashram, and of a charming young playboy king, who loves to hunt. While Kanva is away, Dushyanta catches sight of Shakuntala after he had been chasing down a deer in the nearby forest. Both characters quickly fall in love, marry quickly according to the *gandharva* rites (marriage by seduction and abduction, considered valid in aristocratic circles), soon must part, but anticipate living happily ever after at the royal court. But almost immediately fate intervenes in the form of the irascible hermit Durvasa, who represents the ascetic and spiritual ideal that is in conflict with the courtly hedonism of the young king Dushyanta. Because Shakuntala has been so absorbed in her thoughts of Dushyanta that she forgets to greet him properly, Durvasa curses her to be forgotten in turn by her husband, a curse he only modifies at the insistence of Shakuntala's girl friends to include the possibility that showing a personal token, like the ring the king has given her, will jog his memory. The ring is thus a means of recognition (hence the Sanskrit title of the play *Abhijnanashakuntalam*, literally "The Story of Shakuntala Recognized by a Token"), as it is the king's own signet ring, and as a shared token also symbolizes the marriage bond between them.

But just as Shakuntala, now pregnant, is on her way to reunite with her husband at his royal court, she accidentally loses his signet ring as she is crossing a river, and arrives at court to find that, not only has Dushyanta forgotten about her completely, as the ascetic had sworn he would, but that she has no token with which to jog his memory. Unable to convince him that she is indeed his wife (actually, the youngest of his several wives), Shakuntala lashes out angrily against him in strong language that would have been quite shocking to Indian cultural sensibilities concerning the proper way for a wife to address her husband—so shocking, that only one manuscript tradition (the so-called Bengali recension, not translated below) preserves all of what was probably its original violence:

Wicked man! You see everything through the distorted lens of your
own heart.
Who else would stoop so low? You cover yourself in virtue like a
derelict well, overgrown with weeds.
. . .

I put my trust in the Puru dynasty, and gave myself to a man
With honey in his mouth but poison in his heart!

(Kalidasa 2001: 66)

Now to all appearances heartlessly abandoned by her husband, Shakuntala
leaves the royal court in a paroxysm of anger and anguish, calling upon
Mother Earth to swallow her up. Shortly thereafter, witnesses appear, who
claim that they saw some mysterious luminous female shape sweep down
and carry Shakuntala off as she was bathing in a sacred pool. The specu-
lation that this supernatural appearance was her mother, the nymph
(*apsara*) Menaka who conceived her after being embraced by a lonely
ascetic, seems justified.

At this point in the play, an Indian audience would have easily seen the
analogy of Shakuntala's ordeal of abandonment with that of Sita in the
great Indian epic the *Ramayana* (now familiar to readers of this book via
the animated sequence created by Nina Paley in *Sita Sings the Blues*). This
lends Shakuntala's story an epic grandeur as a drama of abandonment. The
apparently gratuitously abusive treatment of her by the king, followed by
her return to her divine mother Menaka (it is reported that "a curtain of
light / Shaped like a woman, whisked her away" [Kalidasa 2001: 69]), sets
up a clear parallel to the story of Sita, who, after her final ordeal of being
required by Rama to once again prove her purity, calls upon Mother Earth
to swallow her up, and vanishes forever into the womb of her mother the
goddess Bhumi Devi. The parallel with the *Ramayana* continues, when it is
revealed in the last act that Shakuntala has taken refuge in the celestial
hermitage of the Primal Couple Marica and Aditi, and has given birth there
to Dushyanta's son Bharata, just as Sita had taken refuge in the sage
Valmiki's hermitage and given birth to Rama's twin sons Lava and Kusha.
It is this celestial hermitage that will be the place of her entry into the
vanaprastha stage of life, and it is in her new identity as a "forest dweller"
that she will be discovered by her husband several years later, almost
transformed beyond recognition.

Meanwhile Dushyanta, the erstwhile young hero of the hunt and the
bedroom, is beginning a midlife ordeal and transformation of his own. A
fisherman discovers in the belly of a fish he has just caught in the river a
signet ring; he turns it over to the king, who recognizes it as his own, and
then immediately remembers, as the ascetic had predicted, his love for
Shakuntala and their secret marriage. He is then wracked with anguish,

thinks passionately and regretfully of Shakuntala all the time, and finds himself increasingly unable to fulfill properly his duties as king:

> How can I keep track
> Of my subjects,
> When from day to day
> I have no idea
> Which way I am going myself?
>   (Kalidasa 2001: 87)

His midlife ordeal is suddenly interrupted when he is summoned by Matali, the charioteer of the god Indra, and he agrees to risk his life by fighting a horde of demons that have been harassing the gods. In order to put himself fully at Indra's service, he leaves his family, puts his kingdom in the charge of his chief minister, and departs on Matali's flying chariot.

The generative heroic labor that is asked of him (fighting demons on behalf of the gods) has all the hallmarks of a mythologically oriented oneiric drama, involving the ritual testing of the king, his initiation into another stage of life and his acquisition of a new identity. The initiatory drama is extremely compressed, and takes up only a scene at the end of Act VI and the opening scene of Act VII, the main action (the king's battle against the demons) happening off stage between the acts. It is as though the king has been transformed by a powerful and transformative image of himself playing the archetypal role of the human ally of the great god Indra. But this powerful fantasy risks generating a dangerous inflation in him. Fortunately, this does not happen, or at least does not last long. When, after his victory over the demons, the king receives special honors from the god, he receives them with great modesty in the spirit of humble service to the divine. His state has thus gone rapidly from inflation to deflation. He says to Matali at the opening of Act VII, "I only did what Indra asked of me. That hardly seems to merit the special treatment I've received" (Kalidasa 2001: 90). His humility marks the end of his youthful grandiosity and marks his willingness to engage in generative activity as a warrior king fighting the forces of evil.

The last scene of *Shakuntala* takes place in the hermitage of the two divine parents of humanity, Marica and Aditi (roughly equivalent to Adam and Eve in the Judeo-Christian tradition), who live an ascetic life of *vanaprastha*, like the one described in *The Laws of Manu*. Shakuntala herself appears to the king in an ascetic's traditional garb, which he describes, while he himself turns pale with suffering:

> Her robes are dusky, drab,
> Her hair a single braid,
> Her cheeks drawn in by penance—

In that vow of separation
I so callously began.
          (Kalidasa 2001: 98–99)

In a scene that would have astonished the first audience by its dramatic reversal of the usual deference given by a wife to husband, Shakuntala allows Dushyanta to throw himself at her feet and beg for her forgiveness But when he beseeches her to take back the ring, she simply refuses, saying, "I don't trust it now. You wear it, my lord" (Kalidasa 2001: 100). So, free of the curse represented by the ring, their marriage is now on a more equal footing, and Shakuntala is shown as having come into her own as a midlife woman, both in terms of her devotion to ascetic practices and of her unusual feminine self-assertiveness.

In the context of the traditional Hindu association of widened generativity at midlife with what Erikson had called "eventual self-transcendence" or spiritual self-realization, the classic Hindu text the *Bhagavad Gita* has a special place, not only as a core sacred text of Hinduism, but also as the most widely known and appreciated Hindu sacred text in the Western world. The *Gita* is embedded in the vast compendium of epic narrative texts known as the *Mahabharata*, and the two protagonists of this spiritual dialog, Krishna and Arjuna, are warrior heroes who play significant roles elsewhere throughout the epic. Arjuna, a prince and master archer, is one of the five Pandava brothers who, after years of exile, are now about to fight their near relatives the Kauravas at the battle of Kuruksetra in order to regain the kingdom that should be theirs. We should imagine Arjuna, who has a son (Abhimanyu) old enough to fight alongside him, as being at midlife. Krishna, Arjuna's friend, brother-in-law, charioteer, and soon-to-be midlife mentor, is prince of Dwaraka and the chief councilor for the Pandavas.

This embeddedness of the *Gita* in the vast warrior epic the *Mahabharata* will provide us with a key for revisioning what is one of the most unusual midlife transformations in world literature. Although it is usually studied and commented upon for its rich and clear presentation of spiritual teachings concerning yoga and spiritual realization, the *Gita* is also, in its own special way, a wonderful piece of epic narration that presents a vividly dramatic story of a warrior assailed by doubts at midlife, who then undergoes a spiritual transformation thanks to the ministrations and message of his midlife mentor.

The immediate context for Arjuna's transformation on the battlefield is the previous year he spent disguised as a eunuch at the court of King Virata, which Krishna will allude to sarcastically in his first words to him. Symbolically, Arjuna's "playing the eunuch" constitutes a hypermasculine hero's "fall into the feminine" at midlife that will have significant consequences in the *Gita* for Arjuna's core identity, as he shifts from being a warrior only to becoming a yogi who is *also* a warrior. His is an unusual (and at the same time exemplary) midlife spiritual crisis, during which he struggles to give his life a genuinely spiritual orientation in a way that is appropriate to his personal and social situation.

One of the most surprising reversals of expectation in world literature occurs at the opening of the *Bhagavad Gita* section of the *Mahabharata*, where the mighty warrior Arjuna's heroic resolve suddenly crumbles; he lets his bow drop from his hand and refuses to fight, just as the great battle of Kuruksetra is about to begin. His charioteer and advisor Krishna immediately calls him to task in words (*klaibyam ma sma gamah, Partha*) that have been mistranslated repeatedly since Charles Wilkins's first English translation (*The Bhagvat Geeta, or Dialogues of Kreeshna and Arjoon; in Eighteen Lectures; with Notes* [London, 1785]) put them this way: "Yield not thus to unmanliness." The Sanskrit text, when translated literally, however, would be better translated as "do not go into eunuchness" or "do not become a eunuch," and that is more or less how the eminent Sanskritists R.C. Zaehner, in his Oxford University Press translation (1969), and J.A.B. van Buitenen, in his University of Chicago bilingual edition *The Bhagavadgita in the Mahabharata* (1981), finally translated it: "play not the eunuch" and "do not act like a eunuch." This little phrase may sound bizarre, but it is of key symbolic importance for Arjuna's midlife crisis as represented in the *Gita*, and, as we unpack it, we will discover, not only *enantiodromia*, but also shadow anxieties and the resurgence of the feminine.

The *Gita*'s Sanskrit term *klaibyam* (root *klib-*) is also a key term in Ashis Nandy's recent and groundbreaking discussion of the colonial mentality in *The Intimate Enemy* (1984). In the opening chapter "The Psychology of Colonialism", Nandy criticizes the "search for martial Indianness" in nineteenth-century India, which he views critically as a means of "cultural co-optation" based on "identification with the aggressor" (Nandy 1984: 52). He shows how this came to be theorized by the bipolar opposition of *purusatva* (manliness) and *klibatva*, defined as "femininity-in-masculinity . . . perceived as the final negation of a man's political identity, a pathology more dangerous than femininity itself" (Nandy 1984: 9). In this colonial paradigm, "manliness is superior to womanliness [*naritva*], and womanliness in turn to femininity in man" (Nandy 2001: 52). Nandy himself gives a positive valence to *klibatva* and its cognates; for him it represents the despised and stigmatized antithesis of the hypermasculinity represented both by British "manliness" and by the "martial Indianness" that was its colonial reflection.

Nandy seems unaware, however, that this somewhat rare term figures prominently at the opening of the *Bhagavad Gita*, and that it also functions as a key term in the immediate epic textual context of the *Mahabharata* in which the *Gita* is embedded, where it occurs several times, and where it is a major term of epic self-accusation and self-deprecation. In the section of the epic that follows immediately the end of the *Gita*, four great warriors of the opposite side apply the term to themselves one after the other, calling themselves slaves to wealth (since they have been bought off by Duryodhana, the enemy king) and hence only capable of speaking like eunuchs (*klibavat*).

Furthermore, the term, as Krishna applies it to Arjuna specifically at the opening of the *Gita*, is a transparent allusion to the year that Arjuna had spent in the court of King Virata disguised as a eunuch. The *Virataparvan* (the section of the *Mahabharata* that immediately precedes the section in which the *Gita* is embedded) recounts how the five Pandava brothers, along with their common wife Draupadi, after having lost their kingdom in a dicing match and having been required by the terms of their agreement to spend twelve years in exile living in complete secrecy in the forest, had also agreed to spend the thirteenth year living publicly but in disguise. Yudhishthira, the eldest of the five brothers, and the compulsive gambler whose dice-playing lost them the kingdom earlier, continues in character disguised as a Royal Dicing Master for King Virata; the mighty Bhima becomes a chef and cooks curries; the twins Nakula and Sahadeva become stable menials taking care of horses and cows; and Draupadi, their common wife, becomes a chambermaid and hairdresser in the service of the queen. All these are reasonable disguises. But Arjuna's choice is unusual, to say the least:

> Sire, [he says to his elder brother], I am a transvestite [the word used here is *sandaka*, an exact synonym of eunuch], I'll vow, for these big string-scarred arms are hard to hide! I'll hang rings from my ears that sparkle like fire, and my head shall sport a braid, king! I shall be Brhannada [a comic woman's name]. Listen, I'll be a woman, and tell sweet little tales and tell them again and amuse the king and the other folk in the seraglio. I myself shall teach the women in the palace of King Virata to sing, king, and to dance in many ways, and to make music in still others. . . . "I was at Yuddhisthira's place, a maid of Draupadi's; I lived in!" so I'll tell the king if he asks me, Bharata.
>
> (van Buitenen 1978: 29)

Arjuna's almost whimsical assumption of an impotent eunuch's identity will allow him to live among the court ladies for a whole year as a storyteller and dancing master. Adding to the oddity of his decision, he takes on a female name and humorously improvises a history for himself in which he was his own wife's chambermaid! This is the man who will, after a year in the harem (living chastely, as it turns out—his disguise was never intended to give him free run of the harem ladies' sexual favors), dismay his brothers and friends by suddenly refusing to fight at the moment when the battle to regain their kingdom is about to begin. This impulsive move on his part, acted out in full view of the two armies, also means that Arjuna has opened himself up to the charge of behaving like a coward. As Krishna reminds him, dishonor for a warrior is worse than death. This cowardice is clearly the great warrior's *shadow* side—not that it makes Arjuna a coward, but it suggests that all is not strength and valor within his soul. He may justify his startling decision to Krishna with all kinds of arguments, alleging his tremendous feelings of compassion for those who would suffer the consequences of the aftermath of the war. But it is clear that a yellow stain of cowardice suddenly threatens to tarnish his image on the battlefield, and he is not the famous young hero he used to be.

The question is obvious: does Arjuna's "fall into femininity" have anything to do with his impulsive decision not to fight? And is his refusal to fight a "feminine" or an "impotent" gesture? These questions and others are worth asking, if one wishes to link the opening of the *Gita* to the previous Virata episode and to speculate on the psychological effects on Arjuna of living disguised for a whole year as a eunuch in Virata's harem. As we have seen, Ashis Nandy translates *klibatva* as "the femininity in man" (Nandy 1984: 52). Is Arjuna's newly cultivated "inner femininity"— the result of living almost exclusively among women as a "man/woman" in Virata's court—the primary source of his sudden reluctance to fight, and of his being overwhelmed by compassion for those he is duty bound to fight and slay? Is it a case of *enantiodromia*—a replacement in his mind of hypermasculine warrior values with feminine, matriarchal or maternal values that privilege life over victory in battle?

Or is it something else? Nandy's notion of "femininity-in-man"—which Nandy views positively as the androgynous antidote to hypermasculinity— certainly suggests that Jung's theory of the *anima* might prove to be the key to explaining Arjuna's confused state of mind. Jung characterized the manifestations of the unconscious anima as irrational moods such as resentment, touchiness, testiness and sentimentality, which can take a man over completely and paralyze his activity. Arjuna's mood of "despondency" (the traditional title of Book 1 of the *Gita* is "The Despondency of Arjuna") is just such a depressive mood, although it is seemingly based on a sincere feeling of compassion for the lives of those he is about to kill. But Krishna does not admire him for it—quite the contrary: "Abandon this despicable weakness of thy heart, and stand up," Krishna orders him in the words of the 1785 Wilkins translation. So perhaps Arjuna is overtaken by an irrational mood—not by true compassion, but by an anima mood, by something somewhat bogus from the realm of *klibatva*. The plausibility of this interpretation would be reinforced by Jung's idea that a man's anima contains *eros*, the function of relationship, but, as he qualifies significantly, "a certain inferior kind of relatedness" (Jung 1984b: 17). Looked at from this perspective, Arjuna's feelings of compassion for his opponents are not quite real: they derive from an undeveloped, unrealistic and strangely unrelated kind of *eros*, and it is no wonder that Krishna is not very impressed with them.

But our interpretation of Arjuna's mood of despondency need not stop here. After all, Arjuna's irrational mood is also the catalyst for Krishna's teachings in the *Gita* about selfless activity and all the other things that have made the *Gita* a storehouse of spiritual wisdom. It is no good badmouthing a mood that results in things such as these! Arjuna's anima mood also bears the seeds of a remarkable transformation in depth, and this may be because the anima represents not only a personal, but also an archetypal, dimension of the psyche, that is, she is not only a man's personal soulmate, so to speak, but also his bridge to the collective unconscious. Jung believed that coming to terms or "realizing" an archetype usually involved an initial identification with it, so that a man starts to realize the anima by identifying with her, although it is more an unconscious than a deliberately conscious process. Arjuna's hysterical ravings in Book 1, with their wild "femininity in masculinity," can thus be seen as the symptoms of a kind of unconscious anima identification on his part. After a year among the women of Virata's harem, living out his anima-colored "femininity in masculinity" singing, dancing and storytelling, Arjuna viewed the battlefield of Kuruksetra from a totally different perspective from that of the followers of the conventional warrior code (*kshatra-dharma*); he viewed it, not as a place where a glorious victory could be won, but rather as a place where precious lives were going to be destroyed, family relations betrayed, and domestic society corrupted and damaged beyond repair. His sudden decision not to fight involved a radical break with his previous identity as a young, self-assertive hero, and placed in jeopardy the great reputation he had won for himself as a warrior. But, one must emphasize, in the context of Krishna's teachings later in the *Gita* concerning the value of selfless, disinterested action (*karmayoga*), his decision proved to be the catalyst for a total revisioning of the whole idea of activity in the world; it was the necessary prelude to the exposition of the spiritual teachings of Krishna in the next seventeen books of the *Bhagavad Gita*. Anima possessed though Arjuna may have been, he had been led to question the value of conventional patriarchal warrior ethics, and this *enantiodromia* ultimately opened up his mind to a new spiritual vision of life.

The *Bhagavad Gita*, like the *Mahabharata* in which it is embedded, is in all likelihood a composite text that grew over time to encompass the eighteen chapters as we know them now. The author of the earliest version of the text must have deliberately embedded his original *Gita* at a well-chosen point of the *Mahabharata*, just before the onset of the great battle at Kuruksetra. He did his best to create a nearly seamless connection between his text and the preexisting epic text, and by attaching it to the *Mahabharata* must have intended it to reach the widest possible audience—the audience, in fact, of the *Mahabharata* itself, as enormously popular today (witness the wildly successful Indian TV series) as it was throughout the history of India for over two thousand years. The *Gita*'s immediate setting or epic "frame" would thus deserve attention in its own right, both for what it might have to offer in terms of thematic continuity and for the way in which it departs significantly from the epic vision of the *Mahabharata*.

This attention to the *Gita*'s epic frame was first given by the eminent Sanskrit scholar J.A.B. van Buitenen in his trailblazing book *The Bhagavadgita in the Mahabharata* (1981). But van Buitenen was more of a philologist than an interpreter, and so there was only so much he could do in terms of a complete analysis of the *Mahabharata*'s thematic relationship with the *Gita*. Some of what he points out in his excellent introduction is quite suggestive, however. For instance, he notes that "yoga" and the command "to lay on the yokes" (the shout that called for the chariots and their horses to be readied for action) both have their etymological origin in the Sanskrit verb root *yuj*, "to join or link together" (van Buitenen 1981: 17). Thus the epic injunction referring to "the yoking of the horses to the war cars, wagons, and other war equipment" is linked with the idea of yoga as "a self-yoking to a particular effort to win a goal" (van Buitenen 1981: 17). But van Buitenen has a tendency to overplay the continuity of the epic vision of the happy warrior with the more reflective *Gita*'s promotion of spiritual struggle; for him, the *Gita* culminates in Arjuna's "acceptance of *ksatriya* duty and fate," although he does add that "there will be no more happy warriors, only resigned ones" (van Buitenen 1981: 89). Even with this qualification, his conclusion seems a bit shaky, since it would hardly be fair to say that Arjuna has become "a resigned warrior" by the end of the *Gita*; his midlife transformation into a yogi is far more radical than that.

That is why stressing the continuity between the epic vision of the *Mahabharata* and the spiritual vision of the *Gita*, however valuable it proves to be initially, can become misleading. The *Gita*, from its second chapter onwards, quickly moves to subvert the hypermasculine warrior concerns of the epic in order to promote a sublimation of the epic's *kshatra-dharma* (the warrior ethic, especially as a youthful heroic ideal) into the *Gita*'s spiritual discipline of yoga, thus substituting for the warrior's heroic self-assertion on the battlefield the mental fight and generative selfless activity of the yogi. The warrior ethic's perspective is centered on the advantages to the individual warrior of either victory or death on the battlefield. As Krishna reminds Arjuna early on, while he is still attempting (unsuccessfully) to bring Arjuna back to a sense of his duty as a *kshatriya*, battle is a win/win situation for the warrior: "Die and you win heaven. Conquer, and you enjoy the earth" (Prabhavananda and Isherwood 2002: 89).

But a yogi's practice of *karmayoga* is not centered on the ego and its satisfaction, nor does it lead him to cherish the expectation of individual enjoyment here or in the hereafter of the rewards for his actions. *Karmayoga* stresses instead the renunciation of individual enjoyment and personal advantage in the interests of acting effectively and disinterestedly. Yoga thus differs radically from *kshatra-dharma* even as it maintains the latter's emphasis on fearless activity on the battlefield or, in this case, on the battlefield of life.

The immediate effect of the two major epic scenes of the *Mahabharata* that frame the *Gita*—one immediately before the text of the *Gita* begins, and the other immediately after it ends—is to undermine symbolically the hegemonic value of *kshatra-dharma* and hence to justify the advent of yoga as the mature spiritual successor of the youthful warrior ethic. The first of these scenes concerns the announcement of the death of the great warrior Bhisma; it is actually an interruption of the normal chronological sequence of events, since the bard Samjaya begins his narration to the blind king Dhrtarashtra of the events leading up to the battle with the account of the great general Bhisma's death, which occurred near the end of the battle; only when he has finished with this devastating piece of news will he go back to the chronological beginning with a description of the early morning marshaling of the two armies before the battle has begun.

The account of Bhisma's death does not disturb the chronological sequence needlessly or meaninglessly, as this death has high symbolic importance. The ever chaste Bhisma, the Sir Galahad of the *Mahabharata* as well as the commander-in-chief of the enemy Kaurava army, is the most venerable embodiment of the noblest aspects of *kshatra-dharma*. With his death, the warrior code itself has suffered symbolically a terrible blow, as Dhrtarashtra himself seems to realize when, severely shaken by the news, he declares that "Lawlessness, I know now, has prevailed over Law, if the Pandavas still want the kingdom after killing their ancient guru" (van Buitenen 1981: 43). It was Arjuna who had killed Bhisma by taking him literally at his word that he would never raise his weapon against a woman, by cleverly using Sikhandin, a warrior born as a woman but later changed into a man, as a human shield behind which he was able to shoot Bhisma with his arrows. That Sikhandin had been born a woman is a particular affront to the hypermasculine *kshatra-dharma* exemplified by Bhisma, which makes Arjuna's devious procedure all the more obnoxious. But the death of Bhisma symbolically opens the door to something new and as yet undefined, which will be created on the ruins of a warrior ethic that has been shown to be riddled with fatal flaws: treachery, deceit, corruption and greed. With Bhisma's death, and with the symbolic death of the *kshatra-dharma* he embodies, there opens up an abyss of meaninglessness, an ideological vacuum that calls for the creation of a new set of ideals to replace the old ones—ideals to be enunciated by some new guru who would presumably be greater than Bhisma, and would take his place. And this is exactly what happens, as Krishna steps in as Arjuna's midlife mentor with a whole new philosophy of heroic action in the world, which sublimates the *kshatra-dharma* into the spiritual path of yoga.

The second framing scene that comes immediately after the end of the text of the *Bhagavad Gita* reinforces the theme of the discrediting of *kshatra-dharma*. In a seemingly impulsive gesture, which first leaves all his fellow warriors baffled as to its meaning and motivation, the elder Pandava brother Yudhishthira suddenly takes off his armor, puts down his weapons, leaves his chariot and proceeds on foot towards the enemy camp of the Kauravas. (The scene provides an obvious parallel and possibly an inspiration for the opening scene of the *Gita*, when Arjuna inexplicably throws down his bow and refuses to fight.) The Kauravas assume too quickly that Yudhisthira is overcome by fear at the approach of battle, and shout for joy. But Krishna correctly guesses the real reason for this apparently traitorous move, and explains to the Pandavas that their brother Yudhisthira

> will fight his enemies only with the consent of Bhisma, Gautrama, Salya and all his other gurus. It is said that in a former age, when a man openly did battle without first seeking the consent of his betters, he was despised by his betters. But if he did seek their consent and then fought his betters, his victory in battle was assured.
>
> (van Buitenen 1981: 147)

Krishna turns out to be right in his surmise, and we soon see Yudhisthira asking each one of his revered gurus, beginning with Bhisma, for the permission to fight with him and possibly kill him in battle. This moving scene certainly seems intended to demonstrate Yudhisthira's remarkable devotion to the highest ideals of his warrior caste and royal position. But the answer to each one of his petitions to his various revered teachers is uniformly unexpected and shocking. Each guru in turn gives Yudhisthira permission to fight and to kill him if necessary, but each prefaces his consent with bitter words of self-recrimination—words that undermine the nobility of the situation completely—starting with Bhisma, who says "I have been held captive by the Kauravas with their wealth. Hence I can only speak to you like a eunuch (*klibavat*)" (van Buitenen 1981: 149). The potential pathos of the scene is thus undermined by this frank and somewhat cynical self-accusation, as each guru in turn admits how he has been corrupted—made impotent—by Kaurava money. But why do these venerable embodiments of *kshatra-dharma* confess so openly their own moral weakness and unworthiness? Perhaps the author of the original *Gita* saw an opportunity here, and realized that, once again (as with the death of Bhisma), in the epic text into which he wished to insert a new spiritual discourse an ideological vacuum had opened up, and that this vacuum could be filled by the message of Krishna, who, by contrast with Bhisma and the others, was a worthy and uncorrupted guru—in other words, that there was the opportunity to insert into the text of the popular epic a discourse that could take the place of a discredited warrior ethic whose exemplars saw themselves at this crucial juncture as able to speak only "like eunuchs" (*klibavat*).

As we have seen, the opening of the *Gita* will pick up on this key term "eunuch" in the epic scene between Yudhishthira and his gurus, and, taking up the latter's picturesque term of self-disparagement, will use Krishna's quip to Arjuna ("don't start acting like a eunuch *again!*") as a dramatic springboard for developing a discourse dedicated to the idea of yoga as an original transformation and sublimation of *kshatra-dharma* itself, as well as the particular path that Arjuna can follow at midlife in order to deal with his "eunuchness" and sudden faint-heartedness as a warrior.

Alone among all the great warriors of the Mahabharata war, Arjuna proved himself able to challenge the fundamental assumptions of the warrior ethic, namely, that victory is always worth fighting for under any and all circumstances, and that it is the unquestionable duty of the *kshatriya* to fight. He may be seen by Krishna initially as someone who is "thinking like a eunuch," but it is important to emphasize that Arjuna is also the only one of the great warriors who can "think outside the box." Although Krishna winds up either dismissing or refuting Arjuna's heated pacifist arguments in favor of withdrawing from the battlefield, it would be missing the point to claim, as van Buitenen does at one point in his introduction, that Krishna does this simply in order to amass counter-arguments that will persuade Arjuna to backtrack and to accept "the warrior's fate" (van Buitenen 1981: 4). Rather, Arjuna's emotional statements begin the process of a radical *enantiodromia*.

By the end of the *Gita*, Krishna has convinced Arjuna to act as a yogi first and foremost; as regards what he will actually do in battle at Kuruksetra, Krishna, while pointing out the almost irresistible force of karmic disposition and social duty, nevertheless leaves him full freedom to decide upon his future course of action by himself: "Now I have taught you the wisdom which is the secret of secrets. Ponder it carefully. Then act as you think best" (Prabhavananda and Isherwood 2002: 129). Arjuna will choose to fight, of course; this is a foregone conclusion, because the later addition of the *Gita* cannot change the course of the original epic narrative of the *Mahabharata*, where Arjuna already has a preassigned epic role to fulfill as a ruthless warrior. But at this point near the end of the *Gita*, it is clear that he is represented as free to decide whether to fight or not to fight—and, if to fight, in what spirit to fight.

The question then arises: what made Arjuna at the opening of the *Gita* think and act so differently from his brothers, teachers and fellow warriors? What made him capable of thinking "outside the box" of the warrior's unquestioned assumption that a good fight is always to be welcomed? As I have suggested earlier, the answer lies in the year he spent as a eunuch teaching Uttara, the daughter of King Virata, and her ladies in the women's quarters, to dance and sing, and generally keeping them entertained and happy. Arjuna's experience of how women talk and behave when they are by themselves would have gone far beyond the experience of his hyper-masculine fellow warriors, who would mainly have known only how women talk and behave when they are in the presence of men. (It is important—and the *Mahabharata* makes this clear on several occasions—that Arjuna's relationship with the women of Virata's court was at all times proper and chaste; he knew them as a friend and teacher, not as a man—and so knew them *differently*.) In an aristocratic society where there was a fair amount of gender segregation, Arjuna's inside knowledge of women's ways must have been rather unique for a man of his standing and position, and I suggest that enough of these feminine modes of thinking and experiencing the world would have rubbed off on him to make him able to fall into a quasi-feminine anima-inspired way of thinking about such things as war, battle, bloodshed, carnage and the goal of victory at all costs. From his feminine-influenced perspective, engaging in the approaching battle might readily seem a terrible choice to make: better, as Arjuna says to Krishna, to die rather than to kill one's relatives and venerable teachers; better to lose everything than to enjoy the bloodstained fruits of battle; better to be killed by the Kauravas than to act out of greed for kingship and pleasures; better to sue for peace than to bring about the inevitable destruction of family and of dharma (righteousness) itself. In a word, better to protect and foster civil and domestic life, even at the price of humiliating defeat.[3]

Even if Arjuna is depressed and "overcome with [excess of] compassion," his almost hysterical rant does not lack a kind of passionate eloquence. But for Krishna, eloquent as they may seem, his words are ultimately just eunuch talk. This is a harsh judgment, however well intended. What are we, as modern readers, to make of Krishna's position? Jung's concept of the anima as "the feminine-in-man," the unconscious contrasexual subperson-ality that compensates psychologically for a man's dominant conscious masculinity, has provided us a way of appreciating the originality of what Arjuna has to say, as well as a way of sensing its ultimate weakness. Arjuna's ability to abandon the rigid and conventional mindset of the *kshatra-dharma*, to which his fellow warriors cling desperately, even when it is clearly in the process of becoming discredited, can be attributed to the awakening of his anima or unconscious feminine side, thanks to the unusual education he received in the ways of feminine modes of thinking and experiencing in the women's quarters of King Virata's palace. Thanks to his somewhat more conscious feminine side, Arjuna no longer thinks and feels the way another more typically hypermasculine warrior might think and feel. This means that he is a much more interesting and challenging person for Krishna to engage with, since he has one of two things essential for a good student: strongly held personal opinions. Krishna would not have been able to argue fruitfully with one of Arjuna's brothers or fellow warriors, as they were intellectually complacent and satisfied with the conventional answers provided by the warrior ethic; someone who thinks he knows all the answers does not need a teacher, or, at least, will not be interested in accepting anyone as a teacher.

Arjuna also has the second thing required for a good student: he realizes on some level of consciousness that he is in a desperate situation and really needs help. Arjuna is not only *inspired* by his anima or feminine side; he is also more than a little *overwhelmed* by it in the form of emotions he cannot control. Although Arjuna's "thinking outside the box" provided Krishna with a wonderful opportunity for a vigorous dialog with him, there was also something suspect and unbalanced about it. His apparent compassion was based on almost hysterical anima emotion, and in this he cannot be said to be thinking like a woman (women when they think can be as clear and calm as men) but rather to be "thinking like a man trying to think like a woman," that is, his anima has led him into inappropriate and psychologically ungrounded sentimentality and emotionality. There is something not quite right about his feminine wisdom, something *off*, and for Jung this would have to do with the unconscious and unreliable dimensions of a man's inner femininity. As we have seen, Jung believed that the anima contained *eros*, the function of empathic relationship, but in its unmediated form it tends to be an undeveloped, unrealistic and strangely unrelated kind of *eros*. Looked at from this perspective, Arjuna's *eros* has lost contact with the reality of the situation: he is facing relatives and teachers who deserve his compassion (however corrupted by money they may be), but he is also facing them as deadly enemies, who would gladly kill him, his immediate family and his allies. So there is something inappropriate and off base about his declarations of compassion; no wonder Krishna is unimpressed with them.

But for this emotional and anima-driven *eros*, ungrounded and unrealistic as it may be, Arjuna would have been no different from his brothers and teachers. He would have been satisfied with the world as the *kshatra-dharma* represented it, seeing the oncoming battle as a wonderful opportunity to win a kingdom or, failing that, to go to a warrior's heaven. Instead, the imminent battle provided him with a wonderful opportunity for midlife *enantiodromia* through a life-changing conversation with Krishna, which will extend to him the option of living his life from midlife onwards not as a relentlessly self-assertive young hero, but as a yogi, in a spirit of dispassion and disinterested activity leading to spiritual peace and freedom. Without the emotional breakdown that elicited Krishna's insult that he was about to act like a eunuch again, Arjuna would not have been open to Krishna's teachings, which were basically the only solution to an impossible conflict of values that had torn him apart. When it is not possible to resolve such a conflict, the only hope is to rise above it, and that is what Krishna has helped Arjuna to do.

Arjuna is thus presented in the *Gita* and its epic frame as a psychologically complex and troubled midlife individual, whose very complexity led him into a dilemma that he could no longer solve, either on his own, or by relying on conventional social wisdom. But there is still more to be said that is even more problematic about Arjuna's ultimately happy fall into his inner femininity. In distancing himself from the relatively uncomplicated self-confidence of the happy warriors of his entourage he had left himself open to a crisis of confidence in himself as a warrior, and is menaced by being taken over completely by his shadow, which is the antithesis of all his glorified image as a hero; his shadow is the repository of all his repressed fears and cowardice. His openness to feminine modes of feeling, developed during his life as a eunuch in the women's quarters, had made him a more complex individual, whose warrior courage and boldness could no longer be accessed as automatically or as spontaneously as before, now that he had cast an eye into the vision of chaos and destruction that the imminent battle at Kuruksetra had presented to him. His hitherto unquestioned complicity with warrior brutality had been brought to consciousness, and had become problematic for him. So far, so good. But Krishna's discourse on yoga, however enlightening spiritually it was, did not directly address this state of emotional disarray. The way was open for him to become a yogi, no doubt, but the way to go back to being a warrior *as well as* a yogi was not so obvious, since his conflicting emotions allowed for no easy resolution on the purely philosophical and spiritual plane. For that he needed an *emotional* shock that would give him back his warrior courage on a higher plane of awareness. He needed, in short, a transformative image.

For Arjuna, in spite of the intellectual and spiritual enlightenment provided by Krishna's discourses on yoga, can still be imagined, midway through the *Gita*, as remaining in a state of deep emotional confusion and even of emotional trauma. The battlefield of Kuruksetra still proposed death and destruction on an unparalleled scale, and to resume his duty as a warrior would require him to participate wholeheartedly in the process of dealing out this death and destruction. But how would he ever be up to this? His feminine sensibility, heightened and sharpened by his stay at Virata's court as the friend, teacher and companion of the court ladies, had enabled him to ask the original questions that challenged Krishna to teach him the "mystery of mysteries" concerning the ultimate freedom of the soul, but it had also left him in a state where the hypermasculine *kshatra-dharma* could no longer inspire him emotionally as before. At some point in the *Gita*'s composition, the author—or perhaps another and later author— devised a brilliant solution to the dramatic dilemma of an overly sensitive warrior (overly sensitive from the traditional warrior's standpoint, of course) unable to countenance the horror of the killing field of Kuruksetra.

Krishna had given him all the intellectual instruction and spiritual inspiration he needed to become a yogi, but the author sensed at that stage in the elaboration of the text that some crucial element was still missing. His answer was astoundingly original: the evocation of Arjuna's apocalyptic vision of his friend, relative and charioteer Krishna as Lord of the Universe and as the very embodiment of Death and Destruction—a transformative image of cosmic proportions!

To the best of my knowledge, there is no temple anywhere in India dedicated to this terrible cosmic aspect of Krishna, whose description in Book 11 remains perhaps unique in the vast iconography associated with him. Readers cannot forget the gruesome description of his bloody mouths, tusks and the grotesque horror of devouring death represented without restraint. The father of the atomic bomb, J. Robert Oppenheimer, who was an amateur Sanskritist, at the moment of the first flash that opened the Nuclear Age at the Trinity site in New Mexico on July 16, 1945, remembered the *Gita*'s words "the radiance of a thousand suns"[4] and "now I am become Death, the destroyer of worlds."[5] But, memorable as they are in the context of the apocalyptic vision in which they occur, what could be the point of adding such a horrific scene to the otherwise serenely philosophical *Gita*?

I would suggest the following answer: that the dreadful vision of the *Gita*'s eleventh chapter constituted a transformative image that was absolutely necessary in order for Arjuna to regain, on a higher level of consciousness, his warrior's courage and resolve. The vision contained a nightmarish vision of death and destruction, but it was all the same a revelation of the terrible and frightening divine dimension, hitherto unknown to him, of his dear friend and teacher Krishna. If Death and Destruction appear in the form of one's dearest friend and teacher, then they can be accepted, however painfully. In the midst of a terrible dilemma, what Jung called the *transcendent function* provided a transformative image that reconciled the opposites through an original and iconic image of Krishna as Arjuna's dear friend and teacher morphing into the cosmic embodiment of death and destruction.

There is something else about this vision that needs to be highlighted. The vision is divided into two parts of unequal length, and these seem to correspond to what Krishna says when he offers to show Arjuna first of all "the whole universe with all things animate and inert made one within this body of mine," and then, after that, "whatever else you desire to see" (Prabhavananda and Isherwood 2002: 91). The first part of the vision—the radiance of a thousand suns and the entire universe centered in the body of the divine Krishna—clearly corresponds to the first part of what Krishna promised Arjuna could see: "the entire universe," and so on. This part of the vision permeated with light leaves Arjuna "stunned"; the text goes on to say that he then "bowed low in adoration" (Prabhavananda and Isherwood 2002: 92). At this point I believe that we are encouraged by the text to visualize Arjuna no longer looking *up* at Krishna and his cosmic form as he did a moment before, but now rather looking *down* at the ground, head bowed, and then seeing *within* himself, in the depth of his inner consciousness, an *inner* vision. This vision would correspond to the second part of what Krishna promised him: "whatever else you desire to see"—whatever Arjuna desired to see with all the half-conscious yearnings of his deepest need to both see and bear the horror of the vision of the Terrible as an aspect of the cosmic dimension of his friend and mentor Krishna.

This second part of Arjuna's vision is described in the first person, unlike the first part, which is described in the third person. The vision is described *in Arjuna's own words*; it is clearly his own personal vision *of what he desired to see*. Arjuna's description of his own inner apocalyptic vision passes quickly from one fearsome detail to another even more horrific, culminating in Arjuna telling Krishna that

> Licking with your burning tongues, devouring
> All the worlds, you probe the heights of heaven
> With intolerable beams.
>   (Prabhavananda and Isherwood 2002: 94)

At this culminating point Krishna intervenes with his interpretation of the vision:

> I am come as Time, the waster of the peoples
> Ready for that hour that ripens to their ruin.
>   (Prabhavananda and Isherwood 2002: 94)

In conceptual terms, Krishna is simply the allegorical embodiment of Time. But, as regards its grotesque mythological horror, it is something like Job's encounter with the Lord as the Voice Out of the Whirlwind—the vision of the ultimate power and cruelty of the universe represented in horrifying concrete detail. From a Jungian perspective, the second vision is for Arjuna a *compensatory* vision, in that it compensated, with tremendous emotional force, for the mood of compassion that had overwhelmed him at the opening of the *Gita*, and which had made him unfit to function as a warrior. It constitutes a religious experience of the dark side of God. It enables Arjuna to face the worst that can happen on the bloody battlefield of Kuruksetra, because it is an apocalyptic vision that reveals the coming battle in its archetypal dimension as the ultimate fate, not only of the warriors about to engage in battle at Kuruksetra, but also of all living beings faced with annihilation by the Cosmic Destroyer.

Once he has been stunned into a new emotional state of acceptance of Death and Destruction, Krishna quickly defines for Arjuna the practical consequences of his vision:

Therefore, strike. Win kingdom, wealth and glory.
Arjuna, arise, O ambidextrous bowman.
Seem to slay. By me these men are slain already.
You but smite the dead, the doom-devoted heroes,
Jayadratha, Drona, Bhishma, Karna.
Fight, and have no fear. The foe is yours to conquer.
                    (Prabhavananda and Isherwood 2002: 94)

For many readers this may be a rather shocking section of the *Gita*, since Krishna urges upon Arjuna (enthusiastically!) the very murder of the teachers and fellow warriors that Arjuna originally shrank from. But when one keeps in mind the epic frame that establishes Arjuna as a complex personality of a most unusual sort—with unusual human weaknesses but also unusual spiritual potential—then this compensatory vision of the Terrible in the form of Krishna can be seen as having an essential role to play in the spiritual healing of a wounded warrior who, at the beginning of the *Gita*, had foreseen more in the way of approaching murder and mayhem than he could stomach. Now that Arjuna has seen not only the sorrow and the pity of life and death, but also its cosmic implacability and terrible divine grandeur, he can face the apocalypse. In the end, his "eunuch problem" has not been so much resolved as transcended. Having seen, thanks to his awakened feminine consciousness, the dark side of the warrior ethic, he now realizes, thanks to his midlife mentor Krishna's spiritual discourse, that the practice of yoga can become for him the sublimation of warrior energies in a spiritual direction. In Book 11 he has also faced the cosmic—as opposed to the personal—dimension of death and destruction. This vision has jolted him into a frame of mind in which personal gain and loss are no longer the issues. Ego-bound self-assertiveness and youthful heroism are left behind; his transformation at midlife has given him the capacity to act generatively and fearlessly for the welfare of the world as well as for the sake of his own spiritual evolution and self-transcendence.

Notes

1 The poetry of Bhartrihari, translated at various times in the nineteenth century, also became a touchstone for the study and appreciation of classical Indian literature. Mathew V. Spano's essay "Tracking the Hermit's Soul" (2010) demonstrates persuasively how the sequence of poems can be read as illustrating a path of individuation that coincides to a substantial degree with midlife transformation.
2 Johann von Goethe, *West-östlicher Divan* (my translation).
3 Aristocratic ladies in the epic Draupadi could be quite bloodthirsty and ferocious in their desire for revenge, but I imagine that at least some of them can be imagined as not sharing the hypermasculine warrior's supreme confidence in the desirability of victory at any cost.
4 *Bhagavad Gita* 11.12.
5 A mixture of *Bhagavad Gita* 11.32 and 10.34.

Bibliography

Ahl, Frederick. *Sophocles' Oedipus: Evidence and Self-Contradiction.* Ithaca, NY: Cornell University Press, 1991.

Angelou, Maya. *I Know Why the Caged Bird Sings.* New York: Random House, 1969.

Bair, Deirdre. *Jung: A Biography.* Boston: Little, Brown, 2003.

Bennet, E.A. *Meetings with Jung: Conversations Recorded During the Years 1946–1961.* Zurich: Daimon, 1985.

Bly, Robert. *Iron John: A Book About Men.* New York: Vintage, 1992.

Brunton, Paul. *The Wisdom of the Overself.* York Beach, Maine: Weiser, 1983 [1943].

Buitenen, J.A.B. van. *The Mahabharata 4: The Book of Virata; and 5: The Book of the Effort.* Chicago: University of Chicago Press, 1978.

_____, ed. and trans. *The Bhagavadgita in the Mahabharata: A Bilingual Edition.* Chicago: University of Chicago Press, 1981.

Campbell, Joseph, ed. *The Portable Jung.* New York: Penguin, 1976.

Campion, Jane, dir. *The Piano.* DVD. Lion's Gate, 1993.

_____. *Interviews.* Ed. Virginia Wright Wexman. Jackson, MS: University of Mississippi Press, 1999.

Camus, Albert. *The Fall.* Trans. Justin O'Brian. New York: Vintage, 1956.

_____. *Le premier homme* [*The First Man*]. Paris: Gallimard, 1994.

Carotenuto, Aldo. *Jung e la cultura italiana.* Rome: Astrolabio, 1977 [partial translation online at http://www.psychomedia.it/jep/number14/carotenuto.htm, accessed June 3, 2011].

Carr, Barbara. "Goethe and Kurosawa: Faust and the Totality of Human Experience—East and West." *Film and Literature Quarterly* 24.3 (1996), 270–281.

Clay, Jenny Strauss. *The Wrath of Athena: Gods and Men in the Odyssey.* Princeton, NJ: Princeton University Press, 1983.

Conrad, Joseph. *Heart of Darkness.* New York: Everyman's Library Knopf, 1993 [1902].

Craven, Wes, dir. *The Serpent and the Rainbow.* 1988. Video. MCA Home Video, 1988.

Darroch, Robert. *D.H. Lawrence in Australia.* Melbourne: Macmillan, 1981.

de Botton, Alain. *How Proust Can Change Your Life.* New York: Vintage, 1998.

Erikson, Erik H. *Identity and the Life Cycle.* New York: Norton, 1980 [1959].

_____. *The Life Cycle Completed: Extended Version with New Chapters on the Ninth Stage of Development by Joan M. Erikson*. New York: Norton, 1997.

Euripides. *Philoctetes*. Ed. R.C. Jebb. (Greek text and English translation) London: Bristol Classical, 2004 [1898].

_____. *Ten Plays*. Trans. Paul Roche. New York: Signet, 1998.

Fellini, Federico. *Juliet of the Spirits*. Ed. Tullio Kezich. Trans. Howard Greenfield. New York: Orion, 1965.

_____. *8½*. Ed. Charles Affron. New Brunswick, NJ: Rutgers University Press, 1987.

_____. *Fellini on Fellini*. Trans. Isabel Quigly. New York: Da Capo, 1996.

_____, dir. *8½*. DVD. Criterion, 2001.

_____, dir. *Juliet of the Spirits*. DVD. Criterion, 2002.

Fierz-David, Linda. *Dreaming in Red: The Women's Dionysian Initiation Chamber in Pompeii*. Trans. Gladys Phelan. Putnam, CT: Spring, 2005.

Finley, John H., Jr. *Four Stages of Greek Thought*. Stanford, CA: Stanford University Press, 1966.

Fowlie, Wallace. *A Reading of Proust*, 2nd edition. Chicago: University of Chicago Press, 1975.

Freud, Sigmund. *The Interpretation of Dreams*. New York: Basic, 2010.

_____. *On Creativity and the Unconscious*. Ed. Benjamin Nelson. New York: Harper & Row, 1958.

Freud, Sigmund, and C.G. Jung. *The Freud/Jung Letters: The Correspondence Between Sigmund Freud and C.G. Jung*. Abridged edition. Trans. Ralph Manheim and R.F.C. Hull. Ed. William McGuire. Princeton, NJ: Princeton University Press, 1979.

Gay, Peter, ed. *The Freud Reader*. New York: Norton, 1995.

Gennep, Arnold van. *The Rites of Passage*. Trans. Monica B. Vizedom and Gabrielle L. Caffee. Chicago: University of Chicago Press, 1960 [1908].

Girard, René. *The Scapegoat*. Trans. Yvonne Freccero. Baltimore: Johns Hopkins University Press, 1986.

Girard, René, and Mark Anspach. *Oedipus Unbound: Selected Writings on Rivalry and Desire*. Stanford, CA: Stanford University Press, 2004.

Golsan, Richard J. *René Girard and Myth: An Introduction*. New York: Routledge, 2002.

Goux, Jean-Joseph. *Oedipus, Philosopher*. Trans. Catherine Porter. Stanford, CA: Stanford University Press, 1993.

Hart, Josephine. *Damage*. New York:Vintage, 1991.

Hess, Linda. "Rejecting Sita." *Journal of Vaishnava Studies* 12.2 (spring 2004), 29–61.

Hollis, James. *The Middle Passage*. Toronto, ON: Inner City, 1993.

_____. *Finding Meaning in the Second Half of Life*. New York: Gotham/Penguin: 2005.

Homer. *The Odyssey*. Trans. Robert Fitzgerald. Garden City, NJ: Anchor Doubleday, 1963.

_____. *The Odyssey* (Greek text), I and II. Ed. W.B. Stanford. London: Macmillan, 1964.

Joyce, James. *Ulysses*. Ed. Hans Walter Gabler. New York: Random House, 1986 [1922].

Jung, C.G. *Psychology of the Unconscious: A Study of the Transformations and Symbolism of the Libido*. Trans. Beatrice M. Hinkle. London: Routledge & Kegan Paul, 1919.

_____. *Two Essays on Analytical Psychology*. Trans. R.F.C. Hull. New York: Meridian, 1956.

_____. *Psychology and Religion (the Terry Lectures)*. New Haven: Yale University Press, 1960.

_____. *Memories, Dreams, Reflections*. Ed. Aniela Jaffé. Trans. Richard and Clara Winston. New York: Vintage, 1963.

_____. *The Spirit in Man, Art and Literature*. Trans. R.F.C. Hull. Princeton, NJ: Princeton University Press, 1966.

_____. *Alchemical Studies*. Trans. R.F.C. Hull. Princeton, NJ: Princeton University Press, 1968.

_____. *Psychology and Religion, West and East*. Trans. R.F.C. Hull. Princeton, NJ: Princeton University Press, 1969.

_____. *Four Archetypes*. Trans. R.F.C. Hull. Princeton, NJ: Princeton University Press, 1971.

_____. *Letters*, I and II. Ed. Gerhard Adler in collaboration with Aniela Jaffé. Trans. R.F.C. Hull. Princeton, NJ: Princeton University Press, 1975.

_____. *Dream Analysis: Notes of the Seminar Given in 1928–1930*. Ed. William McGuire. Princeton, NJ: Princeton University Press, 1984a.

_____. *Man and His Symbols*. New York: Doubleday, 1984b.

_____. *Nietzsche's Zarathustra: Notes for the Seminar Given in 1934–1939*, I and II. Ed. James L. Jarrett. Princeton, NJ: Princeton University Press, 1988.

_____. *Analytical Psychology: Notes of the Seminar Given in 1925*. Ed. William McGuire. Princeton, NJ: Princeton University Press, 1989a.

_____. *Aspects of the Masculine*. Trans. R.F.C. Hull. Ed. John Beebe. Princeton, NJ: Princeton University Press, 1989b.

_____ Visions: *Notes of a Seminar Given in 1930–1934*. Ed. Claire Douglas. Princeton, NJ: Princeton University Press, 1997.

Kakar, Sudhir, ed. *Identity and Adulthood*. With an introductory lecture by Erik Erikson. New Delhi: Oxford University Press, 1992.

Kalidasa. *The Recognition of Sakuntala*. Trans. W.J. Johnson. Oxford: Oxford University Press, 2001.

Kurosawa, Akira. *Ikiru* (filmscript). Trans. and ed. Donald Ritchie. New York: Simon & Schuster, 1968.

_____, dir. *Ikiru*. DVD. Criterion, 2003.

Lawrence, D.H. *Kangaroo*. London: HarperCollins, 1992 [1923].

Levinson, Daniel J. *The Seasons of a Man's Life*. New York: Ballantine, 1978.

Lucas, George, dir. *Star Wars* (film series 1977–2005). 20th Century Fox.

McGuire, William, ed. *The Freud/Jung Letters*. Princeton, NJ: Princeton University Press, 1989.

Malle, Louis, dir. *Damage*. DVD. New Line Home Video, 1992.

_____, dir. *Mon Oncle d'Amérique*. DVD. New Yorker Video, 2000.

_____, dir. *My Dinner with André*. DVD. Criterion, 2009 [1981].

Marcus, Steven. *The Other Victorians: A Study of Sexuality and Pornography in Mid-Nineteenth Century England*. New York: Basic, 1966.

Molton, Mary Dian, and Lucy Anne Sikes. *Four Eternal Women: Toni Wolff Revisited*. Carmel, CA: Fisher King, 2011.

Morrison, Toni. *Beloved*. New York: Vintage, 2004 [1987].

Nandy, Ashis. *The Intimate Enemy: Loss and Recovery of Self Under Colonialism*. New York: Oxford University Press, 1984.

Narayan, R.K. *My Days*. New York: South Asian, 1996.

_____. *The English Teacher*. London: Vintage, 2001 [1945].

Nicholls, Mike, dir. *Wolf*. Columbia Pictures, 1994.

Noll, Richard. *The Jung Cult: Origins of a Charismatic Movement*. Princeton, NJ: Princeton University Press, 1994.

Olivelle, Patrick, trans. *The Law Code of Manu*. Oxford: Oxford University Press, 2004.

Paley, Nina, dir. *Sita Sings the Blues*. DVD. Filmkaravan, 2009.

Perera, Sylvia Brinton. *Descent to the Goddess: A Way of Initiation for Women*. Toronto: Inner City, 1981.

Petrarch. *The Secret and Related Documents*. Ed. and trans. Carol E. Quillen. London: Bedford/St. Martin's, 2003.

Plasa, Carl, ed. *Toni Morrison*, Columbia Critical Guides. New York: Columbia University Press, 1998.

Plato. *The Symposium*. Trans. Christopher Gill. London and New York: Penguin, 1999.

Prabhavananda, Swami, and Christopher Isherwood, trans. *The Song of God* [*Bhagavad Gita*]. Introduction by Aldous Huxley. New York: Signet, 2002.

Proust, Marcel. *In Search of Lost Time. Volume VI: Time Regained*. Trans. Andreas Mayor and Terence Kilmartin, revised by D.J. Enright. New York: Modern Library, 2003.

Racine, Jean. *Phèdre*. Trans. Margaret Rawlings. New York: Dutton, 1961.

Rutter, Virginia Beane. *Woman Changing Woman*. San Francisco: HarperSanFrancisco: 1994.

Samuels, Andrew, and Bani Shorter and Fred Plaut. *A Critical Dictionary of Jungian Analysis*. London: Routledge & Kegan Paul, 1986.

Shakespeare, William. *As You Like It*. Ed. Albert Gilman. New York: New American Library, 1963.

_____. *The Complete Works*. Ed. G.B. Harrison. New York: Harcourt Brace, 1968.

_____. *Antony and Cleopatra*. Ed. Barbara Everett. New York: Signet, 1984.

Sharp, Daryl. *Personality Types: Jung's Model of Typology*. Toronto, ON: Inner City, 1987.

Shawn, Wallace, and André Gregory. *My Dinner with André (A Screenplay for the Film by Louis Malle)*. New York: Grove Weidenfeld, 1981.

Shay, Jonathan. *Odysseus in America: Combat Trauma and the Trials of Homecoming*. New York: Scribner, 2002.

Shellenbarger, Sue. *The Breaking Point: How Female Midlife Crisis Is Transforming Today's Women*. New York: Holt, 2005.

Shorter, Bani. *An Image Darkly Forming: Women and Initiation*. London: Routledge & Kegan Paul, 1987.

Sophocles. *The Oedipus Cycle*. Trans. Dudley Fitts and Robert Fitzgerald. New York: Harvest, 1977.

_____. *Philoctetes*. Ed. and trans. R.C. Jebb. London: Bristol Classical, 2004 [1898].

Spano, Mathew V. "Hermann Hesse's Use of German Romanticism and Indian Spirituality in the Resolution of His Mid-Life Crisis." Unpublished Rutgers Ph.D. thesis in Comparative Literature, 2002.

_____. "Tracking the Hermit's Soul: A Jungian Reading of Bhartrihari's Satakatraya." Online site http://www.cgjungpage.org (posted October 7, 2010).

Staude, John-Raphael. *The Adult Development of C.G. Jung.* Boston, London and Henley: Routledge & Kegan Paul, 1981.

Stein, Murray. *Transformation: Emergence of the Self.* College Station, TX: Texas A&M University Press, 1998.

_____. *In Midlife: A Jungian Perspective.* Putnam, CT: Spring, 2003 [1983].

Stevenson, Robert Louis. *The Strange Case of Dr. Jekyll and Mr. Hyde.* Ed. Martin Danahay. Peterborough, ON: Broadview, 1999 [1886].

Storr, Anthony. *Jung.* New York and London: Routledge, 1991.

Tacey, David. *Jung and the New Age.* New York and London: Routledge, 2001.

_____. *How to Read Jung.* New York and London: Norton, 2006.

Tolkin, Michael, dir. *The New Age.* Video. Warner Home Video. 1995.

Van Nortwick, Thomas. *Oedipus: The Meaning of a Masculine Life.* Norman: University of Oklahoma Press, 1998.

Verlaine, Paul. *Poèmes Saturniens.* Paris: Le Livre de Poche, 1996.

von Franz, Marie-Louise. *Puer Aeternus: A Psychological Study of the Adult Struggle with the Paradise of Childhood,* 2nd edn. Santa Monica, CA: Sigo, 1972.

Walker, Alice. *Good Night, Willie Lee, I'll See You in the Morning.* New York: Harcourt Brace Jovanovich, 1975.

_____. *Possessing the Secret of Joy.* New York: Harcourt Brace, 1992.

Walker, Steven F. "Literal Truth and Soul-Making Fiction in R.K. Narayan's Novel *The English Teacher*: Jungian Psychology Versus Spiritualist Fantasy." *Weber Studies: An Interdisciplinary Humanities Journal* 6.2 (fall 1987), 43–62.

_____. "Les mythes dans la tragédie: nouvelles perspectives jungiennes." *Proceeding of the XIth Congress of the International Comparative Literature Association* (Paris, 1985), ed. Mario Valdes (New York: Peter Lang, 1990), 87–96.

_____. "Magical Archetypes: Midlife Miracles in *The Satanic Verses*." *Magical Realism: Theory, History, Community,* ed. Lois Parkinson Zamora and Wendy B. Faris (Durham, NC: Duke University Press, 1995), pp. 162–176.

_____. "Mentors, Mixed Messages and the Patriarchal Perplex." A special issue *Examining/Experiencing Masculinities, Mattoid* 54 (summer 1999), 167–184.

_____. *Jung and the Jungians on Myth: An Introduction.* New York and London: Routledge, 2002.

_____. "The Name of the Madeleine: Sign and Symbols of the Mass in Proust's *In Search of Lost Time*." *Religion and the Arts* 7.4 (2003), 389–411.

_____. "Arjuna's Eunuch Problem and the *Gita's* Epic Frame." *American Vedantist* 14.1 (summer 2008), 9–14, and *American Vedantist* 14.2 (fall 2008), 8–16.

Wehr, Gerhard. *Jung: A Biography.* Trans. David M. Weeks. Boston and London: Shambala, 1987.

Wilkins, Charles, trans. *The Bhagvat Geeta, or Dialogues of Kreeshna and Arjoon; in Eighteen Lectures; with Notes.* London: 1785.

Wolkstein, Diane and Kramer, Samuel Noah. *Inanna, Queen of Heaven and Earth.* New York: Harper Perennial, 1983.

Woolf, Virginia. *Books and Portraits*. Ed. Mary Lyon. London: Triad Gafton, 1979.
_____. *Mrs Dalloway*. New York: Harcourt, 2005 [1925].
Zaehner, Robert C., trans. *The Bhagavad-Gita: With a Commentary Based on the Original Sources*. Oxford: Oxford University Press, 1985.

Index